see p.144

For Adelaide Cromwell
Allison Lockwood

ALLISON McCRILLIS LOCKWOOD

AN AMERICAN COMMUNITY IN WORLD WAR II

Copyright © 1993 by Allison McCrillis Lockwood

All rights reserved. No part of this book may be reproduced or utilized in any form or by any means, electronic or mechanical, including photocopying, recording, or by any information storage or retrieval system, without permission in writing from the Publisher. Inquiries should be addressed to the Daily Hampshire Gazette, 115 Conz St., Northampton, MA 01060.

The title of *Touched With Fire* is from a quote by Justice Oliver Wendell Holmes, thrice wounded in the Civil War while serving with the Massachusetts 20th: "Through our great good fortune, in our youth our hearts were touched with fire."

Dedication

Northampton Remembers these 112 who died in military service to their country during the Second World War:

Samuel Adams, William Adams, Edward Allord,
Benjamin J. Angotti, Francis S. Ansanitis,
Rudolph T. Arel, Hyman A. August,
Frederick M. Bailey, Allan R. Bardwell,
Walter A. Bardwell Jr., Julian P. Bubrowski,
Adolph Butor, Edmund J. Cadieux,
Christopher D. Cahill, James S. Campbell,
Daniel Cashman, Lawrence E. Cave,
Neil G. Champoux, William P. Ciekalowski,
Frank Cimini, Alfred H. Conz, George T. Cookman,
Albert Cote, Jeremiah J. Crane, Michael F. Curtin,
Charles Czyzewski, John J. Daley, John J. Daly,
Vernon R. Danforth, Robert L. Darrah,
Donald L. Decelles, Leonard Deinlein,
Parker A. Delaney, Donald M. Ducharme,
Richard E. Ellison, Robert I. Finn, Urban B. Fleming,
Daniel J. Foley, Robert F. Gallivan, William E. Gere,
John E. Gilbert, Francis J. Gleason, Edward Golash,
William E. Gore, Leonard Gougeon,
Henry J. Grochowski, Thomas M. Gutowski,
James L. Hall, Raymond J. Hibbard, James Higgins,
Bernard Jackimczyk, William S. Jackimczyk,
William Kablick, William G. Karparis,
Edward M. Kearns, William A. Kecy, Frank Keefe,
Robert E. Keyes, Aneta Kiley, Robert J. Kinney,
Robert Knight, Albert C. Krukowski,
Charles S. Ksieniewicz, Raymond Lavallee,
Bernard LaFlam, Raymond LeBeau, William E. Leary,
Stanley W. Lipski, Stanislaw Lojko,
Robert W. Loudfoot, Edwin Malinowski,
V.W. McBurnett, Earl McKinley, Jr., Joseph L. Miller,
William W. Montplaisir, Horace E. Morton,
Edward S. Mazuch, William K. Mutter, John F. Netto,
George E. Nolan, John W. O'Brien,
William J. O'Brien, Robert G. O'Connor,
Robert H. O'Shea, Joseph J. Okolo, Wilfred J. Paquette,
Patrick J. Powers, Michael J. Prasol, Arthur P. Pruzynski,
Kazimierz W. Puchalski, William W. Puchalski,
Havelock J. Purseglove, Raymond Racicot, Francis Rice,
Mitchell A. Rutkowski, James J. Ryan,
Edward J. Rydenski, George E. Senuta,
Zigmund Sieruta, Alvin G. Sinclair, Walter J. Siperek,
Charles C. Slater, William H. Smith, Benjamin Spungin,
Willard Straw, Joseph Subocz, Joseph F. Sullivan,
Edward G. Torrey, Jay E. Tremaine, James A. Vaughan,
Bernard F. Wilga, Edward Wong

Contents

Acknowledgements

Preface

Prologue

1. *1937-1940 — The Road Back* page 3
2. *1941 — Already in the War* page 12
3. *1941 — Remember Pearl Harbor* page 18
4. *1941 — A Date That Will Live in Infamy* page 28
5. *1942-1943 — Before We're Through With Them* page 36
6. *1942-1943 — Never Before in the History of Our City* page 52
7. *1943 — The End of the Beginning* page 64
8. *1943 — We Hated to See Those Telegrams* page 76
9. *1944 — The Beginning of the End* page 88
10. *1944 — Some Couldn't Even Remember Their Names* page 102
11. *1944 — People Here Haven't Seen a Thing* page 114
12. *1945 — A Long, Dirty, Bloody Business* page 126
13. *1945 — Welcome Home* page 142
14. *1945-1946 — The Fruits of Victory* page 158

Epilogue page 172

Photo and Graphics Acknowledgements

Index

Acknowledgements

Many people encouraged me as I worked on this, my third book, that endeavors to show how the Second World War affected a single American community, Northampton, Massachusetts. I first tried out the idea on my son, Charles Lockwood, himself the author of six books on urban architecture and cities. He urged me, as did his younger brother John, to pursue my dream.

In 1990, I married my kindred spirit, author-journalist-editor-publisher Richard Garvey whose understanding and appreciation of my effort to re-live WWII has sustained me throughout. I could always go to him for advice and comfort, and I did this.

I owe a special debt to two key persons who opened up my initial avenues of research. Peter DeRose, co-publisher of the *Daily Hampshire Gazette*, granted me access to the old bound volumes of that newspaper for 1941-1947, plus a hideaway in which to study those pages over one whole summer. Elise Bernier-Feeley, Reference Librarian of Forbes Library, Northampton, Massachusetts, introduced me to their World War II Collection instituted by onetime Librarian Joseph Harrison. She also handled my endless stream of reference questions with skill, speed and grace.

Two other always-dependable sources of help were: Robert E. Feeney, Director Military Records Section, Adjutant General's Office of Massachusetts; and Margery Sly, Archivist of Smith College. To these must be added: the staff of Congressman Richard E. Neal; Michael Baron, Librarian at Chicopee Public Library, Chicopee, Massachusetts; Blaise Bisaillon, Director of Forbes Library; O.A. Cooke, Chief Historical Archivist, Director General of History, Department of National Defense, Ottawa, Canada; Mark Richardson, summer-co-op student in the above-named office; Tibby Dennis, Reference Librarian, Forbes Library; Dorothy Frary, Librarian at Edwards Library, Southampton, Massachusetts; and Patricia Tugwell, Librarian, Pentagon Library, U.S. Department of Defense, Arlington, Virginia.

Anna Kwiecinski of Northampton and Patrick O'Keefe of Rockville, Maryland, tirelessly provided names of Northampton young people who took part in and of those who died in WWII, plus leads to surviving kin.

Thanks also to artist Nell Blaine of New York for permission to use the two poems of her deceased friend, onetime Sgt. Howard Griffin; to Jean Cohen for witnessing release-forms for taped interviews; to Maki Harano Hubbard, Ass't. Prof. East Asian Languages, Smith College, for her translation; and to Richard Lee, Executive Director, Hampshire County Chapter, American Red Cross, who opened wartime Director Nancy Trow's files to me.

Many citizens of Northampton taped their wartime recollections while others shared anecdotes, suggested names, dug out old photos and provided leads to persons long since removed from this city. To list them all would require another volume. This book will have to serve as my thank you to them.

The visual aspect of *Touched With Fire* is due to the talent and motivation of graphics-designer Florence DeRose. The text owes much to the painstaking craft of editor Marcy Larmon. Also appreciated is the work of several Gazette staff members, including photographer Brian House; Patricia Luchini who incorporated the manuscript into the *Gazette* system; Rick Richter, who was responsible for the computer-aided publishing; and Nancy Rhoades who functioned as our "message-center" and spent many hours double-checking the index.

Guardian Angel of this book has been Philippa Stromgren, assistant to the co-publishers of the *Gazette,* Peter and Charles DeRose. ''Pip'' kept all of our respective efforts coordinated and — despite all obstacles — ever moving forward. Her dedication, energy and enthusiasm were an inspiration to us all, and, most especially to the author.

Allison McCrillis Lockwood
Northampton, Massachusetts
17 May, 1993

Preface

The Second World War was a watershed experience for the United States. The comfortable political isolationism which followed the First World War was shattered. The Great Depression gave way to an unprecedented industrial growth and an escalating demand for labor. Women and racial minorities found new jobs, freedom and responsibilities. Even the American landscape changed: pastures became airfields, crossroads became cities, and entire industries sprung up in unknown places like Willow Run, Los Alamos and Oak Ridge.

For many Americans, the war would be the most significant landmark of their lives. Young people coming of age physically and mentally became part of a crusade which brought the greatest challenges they would ever face. Many faced personally the horrors of modern war, and their lives were never the same. Some would come to measure all the other events of their lives against their wartime experiences; others, even today, do not talk about the events they survived. Many did not survive; they paid for their country's struggle with their own lives.

In 1986, The Daily Hampshire Gazette published *Children of Paradise*, Allison McCrillis Lockwood's recollection about growing up in New England in the 1920s and 1930s. In 1990 Allison proposed a sequel which would take up where *Children of Paradise* left off. Her idea was to write not just a compilation of local history, but a view of the entire Second World War from the perspective of a single community.

Allison brings to her book a personal understanding of the war. She was 21 when the attack on Pearl Harbor brought America into the conflict. In 1943 she joined the United States Army. She was one of some 3000 men and women from Northampton who went off to war; 112 did not come back. *Touched With Fire* is about those who went to war and those who stayed home to work in defense plants, buy war bonds and take part in scrap drives. The story is a microcosm of what happened in cities and towns all over the United States. The battles and campaigns are here, from Pearl Harbor through North Africa, Normandy, Berlin, and the Pacific Islands to Tokyo Bay, but this is not a military history. It is the story of a community at war as seen through its own eyes.

The illustrations in *Touched With Fire* vary greatly. In some cases the only remaining images of men killed or lost overseas are faded newspaper halftones. In other cases personal photos, treasured by families for 50 years and now published for the first time, show the effects of the passing years. In spite of, or perhaps because of these handicaps, the 300 photos Allison has chosen for the book poignantly recapture the image of the world at war 50 years ago.

Allison's research began with back issues of the Gazette, but she used many other sources, most strikingly her own interviews. Men and women talked freely with her, some relating painful experiences they had never talked about before. It is their voices, and Allison's gift for incorporating them into her narrative, that make reading *Touched With Fire* such a moving experience. During this 50th anniversay of the Second World War, the Gazette is pleased and honored to publish Allison Lockwood's book. More than a story of a community in wartime, it stands as a memorial to those who gave their lives for freedom.

Peter L. DeRose
Co-Publisher, Daily Hampshire Gazette

O Kilroy
Voice in the wind, faintly answering Kilroy, Kilroy
You descended into Hell
And then you died
With a .30 M1 called "Dream Girl"
In your hands,
You rose from the dead
And ascended into heaven;
You are the Trinc we thought of and made real,
The Giant of ourselves, the epic wish,
Invulnerable and vast —
Dogface; ciphered identity —
Maybe you ? or the fellow in the torn fatigues
—or maybe me —
A sacred Name —
That sounds further than the great horn
At which the birds fell dead,
What act too low to be attributed
To you?
To rise to this high point,
A symbol of Desire,
Scribbled on shower-walls
A by word in the machiais of Honshu,
Written in fire across the swastikas —
Born of that martial preference
For plaques, gilt lettering and urns.

Kilroy
by Howard Griffin

Prologue

The Author as a Child

Allison McCrillis in the summer of 1924, in New Brunswick, at her grandparents' home. In the attic, she came upon an old army campaign hat left behind by her namesake.

One of my earliest memories is a soldier's photograph that sat on my mother's desk. In time I would learn this pleasant, earnest young face was that of an uncle I would never know.

Pvt. Allison Sharpe, Royal Canadian Regiment, was killed in the First World War while carrying a litter in the mud, at the battle called Passchendaele, on October 26, 1917. He was 20 years old.

All of the ephemera of Allison's brief life that were cherished first by his mother and then by his sister Sarah — my mother — now belong to me: his schoolbooks, his composition book, his letters home from England and France before his death, the official telegram reporting his death, and even the letter returned to her that his mother had written to him on the evening of the day he was killed by a German shell.

Among these keepsakes are also a few faded photographs taken by my mother with the Brownie box camera she used all her life. One is of myself standing beneath some trees at the old New Brunswick homestead. I appear to be about 4 years old. In front of me I am clutching an old army campaign-type hat left behind by my namesake. Less than two decades later, my mother would be photographing me with that same camera in a military uniform and cap of my own. This symbolizes, it seems to me, the fact that those of us born at the end of the First World War were fated to be the spear-carriers for the second.

On May 17, 1943, three days before Commencement at Smith College, I left Northampton to enter the U.S. Army. I received my diploma in a cardboard tube as I stood at mail call on a company street at Fort Devens, where I underwent basic training. This constituted my graduation. For the next three years, classified as an Army Public Relations Man (*sic*), I would write my way through the Second World War — a sobering experience for a young woman in her early twenties.

Forty-three years later, after a lifetime lived primarily in Washington, D.C., I came back to Northampton where I had been born and reared. On the Sunday afternoon of December 7, 1986, I headed for a ceremony to commemorate the anniversary of this country's entry into World War II following the Japanese attack on Pearl Harbor exactly 45 years earlier.

Killed in World War I

Pvt. Allison Sharpe was killed in action at Passchendaele on October 26, 1917. Author Allison McCrillis Lockwood never knew her uncle, although she is named for him.

Accustomed to crowds during my years in the nation's capital, I hastened to Memorial Hall on Main Street so as to secure a vantage spot from which to view the proceedings. I need not have hurried, for at the brief ceremony led by Mayor David Musante, I proved to be the only spectator. Except for the few participating veterans, a passing policeman and myself, nobody came.

I was dismayed — perhaps depressed is a better word — that the citizens of Northampton had chosen to ignore this recollection of the ominous day that plunged the nation into World War II and changed all our lives forever. It seemed that Northampton had also forgotten all about the more than one hundred citizens of the city who died in that war.

It was at that moment that I determined to try to show what happened to the city itself as the result of World War II, and especially what happened to a representative handful of its 3,000 sons and daughters who went off to that war. This book is the result.

Many historians today view the years 1939-1945 as the greatest cataclysm in human history. The Second World War was fought on six continents and forced approximately 70 million young men to bear arms, primarily through conscription. Around 17 million of them were killed. Non-combatants also perished by the millions, in bombing raids, of starvation and disease, in extermination camps, as hostages and as prisoners of war. Estimates of the total WWII dead run about 50 million altogether. No one will ever know the true figure.

For the United States, the human cost of the war was far less than that for the other major participants. But it was high. A total of 16,353,659 American men and women served in the military. Of these, 407,316 died, including the 292,131 killed in actual combat. There were 670,846 wounded.

A small New England city of 24,794 in 1941, Northampton would pay its share of the price of this war. Besides the 112 who lost their lives, there were 128 wounded — some so seriously that they would die young as a result. Others have had to deal all their lives with the effects of their wounds. Twenty-three young men had to endure the special anguish of prisoners of war, four of them in the merciless hands of the Japanese for three-and-a-half years. Two did not survive this captivity.

There are other wounds of war: memories. And here in Northampton, even today, there are brothers, sisters and widows of this city's WWII dead who are still mourning their loss.

There are old veterans, too, haunted by memories and still trying to deal with their unconsummated grief. Fifty of them agreed to be tape-recorded for this book, while others granted interviews. Two men located said they still could not talk about their WWII experience. One of these men survived torpedoing in the Atlantic; the other somehow came out alive from the Huertgen Forest, called "the Death Factory" by those who fought there. All the others were able and willing to relate their moments of truth.

Uncle's Gravesite

Pvt. Allison Sharpe's grave at Vlamertinghe in Belgium. More than 500,000 Allied soldiers' graves are here in "Flanders Fields" of WWI memory.

"I want you to know," confided a onetime 19-year-old medical corpsman, "that I've shared things with you on this tape that I've never told another human being."

As these veterans spoke, there were awkward pauses, frequent throat clearings and fists opening and closing compulsively. Once a kitchen table began to shake, or so I thought until I realized that it was the man leaning on that table who was shaking. There were tremors in voices, apologies for "being too emotional" and even tears. Both of us wept as a former lieutenant, commissioned on the battlefield in France, related how his friend, who had replaced him as platoon sergeant, was blown away before his eyes by a German shell.

At such moments, certain veterans expressed wonder and something akin to guilt that they had survived when so many of their comrades were killed. "I came through without even a scratch," one of these men murmured. Asked how he would explain this, he answered, "Just lucky, I guess."

Recalled Joanna Hathaway Grimes, who went into Normandy as an Army nurse shortly after D Day: "It was life and death at age 21. We were already dealing with death when we had barely begun to live."

When, near the end of each taping session or interview, the veterans were asked to rank the personal significance of their WWII experience on a scale of 1 to 10, almost without exception their answers were: "Ten! Right at the top!"

The primary reference source for *Touched With Fire* proved to be the old bound volumes of Northampton's newspaper, the Daily Hampshire Gazette. I spent the summer of

1989 perusing these pages, dated October of 1941 through 1947. The story of the war is all there; national and international news, plus reports — often including maps — from the various theaters of war. Also recorded in detail were the daily events of life in wartime Northampton.

A special everyday feature of the Gazette during these war years was a section initially entitled "Reports On The Boys In Service" — soon changed to "News Of Our Men and Women In Uniform." Here appeared articles based on excerpts from letters sent home to parents, together with features on local men and women at war, sent from afar by military public-relations writers like myself. The sad reports of death, wounding or capture were reserved for the front page.

The civilian side of the war rolled out each day on the same pages. Save for some rationing of scarce items, salvage drives, war bond campaigns and elaborate preparations against enemy bombing that never occurred, life in Northampton seems to have continued much as usual, except for the new war-fueled prosperity that finally ended the Great Depression. The WWII experience for most American civilians proved quite different from that overseas, where noncombatants sometimes ended up in the middle of battle itself.

The much-publicized rationing here in America, for example, never remotely approached the deprivation experienced in war-ravaged countries. Most Americans were living better than they had since the Golden Twenties. In 1933, 25.2 percent of the work force was recorded as unemployed, and statisticians today believe the figure was probably even higher. By 1944, the figure was down to 1.2 percent. New cities, industries, fortunes and even a large new middle class were evolving out of the war. The nation was launched on an ever-upward spiral of prosperity destined to continue for more than four decades.

Thus, according to Paul Fussell, author of *Wartime: Understanding Behavior in the Second World War,* the United States never actually experienced the total reality of that war. Today a distinguished professor of English literature at the University of Pennsylvania, Fussell was, during WWII, severely wounded in France as a 20-year-old platoon lieutenant with the 103rd Infantry Division.

For Americans on the homefront, Fussell believes, the war was seen through a haze of public relations, "systematically sanitized and Norman Rockwellized, not to mention Disneyfied." America "has not yet understood what the Second World War was like and has thus been unable to use such understanding to re-interpret and re-define the national reality and to arrive at something like public maturity."

That Fussell's ideal of "public maturity" will ever now be attained is unlikely. Those Americans who did experience WWII are a vanishing breed. Of the 16 million veterans of that war, only nine million are left, and these are rapidly shipping out for the last time. Ten veterans interviewed for this book have not lived to see its publication. The American public, moreover, reads little historical material, while the public schools have so de-emphasized the subject of history that Newsweek magazine recently reported: "Nearly one-third of American 17-year-olds cannot even identify which countries the U.S. fought against in the Second World War."

The Canadian historian James T. Stokesbury writes that "utopia will never arrive. Progress there is and undeniably so. But every step forward ... every solution to one generation's difficulties brings with it a new set. ... World War II certainly created as many problems as it solved; in fact, as most wars seem to do, it may have created more. That does not mean it was not worth fighting, or need not have been fought."

"Evil does exist in the world," believes Stokesbury. "It undeniably existed in Hitler's world of death camps and extermination groups — but without the possibility of evil, there is no true choice and no true freedom. In its basic definition, 'Freedom' means the right to choose one's own way to die. ... The men and women of the free nations who fought World War II chose their own doom. If they could not destroy every evil, they destroyed the most vicious of their day. If it is part of the sadness of the human condition that they could not solve the problems of their children's generation, it is part of the glory of it that they so resolutely faced their own."

Touched with Fire

1937 - 1940 — The Road Back

On a brisk October morning in 1937 my fellow students and I were dismissed from classes at Northampton High School and herded over to our city's nearby opera house and theater, the Academy of Music. We were to view a new anti-war film, "The Road Back," based on a recent novel by German author Erich Maria Remarque.

As I look back, I recall that we were far more pleased at the respite from sessions in Latin and Chemistry than by the prospect of a movie with the solemn thesis that the western nations were once again on the road to war, only one generation after the 1914-1918 conflict still known as "the war to end all wars." Like most teen-agers, in those days we were preoccupied with matters such as pimples, popularity, and the future awaiting us on our graduation from high school in the middle of the Great Depression.

"This generation of Americans has a rendezvous with destiny," President Franklin Roosevelt had proclaimed in his second nomination speech in the summer of 1936. Struggling to be young and carefree during those hard times of the 1930s, we had thought that he meant our care-worn parents; a few years later we discovered that it was ourselves.

Those of us born at the end of the First World War grew up in that strange island of time between the two great wars. The Golden Twenties shaped our childhood; the Great Depression marked our adolescence. And we came of age just in time for our "rendezvous with destiny."

Adolescence is a time of storm and stress at best, but for those few among us who did manage to look beyond the confines of our quiet New England town of Northampton, it seemed as though a world gone mad awaited us. William L. Shirer, an American correspondent in Berlin in the 1930s, would one day label that decade "the nightmare years."

These "nightmare years" began in 1931 when, bent on conquest, Japan marched into the three northern provinces of China, thus launching the 14-year Sino-Japanese War.

In October 1935, likewise in search of empire, the fascist dictator of Italy, Benito Mussolini, zeroed in on Ethiopia in Africa. By January of the following year he was boasting of 10,000 slain Ethiopians, and in May his troops captured Addis Ababa, the capital.

In March of 1936 Adolf Hitler ordered troops into the Rhineland, which had been taken away from Germany by the Treaty of Versailles. "If the French had marched," admitted the Nazi dictator later, "we would have had to withdraw with our tail between our legs." But no one marched, and thus Hitler was free to launch his plan for the conquest of Europe.

1936 also saw the start of the Spanish Civil War, that long struggle between the Republicans and the Fascists. Atrocities were committed on both sides; more than 200,000 people died. On April 26, 1937, the Nazi Condor Legion, sent by Hitler to aid the Spanish Fascists, bombed Guernica, killing more than 1,000 civilians and destroying 70 percent of the city. Such horrors were to become commonplace during the next eight years.

In December 1937, the Japanese entered China's industrial city of Nanking, commencing a four-week-long butchery during which more than 200,000 men, women and children died.

One of the vessels patrolling the Yangtze River, the gunboat U.S.S. *Panay*, had taken

Paradise Pond, Northampton, Massachusetts

While other parts of the world were filled with scenes of war, the people of Northampton enjoyed the tranquil beauty of Paradise Pond.

3

on board a small group of American and European officials and journalists seeking to escape Nanking. On Sunday, December 12, about 28 miles above the city, the *Panay* was attacked by three Japanese bombers and six smaller planes. After two hours of bombs and machine-gunning, she had to be abandoned, and soon sank. One American sailor was killed; 15 people were wounded and 18 were missing. Nine sailors, later decorated, had manned their machine guns until the end — among them Maurice David Rider of Southampton, Mass. A formal apology was later presented by Ambassador Hirosi Saito to U.S. Secretary of State Cordell Hull.

In the United States, all of these disturbing international conflicts caused increasing speculation about inevitable U.S. involvement, along with a corresponding call by many groups for peace. In Northampton, there were periodic parades by Smith College students carrying signs and banners reading "Women's International League for Peace and Freedom," "The New Patriotism Is Peace" and "Don't Fight!" Professor Francis Osborn, their mentor, proclaimed that the aim of his group, the Emergency Peace Campaign, was "to keep the U.S. from going to war and to keep war out of the U.S." In 1936, another Smith College professor, Oliver Larkin, announced a local anti-war essay contest, with a 10 dollar first prize, sponsored by the "American League Against War and Fascism."

Despite the vigorous efforts of President Roosevelt, just returned to the White House for a second term by a landslide vote, the Great Depression was still with us in 1936. There were almost 10 million unemployed in our nation of 128 million people, and in Northampton itself there were still 509 families on relief. A "real drive on the Depression" was to start in July, the President promised, with a sum equal to more than $66 for every person in the nation to be spent through allocations to government agencies such as the Works Projects Administration, the Public Works Administration and the Civilian Conservation Corps, as well as to the Army and the Navy.

In April of 1938, Hitler's troops were welcomed to Vienna and then permitted to take over all of Austria in the so-called *Anschluss*. Mistreatment of Vienna's Jews soon

Rudolph Mathias: Refugee From Hitler's Germany

In the autumn of 1938, a bright, handsome young Jewish refugee from Nazi Germany joined Northampton High School's Class of 1939. He would later serve in the U.S. Army Air Corps as an instructor at Wright Patterson Field.

The Battle of the Atlantic: Nazi U-boats versus Allied Naval Vessels and Supply Ships

The bitter five-year Battle of the Atlantic began September 3, 1939, the day Britain declared war on Germany.

World Leaders

left to right: Franklin D. Roosevelt, President of the United States, 1933-45; Joseph Stalin, Premier of the Union of Soviet Socialist Republics, 1942-53; Benito Mussolini, Fascist Dictator of Italy, 1922-43; Adolf Hitler, Nazi Dictator of Germany, 1934-45. These four men led their nations through the Great Depression and WWII.

The 1938 Hurricane

While Czechoslovakia was being betrayed and turned over to Hitler, Northampton was struck by the savage and unexpected hurricane that hit New England on September 21, 1938. As negotiations went on in Munich, Northampton suffered power outages, floods, and downed trees from 80- to 90-mile-an-hour winds.

followed, and by August Northampton's newspaper, the Daily Hampshire Gazette, was reporting that "more than 1,000 Jews have escaped Austria during the past month." That autumn a refugee from Hitler's Germany itself, Rudolph Mathias, joined our high school Class of 1939. Today, he remembers his senior year in Northampton as a time of "healing over some of the trauma and wounds of persecution and flight."

A copy of Hitler's *Mein Kampf*, in which the Nazi leader had publicly confided his plans for the destruction of Judeo-Christian civilization, was readily available in Northampton's public Forbes Library at this time. The small number of due-dates at the back, however, seemed an indication that few people were reading it. Perhaps Americans were getting enough of *der Fuehrer* in the pages of their newspapers, as well as through the guttural harangues to his German adherents that were beamed to us over radio from Berlin, with intermittent bits of translation by William Shirer. "The March Of Time," a favorite radio program, had even recorded for us the sound of Nazi jackboots marching into Vienna.

Thomas Hogan, a Holyoke schoolboy in 1936, would one day find himself an 18-year-old Marine in the Pacific theater of World War II. He recalled that he followed world events all during the tumultuous 1930s. "I knew there would be a big war, and I fully expected to be in it. Others were much less aware, I think."

At Munich, in September 1938, after considerable negotiation in the interests of "appeasement" (soon to be a dirty word), France and Britain handed Czechoslovakia over to Hitler for dismemberment in order to preserve "peace in our time" as Neville Chamberlain, the British Prime Minister, proclaimed. At that time in Northampton, however, our attention was almost totally distracted by a fearful hurricane on September 21 and the terrible flood that followed. Families were driven from their homes, countless trees were lost and for several weeks many houses were without electricity. We students were back in high school within a couple of days, however, with no cessation of homework, trying to study at night by candle, gaslight, or whatever our harassed parents could provide.

One year later, Remarque's prophecy in *The Road Back* became reality. Hitler's Panzers roared into Poland at 4:45 on the morning of September 1, 1939. On September 3, to keep their treaty commitments, Britain and France declared war on Germany. Screaming headlines in the Gazette proclaimed: "Germany Launches Lightning Attack — Aims To Crush Poland Quickly ... British Forces Soon In Action On Western Front ... Hitler Promises FDR Not To Bomb Cities And Towns ... President Feels U.S. Can Keep Out Of War."

Also on September 3, the British ship S.S. *Athenia* was sunk by a German U-boat 200 miles southwest of Scotland's Outer Hebrides. This was later perceived as the first blow in the epic struggle to become known as the Battle of the Atlantic, which continued throughout the war, as Nazi U-boats sought to cut Britain's supply lifeline by sinking the merchant ships that carried food and war materiel to that beleaguered island.

There were 1,100 civilian passengers aboard the *Athenia*, most of them Canadian but

"Peace In Our Time:"
Neville Chamberlain

Prime Minister Neville Chamberlain of Great Britain announced "peace in our time" after the fateful Munich conference at which France and Britain handed over Czechoslovakia to Hitler. A year later Hitler invaded Poland.

Another World War Begins: September 1, 1939

Picking up the Gazette on their front porches the evening of September 1, 1939, residents of Northampton were greeted by headlines announcing the outbreak of war in Europe, 21 years after the armistice that had ended what was still being called "The World War."

Smith College Professor Survives Torpedoing

Smith College professor Margaret Rooke was among the 1,103 passengers aboard the British liner Athenia, which was sunk by a German U-boat the night of September 3, 1939. The death toll was 112, including 28 U.S. citizens. Prof. Rooke, on the right in this photo, was one of the survivors.

128 of them American — all anxiously seeking to return home and escape the war in Europe. One hundred and twelve passengers died, including 28 Americans. Among the *Athenia's* survivors was Margaret Rooke, a professor of Italian at Smith College. Interviewed on landing at Montreal, she observed, "I didn't feel excited when it happened, but I was frightfully mad at the Huns for getting us right away. I wouldn't have missed the experience for anything." She and the other survivors in their lifeboats had been rescued by British, Norwegian and American ships that hurried to the scene while the *Athenia* heeled sharply and her bow settled in the sea.

By the first of October, Nazi U-boats had sunk 30 British vessels. During the month of September alone, American ships entered our ports with almost a thousand rescued survivors from these sinkings. Before it was through, more than 30,000 British and 5,000 American merchant seamen, plus thousands of sailors from both nations, would die in this deadly contest on the sea. Britain would lose 4,786 merchant ships between 1939 and 1945.

In this period an American trawler captain made news with his report claiming that a large plane, clearly marked with a swastika, had circled his vessel in the Atlantic only 190 miles southeast of Boston. A London photo of young Joseph Kennedy, the American ambassador's son, showed him assisting American citizens intent on getting out of England and returning home.

In Northampton, a local branch of the British War Relief Society opened in a rent-free storefront at 20A Crafts Avenue. Members of this national organization, created to provide clothing, food and other needs to that war-torn nation, wore a handsome enameled pin of red-white-blue that sported a defiant golden lion. Miles of grey-blue yarn were doled out for local women to knit into long, warm mufflers for the Royal Air Force, while other knitters labored over dark-blue "watch caps" for the Royal Navy and olive-drab gloves for the British Army.

After weeks of bombardment and aerial attack, the city of Warsaw finally surrendered to Hitler on September 27. Poland's defeat was noted in Northampton in the big parade marking the opening on October 12, 1939, of the Calvin Coolidge Memorial Bridge across the Connecticut River. A float created by the local Polish Women's Alliance of America featured two young women, in Polish national costume, kneeling by a soldier's grave. In this same parade appeared a highly polished pick-up truck neatly decorated with red, white and blue bunting and American flags. Its sign read: "German-American

Citizens Association."

Despite the ominous events across the sea, many American teen-agers, maturing just in time to become the major players in the coming drama, were still not truly aware of their approaching fate. Life in Northampton continued pretty much as it always had. On September 7, 1939, many of us flocked as usual to the annual Three-County Fair, and a few even made it to the World's Fair in New York. A new Northampton High School under construction was already demonstrating that its final cost would exceed, by at least $30,000, the estimated outlay of $750,000. Edwin Olander, Jr., son of the local state senator of the same name, announced that he would seek the Republican nomination for school committeeman-at-large. The Manse, one of Northampton's oldest and most historic houses, occupied by only two families for many generations, went on the market and many of its precious antique pieces were auctioned off.

When Smith College opened on September 25, 1939, 45 young Northampton women, taking advantage of the full tuition then available to local residents, were in the audience that welcomed Elizabeth Cutter Morrow, class of 1896, as acting president following the retirement of William Allan Neilson.

"Think serenely," she advised us. "Your duty is to study hard to try ... to understand some of the causes that have brought about this frightful conflict ... stretch your minds in every course. ... Be good girls. Learn your lessons. ... Thank God that you are here."

On that same day, the Gazette carried news of the death of 2nd. Lt. Robert O'Connor of Northampton, a 22-year-old Army Air Corps pilot killed in an accident while teaching an Argentinian officer to fly. Photos of handsome young faces like that of O'Connor — men killed in the service of their country — were to become commonplace two years later.

Already the war in Europe was beginning to manifest its ironic effect on the still stark economic situation of the American Depression. A noted New York economic analyst, Merryle Ruckeyser, quoted in the Gazette, referred to what he called "Hitler Prosperity" and warned that the "war-mongers of Europe" would end America's Depression — but only at a high price. Along with the rest of New England, Northampton soon would learn that war is good for business, but you have to invest your sons.

As the year wound down through that glorious New England autumn of 1939, Capt. Leon Lavallee, commanding officer of the local Company G of the Massachusetts National Guard, disclosed that he had been instructed to recruit additional men to bring his unit up to a complement of 79. President Roosevelt was increasing the strength of the Army, Navy, Marine Corps and National Guard units throughout the country, with the National Guard alone expected to reach 235,000 men.

Meanwhile, a group of anti-war mothers in Springfield was urging Northampton women to join them in forming a similar organization. Those interested were invited to a meeting in Springfield on October 3. At the same time, the Gazette was offering a war map of Europe to its readers for only 10 cents. "It will show you just where the bombs are falling, towns are being captured, and ships are being torpedoed," the promotion read. "It will help you understand the radio broadcasts and the articles in the daily press."

***

If 1939 had been a strange and turbulent year, 1940 would prove even more so. One of the strangest events was the publication of a book by Anne Morrow Lindbergh, a distinguished Smith alumna and wife of the national aviation hero, Charles Lindbergh. The title was *The Wave of the Future*, and in it she expressed her thesis that the war in Europe was not, as many people seemed to think, a crusade against the "Forces of Evil." What, she asked, "was pushing behind Nazism? Is it nothing but a 'return to barbarism' to be crushed at all cost by a 'crusade'? Or is it some new, and perhaps even ultimately good, conception of humanity trying to come to birth, often through evil and horrible forms and abortive attempts?" The leaders of Germany, Italy and Russia had "discovered how to use new social and economic forces; very often they have used them badly, but nevertheless they have recognized and used them," she wrote. "They have felt the wave of the future and they have leapt upon it." During the summer of 1940, *The Wave of the Future*

The Fall of Warsaw

After weeks of bombing and artillery bombardment, Warsaw, the capital of Poland, surrendered to the Nazis on September 27, 1939. Polish-Americans in Northampton marked that event with their float in the parade celebrating the opening of the new Calvin Coolidge Memorial Bridge over the Connecticut River on October 12. Entitled "Poland Today," the float featured two young women in Polish national costume kneeling at "the grave of a Polish soldier."

Lt. Robert O'Connor, 1917-1939

The death of Lt. Robert O'Connor, a flight instructor at Randolph Field, Texas, the "West Point of the Air," was a portent of things to come for other young men of Northampton and many communities across the country. O'Connor was killed when a plane piloted by an Argentine Army officer crashed during a routine training flight.

St. Paul's Still Stands

On the night of December 29, 1940, London's famed neo-classical cathedral, designed by Sir Christopher Wren, stood in a sea of flames during a German incendiary-bombing raid. St. Paul's was saved by hard-pressed London firefighters and the cathedral's own heroic air-raid wardens. In this single month of December, 3,793 British civilians were killed.

appalled those Americans who were watching the progress of what is now called the Battle of Britain.

Since the sudden collapse and surrender of France on June 21, Britain had stood alone. Hitler was the master of Europe and now could address himself to the conquest of the small island nation still opposing him across the English Channel.

The Battle of Britain began with what the Nazis called the *Adlerangriff* (Eagle Attack) on August 13, when 1,485 Luftwaffe planes roared in to try to knock out the airdromes of the Royal Air Force (RAF). The German pilots would later admit their surprise at the skill of the young and inexperienced British pilots who rose to meet them. Forty-five German aircraft went down that day — at a cost of 13 RAF fighters. On August 15, 520 German bombers and 1,270 fighters struck; 75 were shot down at a cost of 34 RAF planes. But within a few days, we now know, the RAF had lost its capacity to put men and planes in the air. On August 19 there were no German planes over England; the Luftwaffe, also hard hit, failed to appear. Prime Minister Winston Churchill confided to a colleague that evening: "They are making a big mistake in giving us a respite." It was before the House of Commons the next day that he paid his memorable tribute to the 2,500 pilots of the RAF: "Never in the field of human conflict was so much owed by so many to so few."

Having failed in his plan to destroy Britain's air power, Hitler now made the mistake of turning away from attacking British airdromes, although in fact he had come perilously close to destroying the RAF's ability to fight. Now he started bombing English cities. On September 7, for example, 300 Nazi bombers and 600 fighter-escorts stormed in two waves over the London dock area: 448 Londoners died. By September 17, however, Hitler postponed his invasion of Britain "until further notice."

Now began the "Blitz," — German for "lightning" — during which, night after night, Nazi bombers attacked London and other English cities. Over a seven-month period, 28,859 British civilians would be killed and 40,166 seriously injured.

By this time the RAF was retaliating with attacks on Berlin at night, with one bomb landing smack in the garden of the Nazi Propaganda Minister, Joseph Goebbels. From the German capital, correspondent Shirer described one of these raids: "The concentration of antiaircraft fire was the greatest I've ever seen ... a magnificent, a terrible sight. ...

But not a plane was brought down; not one was even picked up by the searchlights which flashed back and forth frantically across the skies." No Berliners died on that particular night, but some of them did pick up and read the leaflets dropped by the RAF: "The war which Hitler started will go on, and it will last as long as Hitler does."

Here in the United States, on September 16, 1940, an event occurred that now seems to have presaged our own inevitable involvement in the war. On that day, the Selective Service Act became law. There had been a long and tough battle in Congress before the passage of the Burke-Wadsworth Bill, but as one member of the House recalled later, "Every time they bombed London, we gained a vote or two."

Eventually called "the draft," bureaucratic machinery was now organized by the United States government for the registration of 16,500,000 American men between 21 and 35 years of age. By a lottery draft, an Army of 1.4 million men was to be raised through compulsory military induction. Their numbers would be added to those of the regular Army, which in 1939 numbered only 137,000 men. Seventy-one percent of the public supported the new law, since the draftees would serve only one year and were not to be sent outside the Western Hemisphere except to territories of the United States. After October 16, every American man was required to register with his local Selective Service Board on his 21st birthday and henceforth to carry with him his "draft card." First to register in Northampton was Donald Delaney.

Less than a year later, after considerable controversy, the one year of compulsory service would be extended to two-and-a-half years for draftees, men in the regular Army, Reservists and National Guardsmen alike. Thus did the long arm of the federal government reach into our small New England community in a new and sobering way.

Selective Service Board 117 made its headquarters in the old yellow-brick high school, at the corner of South and Main Streets, that had been vacated once the new high school on Elm Street opened that same year. Members of "the draft board," as people called it, included Judge William Welch as chairman, Ted Clapp as clerk, and members Jesse Andre, Alfred Grant, John Nolan and Fred Paulson. As these men organized their local office, it was estimated that 3,570 Northampton men would be registered on October 16.

In November three young men volunteered to be the first draftees sent from North-

Winston Churchill, Prime Minister of Great Britain

Alone in their defiance of Hitler by the summer of 1940, the British people rallied round "Winnie," their charismatic prime minister who offered only "blood, sweat, toil and tears." He warned Hitler: "We shall fight on the beaches, the landing ground ... in the fields ... in the streets ... in the hills. We shall never surrender."

First in Northampton to Register Under the Selective Service Act

On October 16, 1940, Donald Delaney, on the right, was one of 16,500,000 young men between 21-35 who had to register for the draft. Following the example of his older brother, Parker, Delaney enlisted in the U.S. Navy and became a radio man. He survived the war, but his brother was killed when his torpedo-bomber went down off Truk, in the Pacific, in April of 1944.

Willkie vs. Roosevelt: A Tough Campaign

The Republican contender for the presidency in 1940 was Wendell Willkie of Indiana.

The popular vote was close, but Willkie won only 82 electoral votes to Roosevelt's 449.

ampton. They were Edward Garvey, John Krol and Durbin Wells. On the twentieth of the month this trio was given a public farewell and serenaded on the City Hall steps by the Northampton High School Band. Judge Welch himself drove the men to Springfield, followed by "a cavalcade of relatives and friends," the Gazette reported. All three passed their physicals and that same afternoon left for basic training at Fort Devens.

These three soldiers would find themselves serving almost five years: Garvey ended up as a staff sergeant in the 104th Division in the European Theater, where he would earn a Bronze Star; Krol as a technical sergeant in Australia; and Wells as a captain in the quartermaster section of the 13th Air Force in the Pacific.

Another young Northampton man, in the autumn of 1940, was seen driving away from his wedding with a "Conscription Can't Get Me Now" attached to the rear of his car. Before long the bridegroom would learn the error of that belief.

The draft boards exercised enormous power in American communities. Usually consisting of five men, prominent in business and the professions, many were themselves veterans of the First World War. Technically they were federal officials, with letters of appointment from the President, but they served without pay. Their instructions came from Washington, but all decisions concerning individual men were their own responsibility. It was the choices of such men all over the United States that largely determined the composition of our armed forces that would fight in the coming war.

Not all of the draftees passed their physicals in Springfield, although most of them very much wanted to. It seemed to be a matter of masculine pride. The Gazette reported that the highest percentage of "muscularly superior and well-developed types come from the New England states." The newspaper also revealed that, according to a federal report on education in 1942, Northampton ranked high, "with its average adult equipped with 9.4 years of formal education," compared to an average for the nation as a whole of 8.4 years.

Apparently there were no conscientious objectors in Northampton itself, but some showed up in nearby towns. "Boards in some surrounding towns and cities have had to deal with numerous objectors, and these," reported the Gazette on October 4, 1941, "have been sent to Conscientious Objection Camps." Some of them were Jehovah's Witnesses who refused to swear the inductees' oath, just as young Witnesses did in Germany. During the war, 14,000 American men would be imprisoned for resisting the draft. One local case involved a 30-year-old recluse in Chesterfield, a small rural town outside Northampton, who was "opposed to indiscriminate killing of people because of their nationality." Gregory Carhart failed several times to report to the draft board and threatened "to shoot it out with the FBI" if necessary. When, in 1942, his case was finally turned over to the U.S. District Attorney, Carhart failed the physical — thus ending the matter.

In nearby Easthampton, however, a young Jehovah's Witness, Walter Dziubek, the brother of a Marine, was in 1943 sentenced by the Federal Court in Boston to three years in the penitentiary.

In November 1940, President Roosevelt ran for an unprecedented third term. He had to wage a tough campaign against the gravel-voiced but articulate Republican candidate, Wendell Willkie, whose party platform included a strong plank against intervention in the war. FDR defeated Willkie handily in the electoral vote, 449 to 82. The popular vote, however, was close, with 29,263,448 votes to Willkies's 22,336,260. It was perhaps an awareness of Willkie's strength that led the new President, in a speech before a Boston audience packed with Irish-American isolationists on October 30, to make the following declaration that later came back to haunt him: "I give you one more assurance. I have said this before, but I shall say it again and again and again. Your boys are not going to be sent to foreign wars."

That same autumn, Navy Secretary Frank Knox visited the Territory of Hawaii to view our naval installations at Pearl Harbor. On his return to Washington, Knox announced that "the United States has the greatest, the most powerful, and the most effective fleet on the high seas anywhere in the world."

On December 29, 1940, the Nazi Luftwaffe carried out its worst incendiary raid yet, on the City of London's financial district. A wide swathe of fire raged on both sides of the Thames, and many ancient and historic buildings were destroyed, including the Guildhall. Eight of Sir Christopher Wren's churches were destroyed or heavily damaged. Paternoster Row, the book-publishing center, was leveled, and St. Paul's Cathedral was saved only by the fearless diligence of its own crew of firefighters. Civilian deaths in Britain for December alone numbered 3,793.

As that fateful year drew to its close, the picture looked black — at least to those Americans who actually looked across the sea and followed the war news. Britain stood alone against the Nazis, who now dominated the continent of Europe. Japan was on the threshold of dominion over the Far East. China was a virtually helpless giant carved up among the Japanese invaders, Chiang Kai-shek and his corrupt Kuomintang, and the Chinese Communists. Much confused, the American people — including many in Northampton — were now splitting themselves into two groups: the isolationists and the interventionists. There were still many citizens, however, who somehow managed to ignore altogether the possibility that as a nation we were already on the road back to another multi-national conflagration whose name had yet to become familiar to us: World War II.

Future Veterans of Foreign Wars

As Northampton High School's basketball team played their games of the 1938-1939 season, much of Europe and Asia were involved in the deadly game of war. All but two of these young men were to end up in the military services. Charles "Caesar" McDonald, Mitchell Susco, and Challenger Whitham were all wounded in combat. Rudolph Arel was killed in action in Europe on April 13, 1945.

Left to right, back row: Albert Cullen, U.S. Navy; Challenger Whitham, U.S. Army Air Corps. Center Row: Earl Tonet, U.S. Marine Corps; William McDonald, U.S. Coast Guard; Charles McDonald, U.S. Army Paratroops; Donald O'Shea, U.S. Army; Joseph Fungaroli; Ugo Bona, U.S. Merchant Marine; Coach David Wright. Front row: George Adam; Ralph Jabonowski, U.S. Navy; Raymond Kneeland, U.S. Marine Corps; Rudolph Arel, U.S. Army; Edward Kelsey, U.S. Army; Mitchell Susco, U.S. Army.

Company G Leaves Northampton

On January 27, 1941, with their commanding officer, Maj. Leon Lavallee at the head of the column, Company G, 104th Infantry, Massachusetts National Guard, left the National Guard Armory on King Street, headed toward the railroad station.

1941 — Already in the War

"The United States is already in the war and has been for some time," proclaimed Wendell Willkie, the defeated Republican presidential candidate, in November 1941. The nation as a whole was still not ready to accept such statements as truth.

In Northampton, an indication of things to come had been revealed by a photograph in the Daily Hampshire Gazette as early as January 27, 1941. In that photo, members of Company G, 104th Infantry, Massachusetts National Guard, were shown marching out of the Armory on King Street headed for Union Station. In full winter uniform and with Springfield rifles dating from 1903 slung over their shoulders, these young men were bound for Camp Edwards near Falmouth for their one year of compulsory military service. At the head of the company was their commanding officer, Maj. Leon Lavallee. Their regiment had just been federalized, and many of the men — although they did not realize it on that snowy January morning in 1941 — would end up serving almost five years in some of the hottest combat of World War II. After basic training they would be sent to North Carolina on maneuvers. They would return to Camp Edwards on Saturday afternoon, December 6, just one day before the Japanese attacked Pearl Harbor.

Starting in January of 1942, the company would serve first on coastal patrol duty at Portsmouth, N.H., and later at Brunswick, Ga. When the 182nd Regiment was split off from the Yankee Division, certain of the men would find themselves shipped to the Pacific as part of a newly formed task force that would be called the Americal Division (Americans in Caledonia). There is today at Fort Devens, Massachusetts, a museum devoted to that division's exploits during the war out in the Pacific. Others in Company G were to end up in some of the heaviest fighting in the European Theater, where several would be killed in action.

Maj. Lavallee himself would serve in the China-Burma-India Theater for almost two years. Four of his sons would also serve in WWII, and one of these, 1st Sgt. Raymond Lavallee, would die in North Africa in 1943.

On March 1, a contingent of 76 local draftees reported at the train station at 8 a.m. to leave for induction in Springfield. Eight of these men, a shocking percentage, were destined to die in the war that would begin nine months later: Francis Ansanitis, Bernard Jackimczyk, William Jackimczyk, Robert Keyes, William Leary, John Netto, George Nolan and William Puchalski.

From that time on, similar large groups of men would depart at regular intervals, following the ritual Union Station photograph with the old Bay State Hotel in the background.

There was mounting evidence of the approach of war all through 1941 on both the national and international scene. President Roosevelt made one move after another that, according to his critics, was drawing the United States closer to the brink of the conflict.

These had begun in September 1940, when, in answer to Prime Minister Winston Churchill's urgent appeal, Roosevelt agreed to trade 50 "over-age" destroyers to Britain in exchange for 99-year leases on British air and naval bases in the Western Hemisphere.

"The decision for 1941 lies upon the seas," Churchill rightly predicted, and, during that year, those 50 old "tubs" would constitute nearly one-fourth of all the destroyer-escorts available to protect the ship convoys en route to Britain over the Atlantic. These

Down at the Railroad Station

On a cold, snowy morning, friends and relatives of the men of Company G gathered to see them off from Northampton's Union Station. Some of these men would end up serving more than four years, and some would never return.

Maj. Lavallee Says Farewell

Company G's commanding officer, Maj. Leon Lavallee, would not return to Northampton until October of 1945. While members of his onetime company would fight on both the European and Pacific fronts, Lavallee himself ended up in the China-Burma-India Theater. He had four sons in the military. One was killed in North Africa.

The Dummy Tank

To simulate a tank for training purposes during Company G's stay at Brunswick, Georgia, Pvt. Paul Conant built a plywood superstructure on a Jeep. To practice for a gas attack and to force the men to use their gas masks, Conant attached a tear gas bomb to the dummy tank. The driver is Pfc. Larry Houle.

Coastal Patrol: Company G at Portsmouth, N.H.

After being federalized, Company G's first assignment was coastal patrol duty. They were based at Portsmouth, N.H. Pvt. Robert Loudfoot, manning the machine gun, died in France in 1944. His four brothers and his sister also served in the military during WWII.

On Maneuvers

Sgt. Ted Benoit of Company G. He is holding one of the few machine guns issued to his unit.

old destroyers managed to rescue more than a thousand seamen whose ships went down. Nevertheless, at the beginning of 1941 a Gallup Poll disclosed that while 60 percent of the American people favored aid for Britain, 88 percent were still against United States' involvement in the war.

In March, after bitter Congressional debate, H.R. 1776, the "Lend-Lease" law, was enacted. This permitted the President to turn over an initial $7 billion worth of war supplies, rather than merely financial aid, to those nations fighting Hitler. Isolationist Senator Burton K. Wheeler deplored this as a policy destined to "plow under every fourth American boy."

In the spring of 1941 Roosevelt sent U.S. forces into Greenland, and on July 7, 4,095 U.S. Marines landed in Iceland to relieve British troops stationed there guarding against seizure by the Nazis. American naval units had also begun escorting supply ships halfway across their 3,000-mile route to Britain.

On September 4, the destroyer U.S.S. *Greer* and a German U-boat exchanged depth-charges and torpedoes, with no damage to either. Roosevelt ordered that whenever Axis raiders were encountered American naval vessels were to shoot on sight. "The sole responsibility," he declared, "rests upon Germany. There will be no shooting unless Germany continues to seek it."

On October 16, the U.S.S. *Kearney*, part of a British-American-Canadian convoy, was torpedoed off Iceland with 11 men killed. On October 31, the U.S.S. *Reuben James* was sunk, and more than two-thirds of her crew drowned — 115 men in all. These were the first sinkings of U.S. naval vessels doing destroyer-escort convoy duty in the Atlantic. One week later, the Senate voted to repeal the Neutrality Act provisions prohibiting American merchant ships from arming themselves and from entering combat zones.

Between 1939 and 1943, German U-boats would sink 2,452 merchant ships in the Atlantic alone, plus 175 warships. The German Kriegsmarine would lose 696 out of 830 U-boats, and 25,870 out of 40,900 crewmen. Another 5,000 were rescued and became prisoners of war. This was the highest casualty rate — 75 percent overall — of any combat unit of any country in the war. Many Northampton men participated in the Battle of the Atlantic, and some paid with their lives.

In the fateful year of 1941, however, for Americans the war was still to come. For Europeans it was already two years old.

In 1941, this country was a divided nation. The isolationists, Massachusetts Senator David I. Walsh among them, wanted to keep the United States neutral. In September of the previous year, Charles Lindbergh had spearheaded the creation of the America First Committee. An America First chapter was formed in Northampton in June by Professor Carey Jacob of the Smith College Department of Spoken English. Another group, the No Foreign War Committee, was organized in the city that same month.

The interventionists, those who believed that the United States should be aiding Britain far more in her struggle against Hitler, formed organizations such as the Committee to Defend America by Aiding the Allies. On October 13, 1941, at a meeting in the Hotel Northampton, Florence Lyman and Margaret Locke were elected co-chairmen of a local group to be called the Fight For Freedom Committee of Hampshire County. Former First Lady Grace Coolidge, now living in her newly built home, Road Forks, in Northampton, served as honorary chairman. (She confided to a Gazette reporter that the isolationists were calling her an "old-age destroyer.") Other leading citizens lent their support, including Professor Osborn, who only a few years earlier had been busy organizing area college students into Peace Patrols to aid his Emergency Peace Campaign.

Every American public figure was now firing off either warlike or anti-war exhortations. On May 20, President Roosevelt declared an unlimited national emergency. In Des Moines, on September 11, Lindbergh declared in a speech before 7,500 members of America First that "the three most important groups which have been pressing this country toward war are the British, the Jewish, and the Roosevelt administration." The danger posed to this country by the Jews, Lindbergh added, "lies in their large ownership and influence in our motion pictures, our press, our radio and our government." This speech was roundly condemned in Northampton by the Young Progressives Union and the Young Peoples' Forum of the Edwards and First Congregational churches.

A month later, in a speech to the Massachusetts Federation of Women's Clubs, Editor Herbert Agar of the Louisville Courier-Journal called for an immediate declaration of war on those forces "trying to destroy western-world civilization." They were not so much after land, power and money, Agar insisted, as they were for "a revolution against our society — a counter-revolution against the civilization of our western world."

As if in answer to this, on November 27, Professor Jacob warned that "the United States is falling for British propaganda as it did in the last war." In a chapel talk that same month, Smith College President Herbert Davis appealed to all students to "come out and declare where you stand ... whether you are ready to fight or whether you are pacifists ... the real decision which is before your generation. Will you accept the Nazi idolatry or will you resist?"

In this same period Senator Walsh, who was chairman of the Naval Affairs Committee, warned that the U.S. Navy "is not ready to wage a foreign war."

While this battle of words raged, life went on in a relatively quiet way in Northampton just as it did all over the country — but not without signs of impending conflict. A wire story in the Gazette in September reported that British merchant ships picking up war materiel in New York were now bringing bomb rubble from London, as ballast, and that

President Davis of Smith College

Herbert F. Davis, an Englishman with a degree from Oxford, assumed the presidency of Smith College in 1940. Davis seemed caught between the desire to keep the "Smithies" at their studies and the impulse to exhort them to contribute to the war effort.

Grace Coolidge: Former First Lady

After the Coolidges left the White House, they returned to live in Northampton where the former First Lady took part in many community activities. Before this country's involvement in WWII, she advocated help for those embattled nations fighting Hitler, and served as honorary chairman of the Fight for Freedom Committee of Hampshire County.

Charles Lindbergh and America First

As a leading voice of America First – the strong pre-war isolationist movement in the United States – Lindbergh, the aviation hero of the 1920s, exhorted this country to stay out of the Second World War. America First folded suddenly and permanently after the Japanese attacked Pearl Harbor.

The Great Arsenal of Democracy

The Springfield Armory first hired women workers in 1941, as did so-called "defense plants" all over the country.

For American Legs Only

While the legs of women in war-torn Europe went stockingless, American women were buying hosiery made of the new wonder called "nylon." Increasing prosperity, as American factories turned out war materiel for the Allies, made such luxury items obtainable in the U.S. The great American buying binge of WWII had begun.

this was being used as fill in constructing New York's East River Drive. An Air Raid Precaution School opened at Northampton's Smith's Agricultural School in October, and a mock air raid was staged over the town, with four two-motored bombers "nearly destroying" the former high school that now sheltered various municipal offices.

"We must be the great arsenal of democracy," President Roosevelt had declared on December 20, 1940. That is exactly what the industrial might of this country was gearing up to become. In time, we would be able to send enough war materiel to our Allies to supply 2,000 divisions. Our tank output in 1940 totalled 346, but by 1944 would swell to 17,565. Aircraft production during the same period rose from 2,141 to 96,318. World War II would not be just one of fighting men but of engineers and factory workers — and this would be seen nowhere better than in New England.

By 1941, a new prosperity was starting to hit Northampton. Jobs were available at defense plants in Greenfield, Westfield, Holyoke, Springfield and Hartford. "Business In The Pioneer Valley Is Shown Much Improved" reported the Gazette in October. The State Employment Service had placed 144 persons in jobs during the month of October alone, and claims for compensation by the unemployed were reduced by 67 percent from the same month a year before. In November, Gazette readers learned that local banks' "Christmas Clubs" in 1941 would "be the largest ever — $40,000 more than the previous year."

With incomes swelling from new jobs in the "great arsenal of democracy," Americans were swarming into the nation's retail stores bent on a holiday shopping binge. There were "date dresses" in bright red or blue splashed all over at the top with star-shaped glitter. "A soldier beau will have no morale trouble for weeks after he has seen you in one of these," an advertisement promised. Elizabeth Arden was offering a new lipstick shade called "V for Victory." Draftees at Army camps could be sent inflatable pillows, down-filled sleeping bags, silk-lined money bags and portable radios. There was even a board game called Invasion.

For children there were war toys of various kinds, including a pedal-propelled field ambulance with room inside for several doll-sized casualties, and the words U.S. Army Medical Corps painted on its olive-drab sides.

For the first time since the first World War, women were being hired at the Springfield Armory, which took on 14 "to meet the shortage of skilled labor." During this period two Northampton men, Jack FitzGerald and Bob Kinney, took jobs at the Watertown Arsenal. One worked the day shift and the other the night shift. Their shared rented room cost $5 a week, and the bed, used by each in succession, was never made. Before long, both of these young men would enter the Aviation Cadet program and end up as Army Air Corps navigators in the European Theater.

The headlines of the Gazette turned more grim in the closing months of 1941. Ambassador Joseph Grew warned from Tokyo that the American trade embargo of that summer, designed to cut Japan off from her vital oil supplies, might have dire consequences. Grew suspected that the military-dominated and war-oriented Japanese government might soon take drastic action: perhaps even attack the Philippines. And it was clear that any conflict with Japan would soon have broader implications, since on September 27, 1940, Japan had signed the Tripartite Pact, commonly known as the "Axis," with Germany and Italy, obligating each to help the other in case of attack.

"A fundamental disagreement exists between Japan and the United States," a leading Tokyo newspaper, *Nichi Nichi*, was quoted as saying on October 17. The following day came the announcement that Lt. Gen. Hideki Tojo, the war minister, had taken over as Premier from the slightly more moderate Prince Fumimaro Konoye, and was forming a new cabinet "considered friendly to the Axis." Day after day the headlines warned: "Tojo Hits At Encirclement ... Secretary Knox Says Far East Collision Inevitable ... Tojo Says Jap Army Is Prepared For Any Eventuality ... President Quizzing Japs On Aggression ... Washington Awaits Jap Peace Offer" and, on Saturday, December 6, "U.S. Awaits Jap's Next Move In East."

We did not have long to wait.

Lt. Gen. Hideki Tojo of Japan

In October 1941, Tojo became Prime Minister of Japan. Combining this with his positions of War Minister and Chief of Army Staff, he drove his nation relentlessly toward the Second World War. His nickname was "the Razor." Later, as the war turned against Japan, Tojo's position weakened, and he attempted suicide in 1945 after the surrender of his country. He was tried as a war criminal and executed in 1948.

The Allied Blockade of Japan

Fearful of the rise of Japan's planned "Greater East Asia Co-Prosperity Sphere," the American, British and Dutch governments halted exports of oil and iron to that nation — a veritable economic blockade. Japan's military, not content with their long drawn-out war in China, now added western nations to their enemies including, eventually, the U.S.

1941 — Remember Pearl Harbor

December 7, 1941, dawned bright and clear in Hawaii. Those who were there remember it as a typical slow and sleepy Sunday morning, despite recent alerts. Celebrators of the night before were still in their beds, while others were at their breakfasts and looking forward to a day of leisure. Servicemen on duty on "battleship row" in Pearl Harbor, headquarters of the United States Navy's Pacific Fleet, on Ford Island, at Hickam Field, at Wheeler Field and at Schofield Barracks, were either readying themselves to go on duty, or just coming off. Some men had risen early to attend Mass.

Many Navy personnel were ashore for the weekend, so three-quarters of the 780 anti-aircraft guns on board the ships were not manned that day. Only four of the Army's 31 batteries were operational, and their ammunition was safely stored.

Back in January Ambassador Joseph Grew had reported from Tokyo to Washington that Japan might be considering war against the United States. Grew had heard, he said, "a lot of talk around town to the effect that the Japanese, in case of a break with the United States, are planning to go all out in a surprise mass attack on Pearl Harbor.

"I rather guess," Grew had added confidently, "that the boys in Hawaii are not precisely asleep."

On December 7, some of those "boys" who were not destined to die in their cots used pistols, rifles and rocks to fire back at attacking enemy planes.

Two who were not asleep that morning were a couple of young Army privates assigned to part-time duty at the Opana Mobile Radar Station on the northern tip of Oahu. Their "station" was a small truck and their sleeping quarters a tent. Having gone on duty at 4 a.m. as required, they were scheduled to close down at 7 a.m. Instead, they chose to leave the set on in order to practice a while. At 7:02 a.m. an enormous image began to show on their oscilloscope, indicating possibly 50 or more approaching aircraft about 137 miles north of Oahu. The privates telephoned in their finding — "the biggest sightings" they'd ever had. The Army Aircraft Warning Center at Fort Shafter, manned that morning by a pilot with no experience in radar, decided that the sightings merely involved the one dozen B-17s expected at Hickam Field around 8 a.m.

Thus did 353 Japanese high-level bombers, dive bombers and fighter planes, launched in two waves from six carriers about 220 miles north of Oahu, continue unopposed on their way toward Hawaii. Those asleep at Pearl Harbor slept on.

The Japanese pilots aboard Adm. Chuichi Nagumo's carriers had awakened at 5 a.m., showered, dressed, bowed before the shipboard Shinto shrines and eaten breakfast to the sound of soft radio music coming to them from Honolulu. Precisely as planned by Adm. Isoroku Yamamoto, head of the Japanese Navy, their air armada reached Honolulu at 7:53 a.m. Out went the signal from the lead pilot, "Tora! Tora! Tora!" indicating they had caught the American forces completely by surprise.

Through Kolekole pass the first Japanese wave roared in at 7:55 a.m. Their primary targets were the 96 ships of the United States Pacific Fleet tied up at Pearl Harbor along the east side of Ford Island. The *Colorado* was in dry dock back in the United States, but eight other battleships — the *West Virginia*, the *Tennessee*, the *Arizona*, the *Nevada*, the *Oklahoma*, the *California*, the *Maryland* and the *Pennsylvania*, were all there, anchored as close as 500 yards apart. Sitting ducks.

The attack began at once. The first American alert was at 7:58 a.m.: "Air Raid, Pearl

The End of the U.S.S. Arizona

Burned in the memory of every American who remembers December 7, 1941, is this image of the death agony of a great battleship. More than 80 percent of the crew of 1,500 were killed or drowned. Today, the Arizona is a permanent memorial to all who died that day at Pearl Harbor.

Adm. Isoroku Yamamoto

Japan's greatest naval strategist, Yamamoto realized that his country could never win a protracted war with the U.S. The attack at Pearl Harbor was his attempt at a pre-emptive strike to cripple the U.S. Navy and end the war quickly. He might have succeeded except that our carriers were at sea and survived to defeat him at the battle of Midway in June of 1942. Yamamoto died when his plane was shot down on the Western Solomons on April 18, 1943.

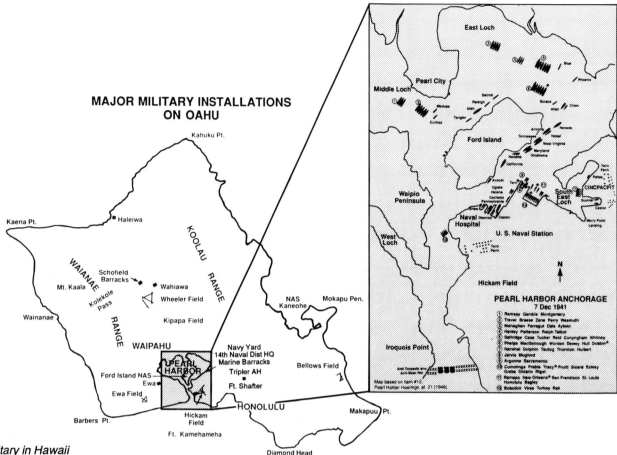

U.S. Military in Hawaii

These maps show the U.S. Army and Navy installations in Hawaii that were subjected to the Japanese surprise attack on Sunday, December 7, 1941.

Harbor. This Is Not Drill!" Loudspeakers aboard the ships took up the warning: "Japs are coming! Japs attacking us! Go to your battle stations! Man your battle stations! This is no shit!"

It was too late. Clusters of torpedoes ripped into the *California* and then the *Oklahoma*, which, after five hits, leaped out of the water, settled back and turned slowly over onto her side with almost 500 men, scarcely roused from sleep, trapped below deck.

An American who witnessed the scene remembered dazed sailors "crawling up her decks by the hundreds, and over her sides as it rolled. They were like ants ... slipping and tumbling down into the water." The Japanese pilots themselves would remember how the sailors swam in a kind of slow motion through the flaming, oil-covered surface of the harbor.

One of those seamen was 21-year-old Jan Kolodziej from Northampton. Slated to go on duty that day, Kolodziej had already risen and was dressed and shaving when the first bomb hit. He was able to get up on deck, fling himself into the water and save his life.

The 29,000-ton *Oklahoma* soon sank, taking down with her many of her crew, both those trapped inside and many who had escaped that fate only to be raked under by her masts and superstructure. Four hundred and forty-seven men died. Rescue crews soon heard tapping from the submerged hull, and by the evening of the following day 32 trapped survivors were rescued. Three men trapped in the hull of the *West Virginia*, it was later learned, did not die until 16 days later.

The greatest losses occurred aboard the 32,600-ton *Arizona*: 1,777 Navy and Marine Corps officers and men. Today the *Arizona* is still officially commissioned and serves as a memorial to all those who died at Pearl Harbor and also as a tomb for those 1,102 men of the ship's company still aboard her.

Wilbur Fisher, a Navy hospital corpsman who after the war joined the staff at the Veteran's Hospital in the Leeds section of Northampton, saw the *Arizona* go up like a big ball of fire. Fisher's main recollection of the Naval Base Hospital following the attack was of "limbs blown off ... the smell of burned flesh — and screams." Sixty percent of all Navy casualties that day were caused by burning oil.

When Gunner's Mate 3rd Class Thaddeus Kozloski arrived back home in Northampton on leave the following April, he described how strong American antiaircraft fire had met the second wave of Japanese planes. He was convinced, Kozloski told the Gazette, that his own light cruiser had definitely accounted for four invading planes. Twenty-nine of the attacking Japanese planes were shot down at Pearl Harbor.

The destroyer U.S.S. *Patterson*, which had just returned from a routine training cruise, was moored north of Ford Island between the *Henley* and the *Ralph Talbot*. Rocked by the falling bombs all around them, the *Patterson's* crew claimed hits on one Japanese plane with their .50-caliber machine gun and another with their five-inch gun. Ordered out of the harbor, "our can ran like a scared hen from hawks, trying to get out into the open sea," recorded Norton Taylor, an Associated Press correspondent aboard. "The Japs were busy with the big fellows, and she escaped unscathed."

Left on shore in the hasty withdrawal, the *Patterson's* skipper, Lt. Cmdr. Frank Walker, used a whaleboat to catch up with his ship.

Shipfitter 3rd Class Zigmund Sieruta of Northampton, serving aboard the *Patterson*, was uninjured in the exchange. Sieruta's personal rendezvous with destiny would come eight months later, when he would become the first Northampton resident to be killed in WWII.

On the far side of Ford Island was another man from Northampton, Seaman 2nd Class Robert Oborne. Oborne had tried five times to enlist in the Navy but had been turned

Wreckage at Wheeler Field

The Japanese attack on Army and Navy air installations on December 7 left 180 aircraft destroyed and 128 others damaged.

Shipmates

Shipfitter 3rd Class Zigmund "Si" Sieruta of Northampton, on the right, with a fellow crew member of the U.S. Patterson. *The* Patterson *escaped to sea during the inferno at Pearl Harbor.*

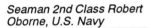

Seaman 2nd Class Robert Oborne, U.S. Navy

"What is the Army doing, doing dive-bomb practice on a Sunday?" young Oborne thought as the Japanese attack began. "Obie" was a member of an aviation utility squadron on Ford Island.

down each time because of a single missing tooth. "That's how strict the physical standards were before the war," he said later. In February 1941, however, he had been accepted, at age 17, by the Navy Reserves and was serving in an aviation utility squadron at Pearl Harbor.

He was assigned to a beach crew that towed targets and tended PBYs, the Catalina "flying boats," and J2Fs, amphibious observation planes. "Nothing very exciting," Oborne recalled. On December 7 he was on watch duty from midnight to 4 a.m. — "Just walking up and down and thinking what I'd rather be doing." Relieved at 4, he and other men of the various watches had had a few hours sleep and were just being picked up by a truck that would take them back to quarters. "We were standing up in the back of that truck, just ready to leave," said Oborne, "when in the distance there were weird sounds like *thump* or *whomp*. Almost at the same time, we saw two planes dive-bombing one of our hangars. 'Boy, what the hell is the Army *doing*,' I thought, 'doing dive-bomb practice on a Sunday? Somebody's going to catch it for using real bombs, too.' Not more than 30 seconds later we realized that this was an actual attack. The planes came in over the south side of the island, dropped the bombs on their battleship targets and then swooped over us, strafing us as they came."

Oborne and his fellow sailors leaped from their truck. "I kept thinking, over and over, 'Don't let me get hit!' but still we all ran for guns ... As the Japanese strafed us, we'd dive under the parked planes, which didn't give all that much protection. At one point we actually saw a submarine periscope about a thousand feet off shore and took potshots at it, too. Then a tin can (i.e. destroyer) came charging down the channel after it and setting off depth charges. All us sailors were cheering. Soon parts of that sub came up, and that was it.

"Probably my worst memory of that day is of the young sailor who ran up to us wanting to help, begging us to let him help, in fact. Suddenly we saw that one of his arms was gone — clean off just below his shoulder ... a bleeding stump ... I was glad I was still alive and grateful to the Lord that I made it through there."

While sailors were trying to mount a response to the Japanese attack on the Pacific

Fleet, men of the Army and Army Air Corps were also struggling to respond to attacks at Hickam and Wheeler fields and at Schofield Barracks.

At Hickam Field, the planes that might have risen to protect the fleet had been parked wingtip to wingtip as protection against possible sabotage. Awaiting the arrival of the 12 B-17s from the mainland, the field was instead systematically savaged — along with personnel on the ground — by the waves of Japanese bombers and fighters.

Tech. Sgt. Armand Bouchard of Northampton, a librarian in the Air Corps, remembered how he emerged from Mass in the chapel wondering why the Army would stage a mock air attack so early on a Sunday morning. Then, spotting the rising sun insignia on the planes zooming in on them, he realized this was not a drill.

One bomb that landed on the enlisted men's mess hall at Hickam killed 35 men and injured many others. One of the injured was Pfc. Earl Rodriguez, a Northampton High School graduate who had decided not to await conscription but had instead enlisted on August 10, 1940. He was wounded in the leg. Back on duty by February, Rodriguez was to be accepted as an aviation cadet and would end up a pilot in Europe.

Pfc. Augie Woicekoski of North Amherst, attached to Hickam Headquarters Squadron, had just left the mess hall and tried to head for the hangars. "The enemy planes started strafing us. Every time there were guys in the open, a plane would make a strafing pass. Everything hit at the same time — pretty soon there was black smoke all over Hickam as well as the harbor." Half of Hickam's aircraft were destroyed or heavily damaged.

With their own 82 aircraft likewise lined up in neat rows, it was now Wheeler Field's turn. So slow were the antiaircraft responses that four Japanese planes flying too low were actually brought down by rifle fire. Pfc. Frank Hayes of Northampton would never forget the line of tents in which a batch of new young recruits were asleep. "Right at the start, planes went down the line of tents — strafing. No one got out. Later, I was on the detail to identify and bury those kids."

At Schofield Barracks, the scene was as chaotic as "an overturned beehive," remembered Pvt. John Wolak, onetime member of the National Guard unit, Company G. He had enlisted in December 1940, and had arrived in Hawaii on March 1, 1941. "I knew there was a war coming on," he recalled, "and I figured I might as well get in on it at the beginning."

On that Sunday morning, Wolak was up, dressed in "suntans" for Mass, and was eating a breakfast of fried eggs in the mess hall when explosions were first heard.

"At first we thought it was a reveille gun," Wolak remembered, "but those weren't fired on Sunday. I never did finish my breakfast. Going out onto the parade ground we saw all these planes, with red circles on the sides, roaring in on us. We thought at first it was some kind of training exercise or simulated combat with practice strafing. They swirled over the PX and the laundry and then came back at us near the mess hall.

"What happened next happened fast, and it was remarkable," recalled Wolak. "This Zero came in. I could actually see the pilot and his shoulders and even the helmet and goggles he was wearing. He waved at me, and almost without thinking I waved back and he soared off. On his second pass, though, I headed back to the mess hall — simulated bullets or not. Anyway, now that guy followed me — firing at me — right till I dived through the screen door. Coming out a couple of minutes later I saw that all the bullet holes were *real*. Those red circles were the rising sun of Japan, and this meant war."

The men of Schofield Barracks that day began their war in the only way that they knew — the Army way. They lined up outside the supply room to sign out M1 rifles. Living targets, the men stood their ground, scattering three times as Zeroes swept over them with a burst of bullets and three times lining up again — each man carefully signing his name and listing the serial number of the weapon he drew.

"Finally," recalled Wolak, "a captain, later killed at Guadalcanal, ran up and yelled, 'You don't have to sign out the guns. This is war!' So we just grabbed guns and fired back as the planes came over.

"One pilot did a queer thing. He just banked off without firing and tipped his wings and waved."

Pfc. Augie Woicekoski, U.S. Army Air Corps.

Woicekoski, top right, is wearing the cap that belongs to the British sailor on his right. On the morning of the attack, Woicekoski was shot at by Japanese pilots strafing hangars at Hickham Field.

Pvt. John Wolak, U.S. Army

Pvt. John Wolak was at Schofield Barracks during the attack. He dodged bullets from a Japanese Zero whose pilot waved at him. "At first we thought it was a reveille gun," he later recalled.

Lt. Dorothy Elkins, U.S. Army Nurse Corps

Lt. Elkins, a recovering patient at Tripler General Hospital, saw the carnage at Pearl Harbor from a hospital porch. Quickly she dressed, and for three days straight attended to a seemingly endless procession of the wounded.

The U.S.S. West Virginia

The "Weevie," as her crew called her, was hit by seven torpedoes. The battleship settled right side up on the bottom of the shallow harbor and oil fires raged in her exposed superstructures for 24 hours.

Wolak's personal saga would take him through the invasion of Kwajalein and then back to Hawaii, where he would serve out the war.

From her vantage point just a few miles northeast of Hickam Field, at Tripler General Hospital, Lt. Dorothy Elkins from Northampton watched horror-struck as the carnage unfolded. An Army nurse who was a patient that day herself, recovering from dental surgery, Elkins was awakened by the sounds of rattling windows and explosions.

"The building was literally rocking. We flowed out onto the hospital's rear porches and saw huge, soaring billows of oily black smoke over Pearl Harbor. We wondered if it was some sort of maneuvers, or a catastrophe. The air was full of planes, and we could see planes in flame on the runways at Hickam."

Elkins thought, "If something terrible is taking place, I had better get dressed. We may be needed." As she made her way down to the nurses' barracks, a fighter-plane swooped low over her. "I saw the pilot clearly. His leather flying helmet, his goggles and white scarf. I even saw the circular red insignia on the wings but didn't realize then what it was. That pilot waved at me, and thinking he was some sort of smart-aleck or someone gone berserk, I thumbed my nose at him as he soared off."

Elkins' first realization of what was actually taking place came with the arrival, 30 or 40 minutes later, of a weapons carrier driven by a haggard, dirty soldier. His vehicle was crammed with burned, bloody and mangled men. "What's going on?" she asked him.

"The damned Japs attacked us," he replied.

"What did they want to do that for?" she remembered saying.

During the three days that followed, nurse Elkins did not even manage a change of clothing. Neither did she eat, drink or sleep. This was due in part to the emergency, but was also because of rumors that Japanese agents had poisoned all food, milk and water on the island.

"How can we care for all these people? When will it end?" Elkins remembered thinking during those three days. The medical staff was exhausted and supplies were running out. A primary task was to prepare morphine solution from tablets and to keep syringes sterilized. "We would use iodine to mark 'M,' and the time morphine was administered,

on the foreheads of the wounded waiting for surgery," she recalled.

Forty years later, at a reunion of Pearl Harbor survivors, a man walked up to Elkins and asked, "Weren't you there at Tripler unloading the wounded off the trucks? Aren't you the nurse who clipped off what was left of my hand?" She was.

For months after the attack at Pearl Harbor, news of servicemen stationed there drifted back to Northampton. The Sieruta family received their son's brief penciled note on a torn scrap of paper in an envelope addressed by someone else: "I am well. Letter to follow."

Other messages were reported in the newspaper. A "heavily censored letter" from Oborne eventually assured his family and friends he had emerged unscathed, as had Charles O'Connell, who was also in the Navy there. Seaman 2nd Class Joseph Shebak, however, was reported injured. "The extent of Shebak's injuries is not known ... the family was asked not to disclose the name of the ship on which he was stationed," reported the Gazette.

Stanley Newell, aboard a fire-fighting barge that had hastened to the aid of the *Arizona* and the *West Virginia* would, the following April, receive a certificate of honor from the Navy Department.

The Japanese score card for December 7 read: four American battleships blown up or sunk; four other battleships damaged; 11 other ships capsized, sunk or disabled. Half the U.S. Fleet, in short, had been knocked out. Fortunately, the carriers of the Pacific Fleet, the *Lexington* and the *Enterprise*, were out at sea that day and thus lived to fight another day. Destroyed on the ground were 167 Navy and Army airplanes, with 128 others damaged. There were 2,403 American dead or missing plus 1,178 wounded.

The Japanese lost 29 planes and five midget submarines. One midget sub had run aground, producing the first Japanese POW of World War II: Ensign Kazua Sakamaki. The Japanese dead numbered 64.

What was it that the Japanese had hoped to accomplish? Their idea seems to have been to undermine American morale and to achieve an impregnable position in the Pacific before the United States was able to retaliate. Such a plan, in fact, had been endorsed in Tokyo at a Supreme War council on September 16, 1941. Japan's Greater East Asia Co-Prosperity Sphere envisioned an economic and political empire that would extend from Manchuria and China to Thailand and New Guinea. The island of Japan, with its growing population, lacked most resources for a modern industrial society and thus needed to import most of its steel, aluminum, oil and iron ore and all of its nickel. Our restrictive trade embargoes had amounted to virtual strangulation.

By the end of 1941, after their triumph at Pearl Harbor, the Japanese could plan to overrun Southeast Asia and build an impregnable defensive ring around their conquests. Following Pearl Harbor there would be a drum-roll of other victories: Hong Kong, Singapore — and the Philippines, where, under the command of Gen. Douglas MacArthur, American troops were stationed. Among them were four soldiers from Northampton: Vernon Danforth, Joseph Miller, William Sniezko and Mitchell Talenda.

On the afternoon of December 8 the Japanese launched a second surprise attack, this time in the Philippines. At Clark Field, 18 out of 35 B-17s, 56 fighters and 25 other planes were destroyed on the ground, wingtip to wingtip just as at Pearl Harbor the previous day. More than half of our air strength in the Philippines was lost.

On December 10, an attack force of 54 Japanese planes destroyed the United States naval base at Cavite Bay just outside Manila. The way was now open for Lt. Gen. Masaharu Homma to land on Luzon and head for Manila, which fell on January 2, 1942. American and Philippine troops had to retreat down the Bataan Peninsula on the western edge of Luzon.

For military security reasons, the American public was not accurately informed concerning events in the Philippines for the next few months. Reports came out of Washington to newspapers all over the country. "Smashing Success Of General MacArthur's Soldiers In A Counter-Attack On The Japs," claimed a War Department announcement reported in the Daily Hampshire Gazette on December 26, 1941. "MacArthur Is On Offensive Drive," the same source reported on February 26, 1942. But as spring came

A Message Home

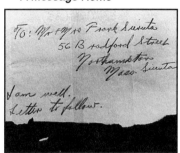

On a scrap of paper, Zigmund "Si" Sieruta tried to get word to his family that he had survived the Japanese attack.

on, some of the bad news began trickling through. Early in April there were hints: "Philippine War Appears About Ended. Defenders Exhausted, Resistance Has Virtually Ceased ... Probability That Defenses On Bataan Overcome." Soon afterward, Gen. MacArthur, his wife and son were whisked off to Australia.

On April 9, 1942, 76,000 starving, ill and exhausted American and Filipino soldiers — "the battling bastards of Bataan" as they had named themselves — finally surrendered and were marched off to imprisonment at Camp O'Donnell. The last remnants of the American forces in the Philippines surrendered at Corregidor on May 6.

Six hundred American and 5,000 to 10,000 Filipino soldiers died of wounds, thirst and hunger, or were bayoneted or beaten to death during that 65-mile march from Mariveles to San Fernando known as the Bataan Death March. Some men were tortured. A few escapees reported these atrocities, but the information would not be released until January 28, 1944, when the British government also released information concerning the atrocities inflicted upon British and Commonwealth prisoners.

At the same time American prisoners were enduring these cruelties, U.S. government officials were declaring, according to the Gazette, that: "Jap Prisoners To Be Treated Well By U.S. Government Has Informed Japan It Will Abide By Geneva Convention Of

Japanese Photos of American POWs

When the Philippines fell to the Japanese in the spring of 1942, their photographers were on hand to record the plight of American POWs. Already weakened by months of starvation rations, many of the men were ill with malaria, dysentery and beriberi. Such photos were not seen in the U.S. until after the war.

1929. Hope Japs Do Likewise." As a matter of fact, the Japanese government had never signed the Geneva Convention. More than 20,000 Americans became Japanese captives when the Philippines fell. Less than 60 percent of them would survive to return home at the war's end.

Today we know that the Philippines had been written off almost from the beginning as a lost cause in the event of a two-ocean war. Navy Secretary Frank Knox had, in effect, established our government's priorities back on January 12, 1942. As the Gazette reported this policy: "No Early Showdown With Jap Fleet. Battle of Atlantic Most Important Of All. Hitler Is The Big Enemy."

In 1942, the Danforth, Miller, Sniezko and Talenda families of Northampton learned only that their sons were prisoners of war.

At first the Japanese would not even reveal the names of their captives. Then in August 1943, cards relayed by the Japanese Imperial Army via the International Red Cross reached the Miller and Talenda families. Sgt. Joseph Miller wrote that he was in "excellent health" and sent "regards to all my friends." Sgt. Mitchell Talenda's card advised his family that he had been wounded at Corregidor and that he was receiving medical care in the camp where he was interned.

We now know that prisoners had been forced to write these cards. American families

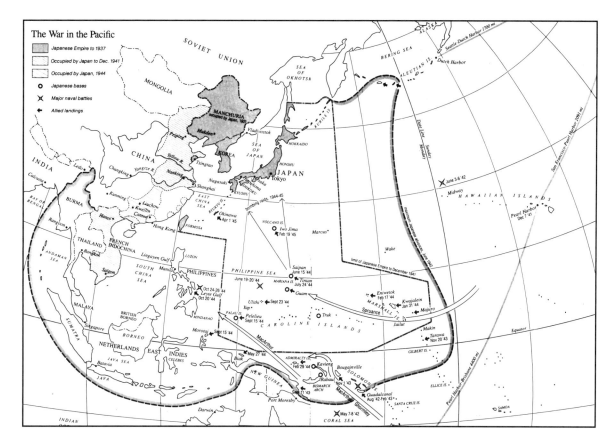

Pacific Theater of War

Following the Japanese attack on Pearl Harbor on December 7 and the declaration of war against the U.S. by Germany and Italy on December 11, this nation faced war on two fronts. The map shows the Pacific Theater.

were thus misled by these and similar cruel hoaxes, such as a report relayed from the Japanese via the Red Cross, and reported by the Associated Press, that prisoners taken at Wake, Gilbert and Guam ... "are well treated. Would like more entertainment and fancier food."

As if in answer to the fate of their brothers, the siblings of the four Northampton Japanese POWs now flocked to the military. Pfc. Blanche Miller, sister of Joseph, served in England and was quoted as saying that her brother's captivity "prompted me to join the Army more than anything else." From the Sniezko family came Lt. Helen Sniezko of the Army Nurse Corps, who served in England, and Pfc. Caroline Sniezko, who served as an "Air Wac" in Colorado. Tech. Sgt. Stanislaw Sniezko would receive the Bronze Star in North Africa and the Silver Star for gallantry in action in the vicinity of St. Laurent sur Mer during the Normandy invasion. Mitchell Talenda's three brothers, Charles, Walter and Edward, would join the service, with Edward Talenda volunteering for the Marines. His motive, he said, was, "to bring Mitch home."

Periodically, following the events of December 7, 1941 and throughout the long war that followed, there were demands for an investigation of what had happened at Pearl Harbor. On January 2, 1942, the Daily Hampshire Gazette announced: "Report On Probe of Pearl Harbor Attack Expected Soon By FDR. President Does Not Know If Findings Will Be Made Public." Two years later, on December 2, 1944, the newspaper revealed: "Washington Takes Some Of Blame For Pearl Harbor Fiasco. Inside story, however, cannot be released until after war, it is claimed, for reasons of military secrecy. Probe to be continued by War and Navy Departments. Demand for congressional investigation now."

To this day this whole subject is still being debated.

Rendezvous with Destiny

Raymond Hibbard in a relaxed moment at home in the 1930s before keeping his "rendezvous with destiny." He enlisted in the United States Marine Corps in 1942 and died on Saipan, June 28, 1944.

1941 — A Date That Will Live in Infamy

On Sunday, December 7, 1941, most Northampton residents flocked to church. Traditional Sunday dinners followed — some of them more bountiful than in previous years due to the town's growing defense-plant prosperity. After dinner there stretched the long, quiet Sunday afternoon with the Giant-Dodgers football game on WOR or the New York Philharmonic over CBS radio. Then there were "The Shadow," the "Jack Benny Show" and Walter Winchell to look forward to in the evening.

Fifty years later it is hard to find anyone then alive who does not remember that sleepy afternoon, or how he or she heard the news — announced first over radio shortly after 2 p.m. — of the debacle at Pearl Harbor.

High School chemistry teacher Allan O'Brien was fortifying himself with a nap when a family member awakened him with the news that the Japanese had attacked. In the years just ahead, serving as a communications officer aboard the destroyer escort U.S.S. *Mosley* in the Atlantic and the Mediterranean, O'Brien would remember with longing that lazy Sunday afternoon.

Pharmacists Leonard and Louis Budgar were at work in the family's drug store at 6 Bridge St. that afternoon. Louis was making up prescriptions in the rear and listening to the radio, while Leonard created chocolate sundaes for 14-year-old Dick Wall and his cousin Dan O'Brien. "Suddenly," Leonard Budgar remembered, "Louis called out, 'The Japanese have attacked Pearl Harbor! Where the hell is *that?*'"

Leonard answered, "I think it's in Alaska." Before long he would be Sgt. Budgar of the 112th Medical Battalion attached to the 37th Division in the South Pacific.

Having grown up with war news, Wall and O'Brien downed their sundaes and ran home, thinking that Northampton might be bombed at any minute.

An 18-year-old member of the class of 1945 at Massachusetts State College in Amherst, Richard Garvey was working as a student reporter under the National Youth Administration program to help earn his tuition. On that afternoon he was covering a meeting of the Winter Sports Council and had slipped out to the men's room. In the corridor, he met a janitor who said to him in a casual tone, "I just heard over the radio that the Japanese have bombed Pearl Harbor." Garvey thought the man must have misinterpreted something and obviously didn't know that Pearl Harbor was a major installation for the Pacific Fleet, or that if something like that ever happened it would mean war. "This," thought Garvey, "is the way rumors get started." It was not until the meeting broke up that he learned the truth of the janitor's "rumor."

That afternoon in Smith College's John M. Greene Hall, a large audience gathered to hear a lecture by the noted Quaker scholar, Professor Emeritus Rufus Jones of Haverford College, also head of the American Friends Service Committee. By this time, the news from Pearl Harbor was on everyone's mind and tongue. "These tragic events today in the Pacific Ocean will probably alter the course of history," James acknowledged with uncommon understatement.

Tucked away in the college library that afternoon was a sophomore, Allison McCrillis, busy on a paper concerning The Gothic Tale of Terror for Katherine Hornbeak's English 19. Overhearing two librarians sharing the news of Pearl Harbor, she never imagined that two years later she herself would be wearing olive drab in the

Allan O'Brien

O'Brien was a U.S. Coast Guard communications officer during WWII. His worst memory was of seeing the Paul Hamilton, a Liberty ship loaded with explosives, sunk off Algiers on April 24, 1944. Attacked by German torpedo planes, the Hamilton vanished under an enormous geyser of water. Lost were 504 soldiers and the ship's crew.

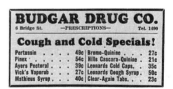

Budgar Drug

This 1941 newspaper ad for the Budgar Drug Store advertises some of the popular home-remedy preparations of the time. Leonard Budgar, who would be a medical corpsman in the Pacific, was in the store making a sundae when the Pearl Harbor attack news came over the radio.

Young Reporter

Richard Garvey, left, former editor and today associate publisher of the Springfield Union News, began his career as a reporter for the Daily Hampshire Gazette in 1943. He received his first byline on a story about a friend of his, Richard Boudway, who had survived a torpedoing in the Atlantic.

Pvt. Thomas Hogan, USMC

In 1941, Hogan, center, barely 18 and in boot camp at Paris Island, hoped the war would last long enough for him to take part in it. He got his wish. He would come close to death on Iwo Jima in 1945.

Earl Tonet

Cpl. Earl Tonet, USMC, right, at New River Marine Base, N.C. Tonet, who later became an officer, survived heavy combat duty in the Pacific.

Allison McCrillis

Allison McCrillis wore her cap and gown as a Smith College senior in May 1943. Six weeks or so after Commencement, McCrillis emerged from basic training at Fort Devens, Mass., a fledgling Army private destined to serve as a "Public Relations Man" until 1946.

yet-to-be established Women's Army Corps.

Ramona Gilligan, a registered nurse, was already in the Army. In 1940 she had answered the call for nurses to administer to the hordes of draftees then serving their one year under the new Selective Service Act. Like the men, Gilligan expected to return to civilian life when her one year was up. On December 7 she was stationed at Fort Bragg, N.C., and attending a dance with an infantry officer when the news of Pearl Harbor came. The following day she volunteered for overseas duty and before long was headed for North Africa. Later she would find herself under fire for months, at Anzio in Italy.

Hugh "Hymie" Crane, who had taken a job making aircraft engines at Pratt and Whitney in Hartford, had brought a Notre Dame classmate home with him for the December 6 weekend. With this friend, Crane and his future wife, Helena Mleczko, and her brother Stanley, went down to the Connecticut River that afternoon to shoot at discarded bottles on the river bank. When they returned to the house, Helena's mother met them on the back porch with the Pearl Harbor news.

"We went into the house and stayed glued to the radio for a long time," Crane recalled. Several years later, he would fight as a Marine in the battle for Okinawa.

Eleven-year-old John Skibiski and his family had been away for the afternoon. Thus he first heard the news as he stretched out on the living room floor after supper to listen to the Jack Benny radio show. "It wasn't until some weeks later, however, when I saw the wrecked and burning ships in the newsreel at the Calvin (Theater) that I fully realized what had happened at Pearl Harbor," Skibiski recalled.

Teen-ager Thomas Hogan was spending his afternoon at the Bijou Theater in Holyoke, watching the Marx Brothers in "A Night at the Opera." Coming out into the dusk, Hogan heard newsboys hawking extras with the reports. "Where the hell is Pearl Harbor?" he thought, and then, he recalled, he hoped "it would last long enough for me to get into it. I got over that, believe me," he added years later, "in the Pacific between 1943 and 1945."

Earl Tonet, a 21-year-old student at Massachusetts State College, was another Northampton youth destined for battle in the Pacific as a Marine. On that Sunday afternoon he and a friend headed for the Calvin Theater, where they planned to see Bing Crosby in "The Birth of the Blues."

"It was shortly after 2 o'clock," Tonet remembered, "when somebody came out of Parnell's Restaurant and spread the news about Pearl Harbor. My friend and I didn't see that movie. Instead, we headed up Main Street to the Food Shoppe and sat over a couple of Cokes while we pondered our future. There was an emptiness, an uncertainty, a fear of the future .... The big question was whether to enlist or wait to be drafted. I knew the draft would get me eventually, so I enlisted in the Marines that July."

Kenneth McKown, who had recently "returned home broke from Indiana Tech," was working at the Veterans Hospital in Leeds. "I was assigned to a very bad ward," he recalled. "The men all had to be fed, and they never spoke. All were veterans of the First World War. There was always a radio on in the ward. One man would sit all day — bent over — his head on his knees with his arms hanging down to the floor. When the news of Pearl Harbor came on, it was incredible. All those guys were very upset. We didn't think they knew anything, but they knew what that news meant. 'I'm ready to go,' one of them said, jumping up. 'I'm ready to go!'"

Suddenly, according to McKown, the bent-over man raised himself. "He grabbed both my hands and looked straight at me. 'You're going to go,' he said. 'I know you're going to go. And whatever you do, don't get into a machine-gun company. Don't let them put you in a machine-gun company.' Then he went back to his usual bent-over position in that chair."

The following summer McKown would enlist in the Army Air Corps and see long service in the Pacific Theater. As an armorer, he would fire machine guns many times.

Besides the men of Company G who had been called up on January 27, there were other Northampton men already in military service. Connie Nanartonis and Dick Holmes, for example, heard the news of the Pearl Harbor attack over the radio in the dayroom of their Royal Canadian Air Force training center at Belleville, Ontario. These two youths, who had worked around LaFleur Airport and earned their pilot licenses, had flown to Montreal early in 1940. Arrested on landing at what had become a military airdrome rather than a municipal airport, Nanartonis and Holmes had been freed when the Canadian authorities discovered they had come to enlist in the RCAF. They were among 8,864 other Americans who went to Canada rather than wait for the United States to be drawn into WWII. Unlike 5,067 who elected to remain in the RCAF after December 7, 1941, Holmes and Nanartonis would return to join the U.S. Army Air Corps.

Another Northampton man, Ed Olander, had volunteered in July 1941 for the naval flight training program. At Corpus Christi, Texas, "they hardly seemed to know what to do with us. There were six musters a day but no airplanes. After Pearl Harbor, however, they soon discovered how and where they would use us." Olander later shot down five

Americans and the Royal Canadian Air Force

Northampton residents Connie Nanartonis, right, and Richard Holmes joined the Royal Canadian Air Force in 1941 and were in training when they heard the Pearl Harbor news. Of the 8,864 young Americans who joined the RCAF, 3,797 returned to the U.S. after Pearl Harbor, including Nanartonis and Holmes, both of whom flew for Uncle Sam in the U.S. Army Air Corps.

Japanese planes to become an "Ace" with the Black Sheep Marine Squadron in the Pacific.

Dan Manning, due for discharge shortly, reported back to Fort Devens that Sunday evening after a weekend at home in Northampton. Customarily, his father had been allowed to drive him right to the barracks. "But not that night," Manning recalled. "Suddenly, everything was very military." Following Officer Candidate School, he would experience some of the fiercest combat in Europe as an officer in the 2nd Infantry Division.

John Qua, who had been drafted on March 1, had just returned to Camp Edwards from infantry maneuvers in North Carolina. His unit had arrived on the afternoon of Saturday, December 6, and many men had only a few months to go before their one year of service would be completed.

"My family had come to visit me," Qua recalled, "and we could hardly believe the news. It was the furthest thing from my mind. I didn't think any nation would have the courage to do such a thing to us." Before long he signed up for pilot training and would serve as a B-17 pilot during some of the 8th Air Force's earliest and toughest air raids over Germany.

Joseph Okolo

Left photo: Joseph Okolo, on the left, Company G, 104th Regiment, 26th Infantry Division, with his sister Blanche, and his brother, Chester, while on furlough before being shipped overseas. He was killed in France on June 15, 1944.

Donald Ducharme

Donald Ducharme, center photo, before the war, at home in Leeds with his dog. He died with all aboard the submarine U.S.S. Amberjack when it disappeared at sea in March of 1943.

Wartime Wedding

Sgt. Alfred "Ted" Conz and his wife Lola, right photo, were married on January 24, 1942. They had just three-and-a-half months together before Conz was shipped out. He was killed when his plane went down somewhere over the Mediterranean or Italy on August 22, 1943.

Also among those who returned to Camp Edwards on December 6 was Pvt. Bernard Begin of Company G, 104th Infantry, 26th Yankee Division. Based on a new Selective Service directive, all men 28 years of age and over were ordered to report the next day to Company G headquarters, where they were to be discharged whether their one year of service was up or not. After their noonday meal at the mess hall, Begin and several others headed for their discharge processing.

They entered on a scene of considerable chaos. The gist of the greeting was "You can forget all those discharges, you guys. There's a war on!"

All the men and women already in service — almost 900,000 in the Army alone — would soon learn that they would be "retained for the duration of the war plus six months."

***

On Monday, the day following the news of the Pearl Harbor disaster, Northampton stores opened as usual, but up and down Main Street the sole topic of conversation was the war. Telephone lines around town remained jammed as anxious friends and relatives exchanged reactions. The Gazette's 1½-inch headline that afternoon read "Congress

Pearl Harbor Headline

Northampton read about Pearl Harbor in the Daily Hampshire Gazette on Monday, December 8, 1941, the day after the attack.

Declares War On Japan. F.D.R. Assails Dastardly Attack on U.S ... A Date Which Will Live In Infamy."

Newspaper readers learned as much as officials in Washington wanted them to know. For example, the paper reported that at Pearl Harbor, one old American battleship had turned over and only one destroyer and two warships were lost. It was also reported, however, that there were approximately 3,000 dead and wounded; also that "Tokyo Says That U.S. Fleet Is Hard Hit. Damage Claimed To Be Such That It Cannot Compete With Intact Japanese Navy."

Local officials had already posted four armed guards at the Calvin Coolidge Memorial Bridge, the only access to Northampton over the Connecticut River, and had also arranged for lighting under the bridge "to prevent sabotage by any Axis sympathizer." Local utility and manufacturing plants were expected to provide their own protection. The water reservoir was to be guarded by armed men who were to "shoot on sight" any suspicious persons. Airplane "spotting posts" were to be manned on a 24-hour basis.

Also in the December 8 Gazette, we read: "763 Japs Arrested In The U.S. Aliens Being Rounded Up By FBI. Hearing Boards To Be Set Up To Pass On Evidence And Future Status." Two Smith College students, Sonoko Okamura of Hawaii and Martha Toda of Great Neck, Long Island, the paper reported, were both U.S. citizens and thus would "not be investigated unless a request for such action is forthcoming from state or federal officials, Chief of Police George J. Bernier reported today."

Professor Otto Kraushaar, chairman of the Smith College Emergency Council, the Gazette reported, spoke before an overflow audience in John M. Greene Hall to make the point that appeasement was not possible and that both Japan and Germany were obviously bent on world conquest.

A large ad on the back page read: "Defend Your Country!" Openings in Regular Army of U.S. for 2,471 New England men during next three months ... accent will be upon the Air Corps — 1,650 vacancies to be filled before December 31." The ad also advised that there were overseas "openings" in Panama, Puerto Rico, Hawaii and the Philippines.

In the December 9 Gazette, members of the local Keep 'Em Flying Committee, under Judge William Welch, announced plans to recruit local youths as "flying cadets" for the Army Air Corps. In the same Gazette was a report emanating from Berlin. An unidentified Nazi spokesman dubbed Roosevelt "father of the war," declaring that "he now has the war he wanted," and attributing Japan's attack to the fact that the American President had "encircled" that nation. "The Shylock in the White House first tried to bluff Japan, then encircle her in every way to prevent her from realizing her national principles and territorial needs." This same spokesman predicted that "now American boys will be plowed under," employing the same reference used by isolationist U.S. Senator Burton K. Wheeler in his warning about Roosevelt's foreign policy back in January.

Charles Lindbergh, oft-quoted leader of the isolationist organization America First,

Recruiting

This recruiting ad appeared in the Daily Hampshire Gazette on December 8, 1941, the day after the attack on Pearl Harbor. Note the irony of the "openings to enlist for" lines about Hawaii and the Philippines. The latter would be conquered by the Japanese with the loss of thousands of American lives.

was reported to be "In Seclusion, Will Not Talk."

On December 10, Northampton held its first air raid alarm test. A number of Smith students, it was reported, had been thrown into "a state of hysteria," and a luncheon at the Alumnae House had been canceled due to a rumor that the Army's nearby Westover Field would be bombed at 3 p.m. The Gazette office was flooded with calls as the rumor spread.

An all-college meeting fired off a telegram to the President pledging "the full-hearted support of the college faculty, staff and students in this struggle against world-wide aggression."

Meanwhile, young men of Northampton were filling the recruiting offices. On December 10 one of them, 19-year-old Francis Rice of Florence, volunteered at the recruiting office in Springfield. Two years later, the report of his death would appear in the Gazette: "Northampton Youth Is Killed In Action In Pacific Naval Battle."

On the same day that Rice enlisted, the S.S. Kresge store on Main Street struck its own blow for liberty by removing all Japanese goods from the counters of the store and announcing that none would be available from then on.

On December 11 the headlines announced that Germany and Italy had declared war on the United States, and vice versa. Thirty-six nations were now in the war.

Northampton's police were keeping a 24-hour-a-day watch on the city's LaFleur Airport to see that a no-flying order was obeyed. Donald Hood, who had taken many children on their first airplane flights, was named commander of the local Civil Air Patrol.

There was already a proposal to set up a wooden Honor Roll in front of Memorial Hall to honor local servicemen. Eventually there would be young women's names there as well.

At the end of December, the Gazette told readers how an 18-year-old who had sneered at some soldiers in a local roadhouse was led outside, garbed in an Army blouse and cap, and then hauled back in to show patrons "how he himself is going to look before long."

Just before Christmas, New England was "Prepared For A Holiday Attack" and there was "stepped up vigilance to offset any possible attempts by enemy air raiders or saboteurs to catch populations off guard."

A popular song launched in this period was "Goodbye Mama, I'm Off To Yokohama." Another song bore the optimistic title "The Sun Will Soon Be Setting on the Land of the Rising Sun."

At December's end, the Gazette quoted Adolph Berle, Assistant Secretary of State: "Everyone thinks that this war is going to be a short picnic. It is not going to be anything of the kind. It is going to be a long, dirty, painful, bloody business."

Francis Rice

A former Sea Scout and Gazette newsboy, 19-year-old Francis Rice enlisted in the U.S. Navy two days after the attack on Pearl Harbor. He died aboard the U.S.S. Atlanta during the Battle of Guadalcanal on November 13, 1942. A shipmate, Frank Yestramski, recalled how young and vulnerable Rice seemed. He had a fine voice; Yestramski remembered him singing "White Christmas" at a party aboard ship.

Gazette Cartoon

This cartoon appeared in the Daily Hampshire Gazette a few days after the attack on Pearl Harbor. We now know just how unready this country was for war in 1941.

1942 - 1943
Before We're Through With Them

"Before we're through with them, the Japanese language will be spoken only in hell," snarled Vice-Admiral William "Bull" Halsey when he sailed into Pearl Harbor after December 7 and surveyed the wreckage of the Pacific Fleet.

On April 18, 1942, the luckless Japanese people would receive their own first taste of modern warfare — to be inflicted primarily upon civilians, as the Japanese themselves had done in China and as would ultimately be done in such large measure throughout WWII.

Operation Shangri-la was the brainchild of President Roosevelt, who felt that an air strike on Tokyo would provide not only a much-needed psychological lift to the American public but also serve as a warning to the Japanese government that the United States was not defeated.

The assignment to bomb Tokyo was entrusted to Lt. Col. James Doolittle of the Army

Air Corps, whose B-25 Mitchell bombers, with their superior fuel capacity, were judged capable of reaching Tokyo from an aircraft carrier 500 miles away, dropping their bombs, and still being able to fly on to land in China.

After one month of training, on April 2, 16 B-25s and their crews sailed out of San Francisco aboard the carrier U.S.S. *Hornet.* They were still 650 miles from Tokyo on April 18 when suddenly they realized they had been spotted by a Japanese naval picket boat. The B-25 bombers were launched immediately. Discovering that enemy aircraft were on the attack, the picket boat captain went below deck and shot himself.

The people of Tokyo were in the middle of a routine air raid drill when the first B-25, with Lt. Carl Wildner of Amherst as lead navigator, roared in at tree-top level. As they flew in, Wildner later recalled, "The people below paid no attention whatsoever,

Battle of Midway

Dive bombers from the U.S.S. Hornet destroy a Japanese heavy cruiser of the Mogami class during the Battle of Midway. The American victory at Midway has been compared to that of Nelson at Trafalgar which permitted Wellington to defeat Napoleon at Waterloo. For the U.S., Midway opened the way to victory at Guadalcanal.

Local Hero

Lt. Carl Wildner was welcomed back from the Pacific at a civic reception on the Amherst town common. He was the navigator in the plane that dropped the first bomb during the legendary Doolittle Raid on Tokyo. Lt. Wildner is shown here with his parents and nephew in August, 1943.

Lt. Gen. Jonathan Wainwright, U.S.A.

Lt. Gen. Wainwright, shown broadcasting surrender instructions over Philippine station KZRH on May 7, 1942, conducted the heroic defense of Bataan and Corregidor. After being forced to surrender to the Japanese on May 6, 1942, he accompanied his men on the Bataan Death March and remained a POW in Manchuria for four years.

Guadalcanal

The largest of the Solomon Islands, Guadalcanal was wrested from the Japanese to keep it from becoming a base for their planned invasion of Australia. The Americans called it "Hell Island," but for the Japanese it was "Death Island."

apparently never suspecting that we were enemy aircraft overhead." So large was the city of Tokyo and its environs, the B-25s were over it for 45 minutes. "Wildner," the Gazette later reported, "believed that they could have burned it all up if they had more planes."

Of the 16 American planes involved in what became known as the "Doolittle Raid," all but one did manage to reach China after the mission, where they either crash-landed or were abandoned in the air by their crews. The sixteenth plane landed in the Soviet Union, where its crew was interned. Eight Americans who had landed in Japan-occupied China were tried for war crimes under a new Japanese law making the bombing of Japanese civilians or non-military targets a capital offense. All eight were sentenced to death, but on review in Tokyo five were instead given life sentences. One of the five died in captivity. The remaining three were executed on October 10, 1942.

On August 16, 1943, Amherst's Lt. Wildner was honored by his townspeople at a ceremony on the town common. According to the Gazette, he wore a decoration called the Order of the Cloud, presented to him by Mme. Chiang Kai-shek, as well as our own nation's Distinguished Flying Cross and the Air Medal.

Although little actual damage had been inflicted on Tokyo by the daring Doolittle Raid, its psychological effect was great — and not just on the American people. With Japan's defensive perimeter having been breached, Japanese military strategists perceived the need for another definitive victory. They turned to New Guinea, the Solomons and New Caledonia to obtain bases from which to attack northern Australia. Most of Australia's military were fighting in North Africa, leaving her vulnerable.

Adm. Yamamoto, the brilliant naval officer who had planned the attack on Pearl Harbor, planned first to seize Tulagi Island in the Solomons for a seaplane base, and also to take the town of Port Moresby on the south side of New Guinea, from which point Australia would be within easy striking distance.

Corregidor had just fallen — our lowest point in the war with Japan — when 72 hours later and 2,800 miles to the southeast the U.S. Navy gave Japan its first real wound in WWII. The Americans had broken an important Japanese code, and they were ready when the enemy invasion force appeared in the Coral Sea. For the first time in naval

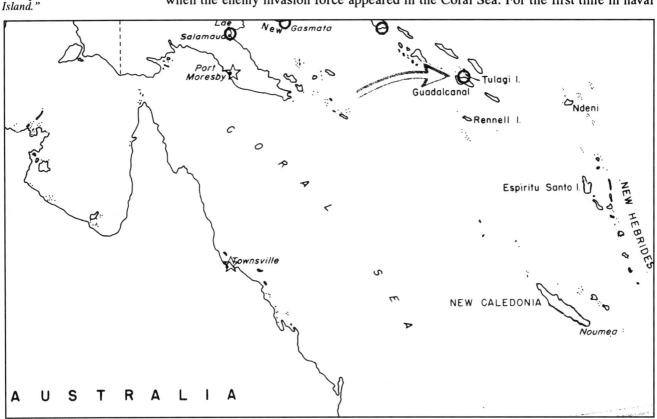

history the surface ships involved never saw each other; the battle was fought entirely by naval and marine aircraft. Thereafter the aircraft carrier was the dominant element in war at sea.

Fought between May 4 and 8, 1942, this Coral Sea action cost the United States dearly but ended in what amounted to a standoff. The Japanese destroyed the carrier U.S.S. *Lexington* and damaged the *Yorktown*, but the Americans damaged the Japanese carriers *Shokaku* and *Zuikaku* sufficiently to keep them from fighting soon afterward at Midway. Above all, the Japanese threat to Australia was lifted, at least for the moment.

One Northampton man who experienced the Battle of the Coral Sea and lived to tell about it was Lt. Irving Davis, the *Lexington's* communications officer. The *Lexington* was attacked by 70 Japanese planes and took two torpedo hits on her port side plus a bomb on her main deck. Nevertheless she was, as Davis later reported, able to steam on at 25 knots. Then, over an hour later, there was "a bad internal explosion below, followed by a series of several small explosions, and then a second large explosion." This last started up fires beyond the crew's control, and word finally came to abandon ship.

Himself among the last to leave the doomed carrier, Davis related how he swam for half an hour before reaching a life raft. Praising the courage and calmness of the crew under fire, "both colored and white," as he put it, and insisting that the retreat was orderly, he expressed his thankfulness "that the sea was calm and that the explosions had frightened away the sharks."

The young officer was "apparently reluctant to talk about the details of the battle and the sinking of the 33,000-ton ship," a Gazette reporter wrote after an interview with Davis, home on leave at the end of July. Davis had obviously concealed much of the worst of his ordeal.

"All the fellows were crying and weeping like young girls, and so was I," another sailor would later be quoted as saying about watching the *Lexington* go under. There were 2,700 survivors; about 200 died.

Japan's only successes in the Battle of the Coral Sea were to secure a seaplane base at Tulagi and to be able to start building an airstrip on a large and forbidding island, off the northeast coast of Australia, with the strange name of Guadalcanal.

Yamamoto had early recognized the need to end the threat of the American carriers that, by virtue of being at sea on December 7, had escaped destruction at Pearl Harbor. He now plotted what he hoped would prove a final confrontation with the United States Navy. As the site of that confrontation he chose the island of Midway, 1,000 miles east of Japan and 1,100 miles west of Hawaii, a desirable base for Japan's perimeter defenses.

On June 4, 1942, alerted once again by the compromised Japanese code, three U.S. aircraft carriers, including the patched-up *Yorktown*, lay in wait with 180 planes at Midway. They were greatly outnumbered, however, by Adm. Yamamoto's four carriers, his 272 aircraft, his 11 battleships and other support vessels.

The Japanese fought off four American air strikes, with two-thirds of the U.S. aircraft repulsed or destroyed in the process. But the fifth strike, carried out by 37 Dauntless dive bombers, won the day. By chance they came on the four Japanese carriers with their flight decks clogged with aircraft just back from hitting Midway and readying to attack the American carriers. Within five minutes, three Japanese carriers were ablaze; the fourth went up six hours later. It was all over by June 6. On June 8, Yamamoto turned homeward.

Only six months after the debacle at Pearl Harbor, the Battle of Midway reversed the whole course of the war in the Pacific.

"U.S. Defense of Midway Sends Japs Staggering," was the Gazette headline on June 6. An Associated Press story declared that "The U.S., toughened and tried by six months of warfare since Pearl Harbor, now seems to have wrested the initiative from Japan in the battle of the Pacific."

Lt. Samuel Adams of Baltimore, who had grown up in Pine Grove in Northampton and graduated from the Naval Academy at Annapolis in 1935, had already seen action in the Atlantic, at Salamaua, Lae, New Guinea, Tulagi Harbor and the Coral Sea. He was one of the pilots responsible for the historic victory at Midway — but it cost him his life. In his effort to score a direct hit on a Japanese cruiser, Adams was seen to dive his plane

Lt. Irving E. Davis, U.S.N.

Radio officer of the U.S.S. Lexington, *he survived the carrier's sinking in the Battle of the Coral Sea. Before the war, Davis worked as a test supervisor at Westinghouse Electric in Springfield.*

Lt. Samuel Adams, U.S.N.

A native of Northampton, Adams graduated from Annapolis in 1935 and became a Navy pilot. Known to his squadron as "the blond Viking," Adams pioneered the steep dive bombing tactics used by the Navy in WWII. He was also credited with locating the Hiryu, *the fourth and last Japanese carrier to be sunk at the Battle of Midway, a blow from which Japan never recovered. Adams was killed during the battle. He is shown here with his sister Anna.*

too low to pull out.

Reported missing in action at first, and then — after many weeks — as killed in action, Adams had distinguished himself by winning the Navy Cross plus two gold stars and the Purple Heart. In 1944, a new destroyer would be named after him and christened at Bath, Maine, by his widow.

Adams' plane was one of more than 100 the Navy lost at Midway. Also lost was one destroyer and the carrier U.S.S. *Yorktown*, hit by three bombs and two torpedoes.

One of the surviving sailors off the *Yorktown* was Electrician's Mate 2nd Class John Londergan of Northampton. Home on leave the following September, he told a Gazette reporter how he had been stationed in a fire control tower during the attack and was "considerably shaken up" but not injured. Certain other *Yorktown* survivors fished from the water by the Japanese met a grisly fate. A torpedo-bomber pilot, for example, was tortured for information and then hacked to death.

The Americans paid a high price at Midway, but for the Japanese the bill was much higher. Four Japanese carriers and her most experienced navy pilots were lost, one heavy cruiser was sunk and another damaged. Approximately 3,500 Japanese died. Midway was the first Japanese naval defeat in modern times; there were others to come.

The first American land offensive in the Pacific was about to take place on Guadalcanal. In due time the Americans would rename it Hell Island; Death Island was how it became known to the Japanese.

Even as the Battle of Midway raged, the Japanese had been busy establishing themselves in the New Guinea-Solomons area. Back in Tokyo the strategists at Imperial General Headquarters were already planning their systems of occupation for Australia and New Zealand. U.S. Army Intelligence reported, somewhat belatedly, that they were also beginning construction of the Guadalcanal air base.

For the Americans, the object of the deadly combat for islands in the Pacific was to secure bases from which to move steadily toward the taking of the Japanese home islands themselves. American strategy involved two main thrusts westward towards Japan: one starting in the Gilbert and Marshall Islands and converging on the Philippines; the other starting from Guadalcanal. But first the island had to be taken.

At dawn on August 7, eight months after Pearl Harbor, the first amphibious invasion made by the United States since the Spanish-American War began. With little difficulty, combat groups of the 1st Marine Division went ashore. Their main objective, the airfield under construction, was taken and named Henderson Field after a Marine pilot killed at Midway. Before it was over the Guadalcanal campaign would claim the lives of 3,000 Americans and, it has been estimated, more than 50,000 Japanese.

Although the initial landing was relatively uneventful, it was followed two days later by a debacle that the Navy labeled the Battle of Savo Island. Those sailors and Marines who fought it, however, would call it "The Battle of the Five Sitting Ducks." Some military historians have called it the worst U.S. naval defeat since 1812. One thousand two hundred seventy American sailors died, and another 709 were wounded. Four Allied cruisers were sunk, and another cruiser and two destroyers were damaged.

The action took place in what was called "the Slot": the sea corridor of the Solomon Islands that runs 400 miles from Bougainville to Guadalcanal. The area was being guarded at its southern gate, between Savo and Guadalcanal, by the *Chicago* and the *Canberra* of Australia. At the northern gate, between Savo and Florida islands, were the *Astoria*, the *Quincy* and the *Vincennes*. All were there to screen the transports and cargo ships from possible attack.

At 10:30 a.m. on August 8, an Australian search plane spotted Japanese warships heading south from Rabaul. Incredible as it now seems, the pilot did not report this finding until he returned from his mission and had tea. The report did not reach Guadalcanal until 7 that evening. The enemy ships were also sighted by a U.S. submarine that reported five ships rather than the actual eight. By the time the Navy brass had erroneously decided that the enemy force intended a seaplane base strike the next day, the Japanese were only five hours away from Guadalcanal.

They entered the sound south of Savo at about 1:30 a.m. and were first spotted only

Electrician's Mate 2nd Class John T. Londergan, U.S.N.

Londergan returned on shore-leave to his native Northampton after surviving the sinking of the carrier U.S.S. Yorktown *at the Battle of Midway.*

4,000 yards away and bearing down by the watch aboard the destroyer U.S.S. *Patterson*. Cmdr. Frank Walker, who had gotten his ship out of Pearl Harbor to fight another day, sent out the alert at 1:43 a.m.: "Warning! Warning! Strange ships entering harbor!" It was already too late.

At 1:55, blinded by a massive enemy searchlight trained on her, the *Patterson* was hit by a large caliber shell that knocked out her number 4 gun and damaged number 3. Three men were killed; seven would be reported missing. One of the *Patterson's* dead was Shipfitter 3rd Class Zigmund Sieruta, ammunition-handler for number 3 gun. He was the first Northampton resident to be killed in WWII.

A graduate of Smith's Agricultural School in 1935, Sieruta had worked as a metalsmith for the Philipp Manufacturing Company in Easthampton until he enlisted in the Navy in 1940. The official telegram informing the Sieruta family of his death, dated August 27, bore three red stars or crosses on it, remembered Felixa Sieruta (Coogan), his

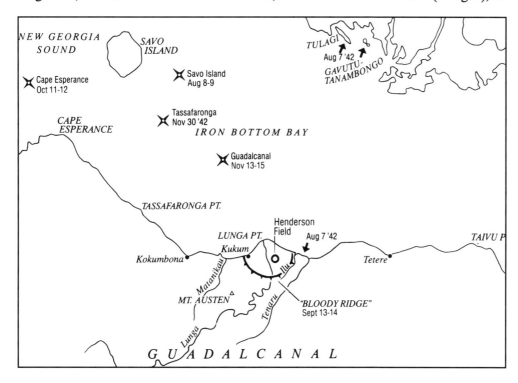

Battle of Savo Island

Dubbed "The Battle of the Five Sitting Ducks" by survivors, this action on August 8/9, 1942, occurred when a Japanese naval force surprised American and Australian vessels positioned to guard "the Slot"—the Solomon Islands sea corridor. Two young Northampton men, Zigmund Sieruta and William Kecy, died during this disaster.

sister, who had answered the doorbell. She signed for it and went into the kitchen.

"My mother was crying. She knew already what this meant," she recalled. The telegram began: "The Navy Department deeply regrets to inform you ..." It closed with: "If not possible to send the remains home they will be interred temporarily in the locality where death occurred and you will be notified accordingly."

On October 16, Nancy Trow, executive secretary of the American Red Cross in Northampton, informed the Sierutas that their son had been buried at sea. One of Felixa's cherished mementoes was the letter written to the family on September 11, 1942, by his shipmates on the *Patterson*.

"In our gang there has been a mutual agreement, that in case anything happened to us, the others would write to their family. Your son was a great man, a real shipmate ... hard to equal ... whose middle name was 'fight'. ... He did his work well and his fighting even better, but working or fighting he was always smiling. ... Your son did not suffer, for which we are all very thankful. He left us instantly. ... This letter is written on behalf of the Carpenter and Shipfitter gang of the U.S.S. *Patterson* and myself.

Sincerely,
    Jack H. Dowlen,
    Robert L. Jackson

Shipfitter Zigmund Sieruta, U.S.N.

Sieruta graduated from Northampton's Smith's Agricultural School in 1937. He was the first serviceman from the city to be killed in WWII. He died at the age of 23 at his battle station, number 3 gun, aboard the U.S.S. Patterson *during the Battle of Savo Island.*

William O. Barth
Gavin Smith
O.A. Gilbert
C.F. Tomlinson
Peter M. Car
E. Graves

P.S. The time and date was 2:05 a.m. Aug. 10 (9 in U.S.), 1942."

A diary (kept against orders) by one *Patterson* crew member recorded some of the horror of that night off Savo Island. "Number 4 gun shelter is a shambles, a shell came in and hit the blower motor and exploded, killed everyone in the room. ... They had to shovel one fellow over the side ... some were blown over the side. ... Number 3 gun is out of commission. ... We are ordered alongside the *Canberra* to take off the wounded. ... The doctors are sure getting a workout, the place looks like a butcher shop. ... We buried our dead, tied them up in a canvas with two shells to hold them down and over the side. Something to look forward to."

Just before daybreak, during the same battle, another young man from Northampton died. Electrician's Mate 3rd Class William Kecy was killed aboard the U.S.S. *Quincy*.

On Guadalcanal, Sgt. Arthur Pope questioned survivors as they returned from the Savo Island disaster about Kecy, whom he had known in the First Baptist Church in Northampton. "An electrician's mate?" they would say, "Forget it! Anyone below decks is gone, gone. They're all gone."

The crew of the *Quincy* had actually managed to hit back at attackers with a few salvos, according to a survivor, but then she was hit by two torpedoes. The forward magazines blew up — and that is how William Kecy met his death.

For some reason, the Japanese now withdrew, leaving the Americans and Australians

Five Young Northampton Men

Left to right:
William Kecy died aboard the U.S.S. Quincy.

Francis Mailloux survived the sinking of the U.S.S. Meredith.

Charles Slater died on the U.S.S. Barton.

Maurice Loiselle survived the sinking of the heavy cruiser U.S.S. Northampton.

Charles Kolodzinski, a downed pilot and prisoner of war, read of the sinking of the U.S.S. Northampton *in a German newspaper.*

to count their losses. The *Astoria,* the *Canberra,* the *Quincy* and the *Vincennes* all now lay in the mud at the bottom of Savo Sound. The sailors began to call it "Ironbottom Bay." The 11,000 Marines already on Guadalcanal were safe for the moment, but they were effectively stranded with enough ammunition for only one week of heavy fighting and enough rations for 37 days.

The American public was not told until later about the Savo Island disaster and thus had assumed that, with the invasion of Guadalcanal, the country was on its way to victory in the Pacific. This was true, but it would take a long time and demand a high price.

On October 15, off the coast of Guadalcanal, the U.S.S. *Meredith* was attacked with bombs and torpedoes from a flight of 27 planes off a Japanese carrier. After only five or 10 minutes, the *Meredith* went down. Those who survived the attack took to life rafts or clung to the sides of overloaded rafts. The water swarmed with feeding sharks.

Of the *Meredith's* crew of 275 men, only 88 survived, one of whom was Electrician's Mate 3rd Class Francis Mailloux of Leeds. During a visit back home in February of the following year, Mailloux gave a graphic description of his ship's fate to a Gazette reporter. He had been blown overboard with shrapnel wounds in his legs and severe arm burns. Still able to swim through the oil-covered water, Mailloux made it to a life raft from which he and others were finally rescued. Two hundred of the *Meredith's* survivors, Mailloux added, were machine-gunned in the water by the Japanese.

Two other Northampton men would die a month later in those same waters off Guadalcanal. Pharmacist's Mate 3rd Class Francis Rice served aboard the U.S.S. *Atlanta* that was shattered during the naval Battle of Guadalcanal. Half the *Atlanta's* crew were killed when she was torpedoed. The other half, burned and mutilated, drifted among greedily feasting sharks while others clung to rafts under a burning sun. Rice is believed to have died on November 12. Ensign Charles Slater, an Annapolis graduate, was aboard the U.S.S. *Barton,* which sank within two minutes after literally being blown apart during the third battle of Savo Island. He was listed as missing in action for more than a year before his parents in Northampton would finally be informed that he had died on November 14.

On November 30, the heavy cruiser U.S.S. *Northampton* went down at Tassafaronga, north of Guadalcanal, with 1st Class Petty Officer Maurice Loiselle among the survivors. Loiselle had first been a member of the U.S.S. *Oklahoma's* crew but had been transferred to the *Northampton* before the *Oklahoma* was sunk at Pearl Harbor.

Back in Northampton on leave the following January, Loiselle gave the Gazette his own account of what it was like to have to abandon a dying ship in the Pacific. He had been separated from the rest of the crew as they slid down the sides of the sinking vessel, he said, and had to escape being sucked down with the *Northampton* as she went under. That night he swam all alone for two hours before being picked up. "It was no picnic,"

Sgt. Arthur Pope

Pictured, left, with a friend on Guadalcanal, where he fought with the Americal Division, Pope left Northampton with Company G on January 27, 1941. He spent 3½ years in the Pacific Theater, ending his tour of duty in 1945 when the Americans recaptured the Philippines.

The U.S.S. Northampton

Known as "Fighting Nora," this heavy cruiser was christened by Grace Coolidge in 1929. The Northampton *was hit by a Japanese torpedo during the Battle of Tassafaronga and sank on November 30, 1942.*

Loiselle recalled. "One guy, after orders came to abandon ship, went down into the engine room and brought out the assistant engineer who had been overcome by steam. The ship's cook swam two hours while towing a disabled shipmate. ... I can't remember all the things that happened that would make the people here at home even more proud of the fellows."

Before she sank, the *Northampton* had seen considerable action in all the Pacific battles and to her crew was known as "Fighting Nora." Far away in Germany, downed American airman Lt. Charles Kolodzinski, a Northampton man who was destined to spend a total of 31 months as a POW, came on a photo in a German newspaper of the U.S.S. *Northampton* and a report of her sinking. He clipped it and pasted it in a notebook where it remains to this day: *"Schwerer Kreuzer Northampton bei einem Gefecht nordlich von Guadalcanal gesunken."*

Almost as if speaking for all these young sailors fighting — and dying, so many of them — in the Pacific, Pharmacist's Mate 2nd Class Thomas Cantwell wrote home to Northampton after many weeks in battle:

"We have had a rugged time for the past several weeks ... sleeping on the deck on gun mounts, on gun shields, under the guns — and always ready. The hard part is not the fighting but the waiting to fight. ... If we have good fighter planes with us they save us a lot of trouble. ... One of the truly great sights of this cruise was the ship shooting all her guns at once. ... I've not been away from my station for more than food in a long time."

He had been at sea 11 months when this was written.

The land fighting on "Hell Island" was just as horrible as that at sea. One hundred miles in length and 50 miles wide at its thickest part, Guadalcanal is the largest of the Solomon Islands. Young Americans and Japanese alike suffered eight months of desperate and vicious fighting, as well as illness and hunger, on that strip of land.

Guadalcanal is remembered by those who survived it — such as Sgt. Arthur Pope — as a hot and steaming green hell that smelled of rotting vegetation. Everything rotted, Pope said; food, equipment, clothing, shoes and human feet. Strange skin diseases erupted and were given names like "jungle rot." There were snakes, scorpions, screeching animals, rain, rats and insects, he recalled. Dysentery was common. Long after the island had been "secured," there were still insane nocturnal *banzai* charges by desperate Japanese. And there were tree-top snipers everywhere.

When he came to Guadalcanal that October, Sgt. Pope was still in his early 20s, a sergeant in the 182nd Infantry Regiment of the Americal Division. He had been a member of National Guard Company G and among those men taken from the 26th, or Yankee Division, and sent to form up a new task force headed for the Pacific.

Before he was through, Pope would spend three-and-a-half years in the Pacific: five months on Guadalcanal, a year on Bougainville, and finally as part of the invasion and recapture of the Philippines. He returned to Northampton at age 25 — "yellow as a lemon" from atabrine and weighing only 114 pounds.

"There were a lot of good times out there as well as bad ones and some I'd never want to do again," he recalled years later. "I always figured we were winning, taking one island after another like notches in a belt. I never got hit — just lucky I guess, so I was never sent home. I just stayed out there. I thought they'd forgot us out there."

Pope's memories center around the jungle patrols he had to make in an effort to determine what the Japanese were going to do next. There were the snipers: "You never knew where one would be, so we'd spray the trees with a machine gun. ... Sometimes we'd lose three or four men on patrol, and then three or four days later we had to go out to bring the bodies back to the graves-registration guys. By that time the bodies were already badly decomposed, and we'd have to bring them back on an overhead rack on a Jeep. There's not much left of a body in that heat, they just sort of collapse. It was awful.

"I remember one weird incident. We were out on patrol — a dozen or so of us — when we heard what sounded like the whole Japanese army coming down along the trail. We always moved in silence, but they always made a lot of noise with gear hung all over them and clanking like cowbells as they moved. Very noisy; this time we could even hear them talking. We got off to one side and hunkered down as flat as we could. I hoped nobody'd sneeze. There were about a hundred of them and 16 of us. We'd have been wiped out. They were headed for our sector, so we beat them back and got ready for them."

Pope also recalled the *banzai* charges: "First they would race back and forth out in front of us, trying to draw our fire so they could know where we were. They'd scream things like ''Merican you die tonight' — everything to get us nervous and scared. They were good soldiers until you took out their non-coms and officers. We took four or five prisoners one day. You had to strip them first, because some had grenades hidden on them, and then we'd throw their clothing back at them. There was one crack division on Guadalcanal that was in on the 'rape of Nanking' where Japanese troops killed all those Chinese civilians. Their commander committed *hara-kiri* rather than surrender. He wasn't used to losing, I guess."

Sgt. James Grogan of Northampton would be awarded the Soldier's Medal "for Heroism at Guadalcanal in rescuing a comrade from drowning, at great personal risk to himself, on February 5, 1943."

Some Northampton men never left Guadalcanal. Death came early to Sgt. Neil Champoux of the Marine Corps, on September 15, as the Marines battled for the airstrip that became Henderson Field.

Sgt. James Grogan

He won the Soldier's Medal on Guadalcanal.

After the Battle

This is how a weary young infantryman looked leaving the line after 21 days of combat on Guadalcanal.

Pvt. Francis Ansanitis died on November 21. A fellow soldier later told his family, "His head was blown off. He died instantly and without pain." Civilians perhaps cannot understand why a serviceman would consider relating this detail to be a kindness, but any combat veteran would.

When the official telegram came to the Ansanitis home in Florence, it was Ansanitis' mother who received it. Born in Lithuania, she could speak English but not read it and thus had to ask the Western Union delivery boy to read it to her. In disbelief she carried the telegram to a neighbor to hear it read again. On his last furlough home, Ansanitis had confided to his friend, William Sieruta, as they shook hands: "Well, Bill, this is my last trip here. I won't be coming back."

William Puchalski, a friend of his would one day tell his family, was shot and killed instantly by one of the Japanese snipers tied high up in a coconut tree. Marine Pvt. William Noble wrote home that he had spoken to Puchalski the morning of the day he was killed. A buddy of Puchalski's sent his family a photo of his crude grave with its rough white wooden cross. It was the only photo of its kind to show up in the Gazette during the war.

Sgt. Michael Florio, the Gazette reported, had been struck in the knee by a rifle bullet, in the thigh by fragments of a hand grenade and in the ankle by a 90 mm. mortar shell. The newspaper went on to report that Florio, who was among those who had left Northampton with the National Guard in January 1941, was aided under fire by his brother Vito, a private in the same outfit, who carried him to safety on a stretcher improvised from a shelter-half. Florio would lose the badly injured leg. He was later quoted recalling his arrival on Guadalcanal on November 11, 1942: "It was Armistice Day, but it didn't look much like it there."

* * *

Just as the war in the Pacific, in late 1942, finally seemed to be swinging in our favor, so did the deadly duel in the Atlantic between the submarines of the Nazi Kriegsmarine and the Allied supply ships.

"U.S. Slowly Winning Main Campaign In the Atlantic," the Gazette proclaimed at the end of the year. "Steadily Increasing Production of Both War and Merchant Ships To Clinch the Ultimate Victory."

It was, historians point out, the failure of both the Japanese and the Nazi leaders to assess the industrial potential of this country that played a major role in their defeat. Between September 1939 and May 1943 the Allies had 2,452 merchant ships sunk — nearly 13 million gross register tons — as well as 175 warships. At certain low points — November 1942, for example, when 509,000 tons were sunk — it had seemed that Britain might be conquered. Instrumental in preventing this was our capacity in the United States to turn out Liberty Ships and tankers enough to surmount such devastation. German U-boat losses of about 15 per month, moreover, steadily weakened the Kriegsmarine. By May 1943, Adm. Karl Doenitz of the German Navy admitted later, "We had lost the Battle of the Atlantic."

While Americans were fighting, suffering and dying in the Pacific theater, sailors and Merchant Marines were facing death on the sea lanes carrying the war materiel and much-needed food and medical supplies to Britain and to the Soviet Union, which had

News from the Front

Pvt. William Puchalski died on Guadalcanal on December 12, 1942.

Marine Sgt. Neil Champoux, left, died on Guadalcanal during the struggle for the airstrip later known as Henderson Field.

Pvt. Francis Ansanitis, center, killed in action on Guadalcanal, November 21, 1942.

Seaman and Radioman Charles Hayes, right, survived his second sinking on the deadly Murmansk Run to the U.S.S.R.

joined the Allies after the Nazis Panzer units roared over the Russian border on June 22, 1941. The most deadly and dreaded route was between Iceland and the Russian cities of Murmansk and Archangel on the Arctic Ocean, known as the "Murmansk Run."

When 18-year-old Charles Hayes, a Radioman 3rd Class and also Seaman 1st Class, spent his shore leave in Northampton in the autumn of 1942, he described for the Gazette his own experiences on "the Murmansk Run." Something of what it meant to have been torpedoed twice within one month in the North Atlantic shows up in the youthful but drawn face in the accompanying photograph.

On his first voyage and only in his 17th year, as a Navy gunner and radioman, Hayes and the rest of the crew on his merchant vessel had been subjected to six days and nights of machine gunning and cannonading by Luftwaffe planes as well as constant harassment by submarines. He was manning his 50-caliber machine gun when a Junker 88 roared in and scored a direct bomb hit. The order came to abandon ship. An English escort ship rescued survivors, including Hayes, from the icy Arctic water, and carried them into Murmansk.

After a brief rest in the Russian city, Hayes was ordered back to Iceland. On this, his second voyage, his ship was torpedoed by a German submarine. This time he went over the side into a lifeboat, which capsized when a second torpedo hit the ship. Fifty-five of the 60 men in that lifeboat died in the freezing water. Hayes was one of the five survivors. Adrift on wreckage for two-and-a-half hours, the nearly frozen and oil-soaked five were picked up by a French corvette and taken to safety.

As soon as his shore leave in Northampton was up, Hayes assured the Gazette reporter, he would be "going after them again."

Between March 1941 and October 1945, 16,529,791 tons of military cargo were carried to the beleaguered Russians over the Murmansk Run: trucks, jeeps, locomotives, rails, gasoline, tanks, aircraft and boots. During the 24-hour-long days in summer, the convoys offered German submarines an easy target. Death in those waters came quickly because of the intense cold, and the route became the grave of many good men. One of them, whose death was reported in January of 1943, was Petty Officer Joseph Subocz of Northampton.

Subocz had visited his onetime elementary schoolteacher Rachel Osgood of Florence just before his last voyage. A short man, he was still called "Little Joe" even in the Merchant Marine, he told her. He was philosophical concerning the dangers he had yet to face. "The way we figure it, if your number is up, you go," he said. "If we are carrying explosives and we are torpedoed, we'll never know what hit us."

Also in 1943, Cadet Midshipman Donald Fennessey's ship, the S.S. *James Smith*, a Liberty ship, was torpedoed in a convoy bound for Brazil. The deck looked "like a perforated tin can," Fennessey recalled afterward. Six merchant seamen and five Navy men died.

Fighting as sailors in the U.S. Navy in this Battle of the Atlantic were other young men of Northampton, including Yeoman Richard Boudway, who spent 20 hours clinging to the side of a raft in a howling Atlantic storm after his Coast Guard cutter sank. Boudway had seen his crew mates swept overboard and was himself almost trapped below deck in his attempt to save the men's pay accounts and service records. Diving from the sinking ship he then had to swim 300 yards to a raft. After 18 hours, the survivors spotted a Navy blimp passing overhead — but it did not see them. A ship in a passing convoy finally caught sight of them and radioed the blimp to drop smoke bombs to mark their position. A Coast Guard cutter picked them up and delivered them to the nearest port, where Boudway spent many days recovering from exhaustion and exposure.

Carpenter's Mate 2nd Class Raymond LaBarge, who had worked at the Springfield Armory making rifles before enlisting, joined the destroyer U.S.S. *Thomas* when she was commissioned on November 21, 1943, at the Norfolk Navy Yard.

These little destroyers were the killer-watchdogs that protected merchant vessels and heavily laden troopships by detecting U-boats and attacking them with their guns and depth charges. "Oh, boy! how those little destroyers would roll!" goes a line in a poem written in their honor. "They'd stand on their ends like an up-ended bowl. They'd plunge

On Active Duty At Sea

Joseph Subocz, a petty officer in the Merchant Marine, died on the Murmansk Run.

Yeoman Richard Boudway survived 20 hours on a raft in a raging Atlantic storm after his ship went down.

Carpenter's Mate 2nd Class Raymond LaBarge, kneeling center front, was "commended at mast" for making repairs to the hull of the U.S.S. Thomas *during a violent storm.*

into seas, and you'd think they were gone. They'd tremble all over, and then they'd plunge on."

On March 10, 1944, when the *Thomas* was on destroyer-escort duty in the Atlantic, LaBarge was "commended at mast" for having made emergency repairs to the hull, in a raging storm, held fast only by a lifeline. On July 5, 1944, south of Newfoundland, the *Thomas* rammed and sank the German U-233 loaded with mines thought to be destined for the harbor entrances at either Halifax or New York. The 1,600-ton U-233 was ripped almost in half and sank rapidly — but not before 29 of her crew were hauled from the sea, including Kapitan Leutnant Hans Steen.

Earlier, during the invasion of Italy, LaBarge had played the role of his ship's French interpreter when they had to negotiate with the Free French in North Africa for fresh water and torpedoes, and again in the Mediterranean, prior to the Allied invasion of Italy, when the *Thomas* had to make contact with small fishing boats. On his last voyage aboard the *Thomas*, LaBarge was blinded for 21 days as the result of gun-flash. Disqualified by this injury for sea duty, he was next sent to Okinawa in the Pacific, where he was again wounded.

Not entering the Merchant Marines until December 1943, 18-year-old Cecil Clark of Northampton experienced a different war. It started with long months in the South Pacific aboard a tanker that would pick up gasoline at Caribbean refineries, run it through the Panama Canal and then deliver it to ships of all types — destroyers, cruisers and submarines.

"The Pacific is big and lonely," Clark recalled. He remembered young sailors looking like castaways who had to man great concrete storage tankers "alone on some godforsaken little island." He wondered if "loneliness, the fear of being left behind, and homesickness are not among the greatest tortures of war."

Clark's later voyages would carry him to the Florida Islands, Guadalcanal and Tulagi, the Fiji and the Marshall islands, Curacao, Aruba, Panama and the Christmas Islands,

Cecil Clark, U.S. Merchant Marine

Cecil Clark, second from left, age 18, with his crew mates.

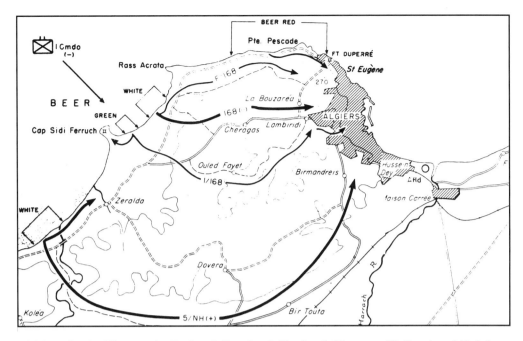

Operation Torch

On November 8, 1942, Operation Torch, the largest amphibious invasion in history up to that point, involved more than 100,000 American and British troops and was intended to drive Axis forces out of North Africa.

Africa, Spain, Venezuela, Iceland, Scotland, England, Norway, Holland and Belgium. "I crossed the International Date Line, the Arctic Circle and the equator," he said years later, "I met many brave young men, some of whom never came home. I was lucky — and did get home. And I was only 20 years old when I got there."

Had the men of the U.S. Navy and the U.S. Merchant Marine not won this war of the supply lines in both the Atlantic and Pacific, the outcome of World War II might have been very different. It was their courage and heroism that enabled other young men to fight on land, sea and in the air and to win. Courage and fidelity are vital, but American troops also had the advantage of never-ending quantities of food, ammunition, equipment and medical supplies. Not until 1988 did Congress pass Public Law 95-202 that at long last recognized the Merchant Marines as veterans of WWII. These men finally received the official discharges, medals, awards and benefits due them.

Armistice Negotiations

Col. Hobart Gay, U.S.A., on the right, arrives at Fedala in North Africa on November 11, 1942, to negotiate an armistice with French troops who have decided to favor the Allies after a period of indecision.

***

Meanwhile, on the European front, the Allies' first ground offensive against the Axis powers of Germany and of Italy began in North Africa on November 8, 1942. Since 1940, British forces had been fighting first the Italians and then the legendary German Afrika Korps under Gen. Erwin Rommel for control of the empire's lifeline through the Mediterranean and, more importantly, access to the oil fields of the Persian Gulf. The invasion of North Africa, code-named Operation Torch, would provide the Allies a position from which to strike at Rommel's forces from the rear. This was also the best response that Britain and the United States were able to make to the Soviet Union's demand for a second front. It would prove to be a tough testing ground for equipment, tactics and soldiers alike.

Operation Torch was entrusted to British Adm. Sir John Cunningham and a still obscure American lieutenant general named Dwight D. Eisenhower. "Torch" consisted of three separate forces: 35,000 Americans who sailed directly from the United States to French Morocco; 39,000 Americans who embarked from Britain with the intent to take Oran in western Algeria; and a combined force of 10,000 Americans and 23,000 British who sailed out of Britain to capture Algiers. The U.S. and British navies together transported and protected all these forces. This was the largest amphibious invasion thus far in the history of warfare: 300 warships, 370 merchant ships and more than 107,000 men.

At first the experienced German troops of the Afrika Korps gave the green American troops a difficult time. Maneuvers on their home soil, moreover, had not prepared the Americans for the terrors of the dreaded Stuka dive bomber, the German 88 artillery piece or the hardships of the North African terrain. In February 1943, Rommel drove a bulge into the Allied lines at Kasserine Pass and routed the Americans, 2,400 of whom would spend a long time as POWs in Germany.

One of these prisoners was Pfc. Joseph Gesiorek of Northampton, a member of a

Lt. Ramona Gilligan, U.S.A Nurse Corps.

Lt. Ramona Gilligan volunteered for active duty after Pearl Harbor. Arriving in Casablanca in May 1943, she was assigned first to a station hospital just outside the city, and then to a prisoner-of-war camp at Berrechid where she helped care for wounded German and Italian soldiers.

medical unit captured on February 19, 1943. He had enlisted in 1940; he would be a prisoner in Germany at Stalag 3B until his liberation on June 8, 1945.

Northampton was also represented in North Africa by Cpls. Chester Switalski and Julian Bubrowski, both wounded there in 1943. Sgt. Lenwood Choquette, a paratrooper, the first man from Northampton to wear the coveted wings and boots of this profession, was in on the capture of Tafaraoui airdrome near Oran, which then had to be defended against an attack by the French Foreign Legion — as the French had not yet decided whose side they were on. Later, Choquette would fight alongside the French Zouaves in an engagement that won his 509th parachute battalion the right to wear the Zouaves' insignia, *"Suis Ty Reste"* on their right breast pockets. His unit would end up in Italy, where he would be wounded at Venafro and would recover in time to take part in the Allied landing at Anzio.

In October 1943, Tech. Sgt. John Chereski, a radio gunner aboard a B-25, completed 50 missions flying out of North Africa. His two toughest involved a sea sweep off the coast of Cape Bon on April 30, where his crew bombed and sank a 350-foot destroyer, and a raid on vital railroad marshalling yards in Italy on September 30 that won them a special commendation from Gen. Doolittle, now in command of Chereski's Air Force unit.

Lt. Ramona Gilligan of the Army Nurse Corps, who had volunteered for overseas duty after Pearl Harbor, landed at Fidela Beach near Casablanca in May 1943. Her first assignment was with a station hospital on the outskirts of that city, but after a few months she was put on "detached service" at a prisoner-of-war camp at Berrechid. There U.S. Army doctors and nurses worked alongside Afrika Korps army doctors and medical corpsmen in caring for wounded German and Italian prisoners. All the staff lived in tents, and in the evenings there would float out over the whole prison compound the voice of an Italian POW singing operatic arias. On Sundays, Mass was said for Roman Catholic captors and captives alike by a German chaplain. When these prisoners were exchanged for American wounded, Gilligan was on the hospital train with her German patients, who called out *"Aufwiedersehen, Schwester,* (sister) *Aufwiedersehen."* On hearing these German farewells, an American M.P. walked up to Gilligan and sneered, "Are they friends of yours, Lieutenant?"

Marrakech Encounter

Halfway around the world from home, Lt. Ramona Gilligan, right, and Lt. Francis Sheehey, center, U.S.A. Air Corps and former Northampton newsman, enjoy a chance meeting in Marrakech. The other person in the photo is unidentified.

Gilligan's next assignment was at Marrakech in the French-American Hospital, where she gave emergency shots against a bubonic plague threat. Into her dispensary one day walked one of the best known young men of Northampton, Francis Sheehey, formerly a reporter with the Springfield Daily News and now a B-17 pilot with the Army Air Corps. Sheehey had suffered a burn in a routine airplane mishap and had come in to have it dressed before heading out on a mission. There was just time for a photo, dinner and some reminiscences about Northampton before he took off.

Rommel and the Afrika Korps were in effect defeated when, with only a few hundred tanks left, little ammunition, virtually no fuel and no air cover, they were forced to cease attacks on the Allied armies. "The Desert Fox," as Rommel was known, in ill health, left North Africa for good on March 9, 1943. Suspected of complicity in the July 20, 1944 plot against Hitler, he was allowed to commit suicide on October 14 to save the lives of his wife and son.

Following Rommel's departure from North Africa, sporadic fighting continued for a time, but the combat that for the Americans had begun with Operation Torch on November 8, 1942, ended with the final surrender of German and Italian forces on May 13, 1943. This was, in fact, the first complete Allied victory over the Axis in WWII. The defeat of Rommel, together with the hard-won victories at Midway and Guadalcanal in 1942, dulled somewhat the shame for Americans of the Pearl Harbor debacle. But there were two-and-a-half hard years still ahead.

Killed in Action

Pvt. Edward Mazuch, USMC, after completing "boot camp" at Parris Island, S.C. He became a "paramarine," and in 1944, took part in a raid behind enemy lines during the Bougainville invasion. He would be killed in action on Iwo Jima on February 22, 1945.

Off to War

During the early months of the war, draftees were assembled in the morning at the high school, where they were subjected to patriotic speeches and music. Then they marched behind the high school band to the train station. Finally, several groups of draftees rebelled and insisted that they be allowed to report directly to the station with their families and friends to see them off — minus the show-biz.

1942 -1943
Never Before in the History of Our City

On the sixth of January, 1942, attorney Walter W. O'Donnell was sworn in as the 30th mayor of Northampton. In his inaugural speech O'Donnell warned citizens that his administration was "entering office at a time when the world is facing fast-changing conditions which may make it essential for us to take steps which have never before been necessary in the history of our city."

Mayor O'Donnell was leading up to the likely necessity of a hike in taxes, but his words proved more prophetic than he realized. After Pearl Harbor, life would never again be the same in any American community, including Northampton.

The Japanese attack at Pearl Harbor — at first apparently a victory of heroic proportions — proved in the end to be a monumental blunder. Instead of demoralizing the seriously divided American public as intended, its effect was to unify and energize the nation as never before. All of the bitter dissension and wrangling between isolationists and interventionists vanished after December 7. Even the isolationist Sen. Burton K. Wheeler would declare: "The only thing to do now is to lick the hell out of them."

One of the earliest concerns in communities all over the country was that of "enemy aliens" — people not yet American citizens, of German, Japanese or Italian birth. The Smith Act, or Alien Registration Act, passed on June 28, 1940, had provided for the registration and fingerprinting of all aliens living in the United States. In February 1942, the Department of Justice office in Boston sent Immigrant Inspector Joseph E. Geary to assist in the registration of several hundred so-called enemy aliens residing in Northampton.

"All citizens or subjects of Germany, Japan and Italy over 14 years of age must register and bring with them three unmounted photographs," it was announced in the Gazette. Punishment for failure to register, it was warned, could include possible internment for the duration of the war.

These same "enemy aliens" were soon directed to turn in all of their firearms, radios and cameras to the local police. By February 27, several cameras and shortwave radios had come in, but "no guns as yet," according to Chief of Police George Bernier. Only about 172 of an estimated 300 aliens of enemy countries had registered at the local post office by March 2. Delinquents were warned again that possible "apprehension, detention and internment for the duration of the war" awaited them.

The following October, U.S. Attorney General Francis Biddle restored to Italian-born citizens in the United States their "freedom of pre-war status" and also lifted the stigma of "enemy alien." There were 337 Italians affected by this decision in Northampton alone. Biddle gave as his reason that Italian immigrants and native-born Italian-Americans alike had demonstrated their loyalty to the United States.

This was a far cry from the treatment accorded both foreign-born and native Japanese-Americans, most of them living in the western states. More than 110,000 people from California, Washington, Oregon and Arizona were moved to what were euphemistically called relocation camps at 10 centers in western states plus two in Arkansas. Seventy thousand of these internees were *Nisei*, or American citizens born in the United States; another 40,000 were *Issei* who had lived here from 20 to 40 years but were nevertheless ineligible for citizenship. The first Japanese internees would not be set free until 1944, when they would emerge to find their jobs, farms, businesses and homes in other hands.

Mayor Walter O'Donnell

Northampton's chief executive from 1942 until his death on January 10, 1944, at age 46.

It would be almost half a century in the future before this injustice would finally be acknowledged and any attempt made at reparation.

After Pearl Harbor, if the people of Northampton needed any further inspiration to launch war on the home front, they got it on January 9 in a front-page article in the Gazette: "The contention that the United States cannot be invaded is as much a myth as that ... Singapore and Pearl Harbor were impregnable." Thus, despite the two great oceans that lay between our continent and Germany and Japan, the citizens of Northampton now organized for civilian defense.

A Committee on Public Safety, with attorney Edward O'Brien at its head, had already been set up. There would be provision for the "conduct of blackouts, air raid warnings and other civilian defense activities, and the appointment, training, and equipping of volunteer, unpaid protection units."

On February 28, there was a mass Meeting for Morale in Northampton "to build civilian morale and awaken local residents to the dangers confronting America." An elaborate air raid precaution network was formed, with Franklin King, Jr. at its head as chief air raid warden. Later, when he joined the Massachusetts State Guard, King's replacement would be Mary Phillips Bailey. A mass swearing-in ceremony for civilian defense personnel was staged at Look Park on May 20, 1942, complete with presentation of wardens' armbands and certificates, plus patriotic music by the American Legion Band and vocal soloist Esther Strong.

More than 2,000 Northampton residents, both men and women, would serve as air raid wardens, including 25 nuns from the teaching order of Sisters of St. Joseph. One local warden, Eleanor Lincoln, a professor of English at Smith College, recalled her lonely patrols in the college area equipped only with a flashlight covered over with red paper, making her way through the inky darkness as she looked for cracks of forbidden light in the houses on her route.

Frequent tests were held to see if the air raid sirens worked and how fast and efficiently firefighters and medical-aid personnel could respond. In January 1942, a few Main Street merchants were still putting business first and not participating in the practice blackouts, and there was a brief confrontation as to where the responsibility for enforcement lay. "I'm the chief of police," declared Chief Bernier to a Gazette reporter, "and whether the Civilian Defense bunch likes it or not, I'm going to enforce the blackouts!" The next day a brief item appeared in the newspaper to the effect that there was "no rift" between the two organizations.

Police Chief George Bernier

Head of Northampton's police force for 27 years, beginning in October, 1940.

"Relocation Center"

Japanese-American "evacuees" arriving at the Colorado River Evacuation Center, Poston, Arizona, in the summer of 1942. Ironically, some 20,000 young Japanese-Americans served in our armed forces in both the Pacific and European theaters. The Legendary "Go For Broke" 442nd Combat Team, 9,000 strong, received more awards for valor (based on its size) than any other American unit in WWII.

Civilians Help Out

Members of the Northampton Revolver Club in their new wartime role of Auxiliary Police designed to aid local police in the event of air raids.

Householders were urged to prepare one room for use as emergency living quarters, and a special course was offered to train one member of each family in blackout and air raid procedures. One such "household warden" was Grace Coolidge. Special cloth and tape were being sold for blackout curtains, and LaFleur Bros. on King Street advertised "blackout paint ... developed and used in London."

The Northampton Report Center, in charge of all civilian defense and rescue work, was located in the former high school building. Chief Air Raid Warden King presided over the entire setup, including a staff of 120 telephone operators, two map plotters and four managers; also, 53 auxiliary firemen and 70 auxiliary police with helmets and white nightsticks, who had "regular police powers while on duty and displaying their badge." Most were members of the Northampton Revolver Club. Chief Bernier, at one point, had to advise them that their badges were to be worn only on duty.

There were also 36 men in the "rescue squad," 36 road-repair crewmen, three in the bomb reconnaissance squad to deal with unexploded bombs, and four on the blackout committee.

Dorothy Miller was a schoolteacher during this time. She recalls her duties in the Hampshire County Courthouse basement, from which any damage to that building was to be reported. "I did this one whole year early in the war. The headquarters was manned around the clock, and my shift was from 5 to 10 p.m. one evening each week. There were two telephones and always two wardens on duty in case bombing incidents occurred."

In April the Gazette reported news from the War Department: "New England Warned Of Possible Landings From Submarines" and "Parachute Troops May Land In New England Bent on Sabotage." Civilian anxiety was further heightened by reports in September from Oregon that an incendiary bomb, believed to be of Japanese origin, had dug a foot-deep crater there and set the forest around it on fire. Little wonder then, that "suspicious lights on Mt. Tom and the Holyoke Range" would require investigation, and that the Holyoke and Easthampton police were alerted that these lights might be "signals as to the activity of planes at Westover Field."

Northampton's elaborate civil defense apparatus was not, apparently, being taken too seriously by local servicemen and women home on leave. In September, a Massachusetts Public Safety Committee warning was issued reminding them that military personnel were subject to all civil defense regulations. Ironically, when Fire Chief Thomas W. Hurley, Sr., that same month, requested auxiliary fire equipment, including steel helmets and gas masks, the Office of Civilian Defense in Washington informed him that Northampton was "not a possible military objective of prime importance."

The Aircraft Warning Service in Northampton, headed by attorney Merrill Torrey, was also organized in 1942. The first "plane spotters" were stationed on the Calvin

Public Safety News

This logo for the Committee on Public Safety spotlighted a weekly civilian-defense news and information column in the Daily Hampshire Gazette.

Plane-spotter Shelter

Designed and built by students at Smith's Agricultural School, the shelter protected enemy-airplane spotters in Williamsburg from the cold.

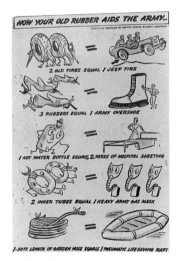

Wartime Poster

Civilians were taught how the rubber they were salvaging would aid the army.

Coolidge Memorial Bridge, but other undisclosed posts soon sprang up in and around Northampton. Spotters, who worked regular shifts, telephoned to Boston concerning each aircraft they sighted — except for the Navy training planes out of LaFleur Airport. These spotters were housewives, businessmen, Smith college students and even a few grade-school children. The Gazette reported that those on duty in nearby Williamsburg enjoyed the warmth and comfort of a "streamlined plane-spotters' station," heated by a wood stove.

A vitally important civilian war effort carried on in Northampton, as in communities all over the country, was salvage drives. Heading the local campaigns were District Salvage Director Edward J. Gare, Jr., and Northampton City Salvage Director Sidney F. Smith. These never-ending drives sought rubber, primarily in the form of old tires; scrap metal of every description, including old license plates; carefully strained fat which went into explosives, medications, and camouflage paints; tin cans, which had to be washed, the ends removed, and then flattened; used paper, which went largely into cartons in which to ship military supplies around the world; rags for the making of paper; old silk stockings used to make powder bags to contain charges for heavy caliber guns; and even human hair — "unpermanented and unbleached" — for use as cross-hairs in the Norden bombsight and in hygrometers. Eight-year-old Nathalie Witty, a fourth grader at Bridge Street School, gave her two 25-inch braids for this purpose.

On one banner collection day in Northampton — June 15, 1942 — 15,000 pounds of metal were collected plus 500 pounds of rubber and a half ton of rags. The total for 1942 was: 285,215 pounds of scrap metal; 14,180 pounds of rubber; 23,775 pounds of rags; and 59,260 pounds of tin cans. Eight-year-old Billy Sicard reportedly had collected 96 pounds of rubber in his wagon; tailor Martin Paddock had donated his old automobile. "We made a great start during 1942," reported local Salvage Director Smith, "We must keep on through 1943."

The children of Northampton played an important part in the scrap metal effort by collecting large piles in their various school yards. Northampton's old voting machines, the first mechanical voting machines in the United States, went to the scrap drive, as did 360 tons of the city's old street car tracks and the old WWI Krupp cannon from the courthouse lawn. The German cannon was cut up with acetylene torches, and Kaiser Wilhelm struck one last blow when a concealed spring was suddenly released and soared across Main Street to hit the Nonotuck Bank building near the corner. "Get the iron out of your basement," read one scrap drive appeal. "Half of every tank, gun and ship is made from scrap iron and steel."

And of course there were the numerous war-time restrictions of consumer goods. With Japan's seizure of Southeast Asia there was no more raw rubber imported, and thus tire purchases were severely cut back. "Re-capping" and "re-treading" were terms now added to the WWII vocabulary. Condoms, however, were reportedly not restricted. Gas Rationing Boards were set up to control the use of gasoline for automobiles. Eighty-five percent of all drivers received an "A" sticker for four gallons per week. (In August the following year this was reduced to three as so much gasoline was disappearing into the black market.) "B" and "C" stickers went to drivers engaged in government work, medical service or crucial deliveries. A 35-mph speed limit was imposed to cut back on both rubber and gas consumption. Spare parts, antifreeze and batteries were also hard to get.

Some motorists chose to store their cars for the duration, and during 1942 about 36 license plates were returned to the Registry of Motor Vehicles each week. Only 4,500 cars were registered in Northampton during 1942, compared to 9,900 the previous year. One bonus of the gasoline rationing was that the highways were now virtually free of accidents, according to the Gazette.

In July, bogus gas ration books were first discovered on sale in the city for $1.50 each.

Food restrictions also began early in 1942. Sugar-rationing registration took place between May 4 and 7, with local teachers working six-hour days on the enrollment — a chore they would continue to perform when rationing also was applied to meat, canned goods, coffee, lard, jams and jellies, and butter.

City Agricultural Agent Allen Leland warned storekeepers against forcing customers to purchase other products in order to obtain butter. Lines for butter became a common sight, especially on Friday evenings and Saturday mornings, particularly in front of the S.K. Ames Butter-and-Egg shop on Main Street. So complicated did the rationing system become that a "ration school" was organized for grocers. Price controls by the Office of Price Administration (OPA) in Washington further complicated the local scene.

Each week the Gazette would print a chart prepared by the National War Price and

Local Girl Gives Long Tresses to Help Uncle Sam

Eight-year-old Nathalie Witty gave her two 25-inch braids to the war effort, to be used in the manufacture of hygrometers — sensitive instruments that indicated atmospheric changes.

School Scrap Drives

Helen and Violet Wong, whose family owned the Pagoda Restaurant, stand before the pile of metal scrap collected by students of Hawley Grammar School. Edward Wong, an older brother of the two little girls, died aboard the U.S.S. Princeton *off Saipan in July of 1944.*

Rationing Board, plus a "ration calendar" indicating the number of "points" required for various items. Ration books contained points stamps for each household member. Before long, handsome leather cases were devised for these books, and some owners even had theirs imprinted in gold with their name or initials. Residents had to be warned, however, not to keep using the ration books of men and women who had departed for military service.

American consumers may have felt pinched, but they never knew anything remotely resembling the rationing hardships endured, for example, in Britain. According to a Gazette report in 1944, American meat consumption actually rose during the war to a per capita rate of 158 pounds per year — the highest since 1908. Unrationed dairy products, plus cereals, fresh vegetables and fruit were all in plentiful supply.

With the nation at war, the draft went into high gear. On March 18 the Gazette published an entire page of the names of all local men registered, together with their draft numbers. Then followed the first draft lottery of the war — a step toward classification of about nine million men for possible military service. The number-one Northampton man was Richard Kinner. He would return safely from the Army in December 1945, after three years of service that had made him a sergeant and taken him, finally, to Germany, where he worked on electric railway engines.

Wartime Rationing

"Butter Late Than Never." Butter was added to the list of rationed food items in the U.S.

The batches of draftees began to swell in size, with more than 90 leaving Northampton December 26, including two sets of brothers, Robert and Joseph Moriarty and Pat and John Sullivan. In these early months of the war, elaborate public farewells were staged by townspeople. The men would be assembled at 6:30 a.m. in the auditorium of the old high school and subjected to a speech by the mayor followed by a patriotic song or two. To the tunes of the Northampton High School Band, the draftees were then marched down Main Street to the railroad station, where a group photo always was taken. Each

Mrs. Coolidge Volunteers

Former First Lady Grace Coolidge, right, with a basket at her feet, was one of a group of volunteers who handed out small going-away gifts to departing draftees.

Rendezvous With Destiny

Approximately 3,000 young men and women left Northampton for WWII. Representative of them is this young unknown draftee waiting to board the train for his "rendezvous with destiny."

Final Goodbyes

Relatives always gathered at the station to say goodbye to their sons, brothers and husbands.

draftee was handed a departing gift of a book and a pack of cigarettes by volunteers — one of whom was Grace Coolidge, who seldom failed to appear. Eventually, the draftees began to rebel against all the hoopla at the high school and demanded to be allowed to go directly to the station.

The Hampshire Book Shop in this period advertised "armor for our fighting men ... shields of faith — New Testaments or Catholic Prayer Books with Plated Steel covers." Carried in the vest pocket, it was claimed, these were "a protection and sometimes deflect flak, bullets or pieces of shrapnel." The pages themselves proved useful for rolling cigarettes.

Interestingly, the local birthrate began zooming right after the draft was instituted in 1940 — and kept on climbing all through the war: 616 births in 1941; 696 in 1942; 741 in 1943 (including four sets of twins); 773 in 1944; 842 in 1945; and in that post-war peak year of 1946, 1,084. The marriage rate that precipitated all these births, in an age when unmarried mothers were uncommon, was likewise phenomenal.

The lives of American women were changed in many ways during the Second World War, not the least of which was the urgent need for them to alleviate the shortage of labor caused by the departure of millions of men. Cooley Dickinson Hospital was short of nurses, and the State Hospital and the Veterans' Hospital in Leeds were desperately short of attendants. The Veterans' Hospital announced that women would be accepted as attendants and offered living quarters and a starting wage of $26 a week for the inexperienced. The following year, 85 officers and enlisted U.S. Army men had to be brought in to alleviate the labor shortage there.

When enough men and boys could not be found for work in the nearby onion and potato fields, students from Smith College and the Northampton School for Girls were recruited. Smith students also now had to "stand ready to give one hour of service a day to the college without remuneration, in the hope," said the Board of Trustees, "that an additional fee to meet the rising cost of living may thus be avoided."

The need for women to move into actual "war work" was reported in the Gazette in March 1942. "Millions of Women Must Be Shifted to War Work ... 15,600,000 Housewives Between 18 and 44 Constitute a Reserve Pool to Draw On." A voluntary registration of women with the U.S. Employment Service Office was held in Northampton in October, headed by Frederick Hawkes, local manager of the War Manpower Commission. By December 17, 4,215 women had filed. Of these, 639 who had no children volunteered for factory work. Smith's Agricultural School was now conducting courses for women interested in defense work, and some of their trainees were already working

The Women Take Over

"We will have to bring large numbers of women, not usually in the labor market, into factory employment," announced the female Secretary of Labor, Frances Perkins, early in 1942. Cartoons like this one were designed to popularize this concept.

War Work

Helen Jason, who would later become Helen Driscoll, and her car-pool companions drove back and forth to their work at Springfield Ordnance in her "new" second-hand Pontiac.

at the U.S. Armory, American Bosch, Indian Motocycle in Springfield and the Perkins Machine and Gear Company in West Springfield; others were at Worthington Pump and Machinery Corporation in Holyoke and at Stevens Arms in Chicopee Falls. The Armory pleaded for skilled help, with openings for everything from "barrel chamberers to routers," with salaries ranging from $5.68 to $11.60 per day.

A breakdown of daily wages for "learners" for a 48-hour week at the Armory appeared in the Gazette in August: $5.28 for men; $3.36 for boys; and $3.12 for women. By 1943, unskilled women started at $4.88 a day. And it was reported that Marion LoCoco of Leverett was granted a taxicab driver's license — "undoubtedly because of the shortage of men available."

Urgent appeals from Washington, D.C., for stenographers, typists and secretaries brought regularly scheduled Civil Service representatives to the city's post office. Helen Jason, a recent graduate of Northampton Commercial College, took their examination and almost immediately received a telegram offering her an appointment in Washington with the United States Navy. When family considerations required her to seek an appointment closer to home, she was assigned to be secretary to Brigadier-General George Drury, Chief of the Springfield Ordnance District. "We took care of all military contracts for the whole Springfield-Hartford area ... dealing with every aspect of armament including guns and parts for tanks and airplanes," she recalled. "Military security was tight, so we were all fingerprinted and wore badges that were checked by guards at all the doors."

Citizens engaged in defense work received carefully allotted extra gallons of gasoline, and Jason's father bought her a used Pontiac for $275 from friends in Hadley and taught her how to drive it. She recruited a car pool of other women at Springfield Ordnance. "All in all," she recalled, "we had a good time — a friendly bunch. We worked six days a week, so each passenger chipped in 25 cents a day for gasoline."

It was during this period that Jason met Earl McKinley, a soldier then attending

Amherst College in a group selected to be sent to West Point for officer training. The couple met in the Atkins apple orchard in South Amherst, where local young people volunteered on Sundays to help pick the apple crop for the orchard owner so desperately short of help.

"Earl and I dated for over a year and then were married before he went overseas," she remembered. "He ended up at the Battle of the Bulge in December of 1944. I didn't know this until later. What I got was a telegram, two days before Christmas, informing me that he was 'missing in action.' I went to work as usual, and when friends would tell me how sorry they were, I told them, 'No, he's alive, I'm certain.' A week and a half later I learned that he had been killed in action. Eventually I found out that he had been captured by the Germans and died, together with other American POWs, when our planes unknowingly bombed the area where they were being held."

Putting Out the Call

Typical wartime ad seeking women for factory work. Some middle-class Northampton matrons took such jobs against the wishes of their husbands.

Juliette Tomlinson also commuted for "war work" from Northampton each day, but to a job of quite a different sort. She worked on components of aircraft engines for Pratt and Whitney at their newly constructed Plant M in East Longmeadow. A "model of modern design and construction," Plant M covered the same area as had the entire Pratt and Whitney Aircraft manufacturing division in Hartford before the war.

"I needed a job, and we were extremely well paid — between $50 and $60 a week as I recall," she says. The huge plant turned out crankshafts, links, propeller shafts and master rods. Tomlinson inspected master rods. "The other items were probably too heavy for the women, most of whom seemed to be in their 40s," she recalled.

Like Helen Jason, Tomlinson drove a car pool back and forth each day. Assigned to the 3-11 p.m. shift, she left Northampton at two p.m. and proceeded to Holyoke, where she would pick up four nurses who also worked at Plant M. Part of their daily routine was stopping around midnight, en route home, for something to eat. "Home around 2 a.m. meant falling into bed to be ready for the next day," she recalled. "I can't remember much social life. With a six-day week, and those odd hours, one slept a lot."

That summer, the Navy decided to follow the lead of the Women's Army Corps (WAC), established on May 15, 1942. In July, Northampton learned from the Gazette that Smith College had been chosen as a training site for officers of the Women's Naval Auxiliary. The popular name "WAVES" came from "Women Accepted for Voluntary Emergency Service."

The first contingent of future officers arrived that autumn. "Nine Hundred Trainees Flow In, Special Buses From Railroad Station All Day Long," reported the Gazette on October 7. They established their headquarters in the wing of Smith's Alumnae House and soon billeted 400 women in Capen, Northrup and Gillett, residential houses on campus. Five hundred more roomed at the Hotel Northampton, where all the WAVES were fed. The hotel's Wiggins Tavern was taken over for the Officers' Mess. On the last night it was open to civilians, a crowd of Smith students dined there and sang "There's A Tavern In The Town" by way of farewell to a favorite spot.

Although Army women were sent into all foreign theaters, Sen. David Walsh of Massachusetts had for some reason argued against Navy women being sent overseas. This proviso stuck. But before the unit closed down in January 1945, 9,000 WAVES officers trained in Northampton had reported for duty at posts all over the United States and in Hawaii.

The WAVES became a familiar sight as they marched to and from mess at the hotel. John Skibiski recalled mischievously firing snowballs at them from his yard at the corner of State and what was then called Park Street. Other Northampton residents recall the women singing a song, written by two WAVES, as they marched through the streets:

> "North, South, East and West
> We're marching as one.
> We are here to serve our country
> 'Til the war is done
> Heads uplifted proudly for the Navy Blue and Gold
> We cannot do the fighting
> But tradition we uphold

As we swing along with our purpose strong
Bearing our ensign high
To oppressors now our challenge we have hurled
We will free our Navy's men
Who will free the world."

WAVES

A familiar sight on Northampton's streets during the war were batches of WAVES officer trainees marching to and from their meals at the Hotel Northampton.

The WAVES' uniforms — designed by Mainbocher — were meticulously altered and fitted by the supplier, Filene's of Boston. This was done by 15 dressmakers working in a garage they had taken over at 141 King Street. The first detail, en route to their fittings, marched in the wrong direction, and Officer Frank Zaborowski of the Northampton police force had to intervene and head them the right way.

Capt. Herbert Underwood, the commanding officer of the midshipmen's school, and his wife lived graciously in Mrs. Coolidge's home on Ward Avenue, which she had turned over to the Navy for the duration. Naval officers assigned to the school, however, discovered an acute housing shortage on their arrival here. This problem would ease, as time went on, when the original male officers were replaced by the first women graduates, one of whom was Margaret Clifford. A math teacher at Northampton High School, she was the first woman from Hampshire County to enter the WAVES.

Lt. Clifford's first post was that of company commander and drill instructor for Gillett House. This was followed by her role of 1st Regimental Commander of the U.S. Naval Training Station at Hunter College in New York, where classes of 5,000 enlisted women at a time were put through a three-month training course. Her last duty was in Washington, D.C. with the Far Eastern Section of Naval Intelligence.

She recalled that during her time in Northampton people would park their cars along Park and Gothic Streets during the noon hour to watch the WAVES marching to and from the Hotel Northampton. "I couldn't smile at people I knew," she said, "but I would wink at them as I marched by."

The WAVES enjoyed the benefits of USO rooms on the second floor of the old YMCA on King Street, complete with a kitchenette. An article in the Gazette made the claim that this USO was the first "for women only" in the United States, if not the world.

As many as 3,500 to 4,000 pieces of Navy mail were now flowing into Northampton every day, with outgoing mail just as heavy. A special substation was set up to handle it. Cancellations topped 100,000 pieces daily around Christmas.

Despite the inspiration of all these young women striding around Northampton in their Navy-blue designer uniforms, the majority of the town's female volunteers, the Gazette would observe, chose the Army as their branch of service instead — some of them, possibly, because they would not be denied overseas duty. By September 1944, 62 young women of the city were serving as WACS. The first two enlistees for the Women's Army Auxiliary Corps (later the Women's Army Corps after the women were sworn into the Army itself in August 1943) were Ruth Banister and Lucille Hood, who left Northampton on September 5, 1942. Their original assignments were motorcorps duty, and an early Gazette story concerned their greeting to the third Northampton volunteer, Shirley Pomeroy: "LOOK at our hands!"

It is a sad fact that it took the Second World War to end the Great Depression, but that is what happened in this small New England city of some 24,000 people. Local citizens

Northampton Women Enlist

The first two Northampton women to enlist in the Woman's Army Corps were Ruth Banister, left, and Lucille Hood. Banister became a finance officer; Hood the Fort Devens motor pool dispatcher.

In the group photo taken during basic training at Fort Des Moines, Iowa, Hood is second from left, back row, with Banister on her left.

would complain about crowded shops and waiting lines at restaurants due to the influx of the young women in blue, but their pain was somewhat relieved by the fact that the WAVES were spending more than $70,000 a month in Northampton. Defense-plant jobs also continued to swell local incomes. In fact, a report from a data bank in New York pointed out that the city had been the "leading sales market last year," with more disposable income available to the average resident than was the case generally throughout the country. The average worker in Northampton was reported to have an annual income of $1,176, "1.07 times as large as the $1,100 Massachusetts' average and 1.35 times as large as the $871 national figure."

Retail sales in Northampton were at a new high, with $14,583,000 having been spent in 1941, representing ".026 percent of the nation's ... and .65 percent of Massachusetts' retail business." Welfare costs in 1941 had dropped $32,000 below those of 1940, with the case load dropping from 264 in 1940 to 136 in 1941. Another wartime benefit to Northampton was a reduction in crime, although this was somewhat affected when "a pair of polite young men under 24," as the Gazette described them, robbed the Florence Savings Bank of about $13,000 in March 1942.

The Gazette also carried several interesting international reports in 1942. In October, one revealed that "tens of thousands of Polish Jews had been exterminated" as reported by Premier Wladyslaw Sikorski of the Polish government-in-exile in London. Prime Minister Churchill denounced "the systematic cruelties to which the Jewish people, men, women and children, have been exposed under the Nazi regime (as) among the most terrible events of history," and said such acts "have placed an indelible stain on all those who perpetrate and instigate them." Twenty-six Allied nations had first united against Hitler on January 1, 1942, and these "United Nations" issued a condemnation in December warning that the cold-blooded extermination of the Jews "shall not escape retribution" and that the Nazis were believed to be "carrying into effect Hitler's oft-reported intention to exterminate the Jewish people in Europe." Despite these reports, many people today claim that they knew nothing back then of the Holocaust.

Smith College students, pressed by President Davis to take a stand concerning the war,

Smith Graduate Joins WAVES

Lt. Elizabeth Gallaher graduated from Smith College in 1944. After completing her training with the WAVES unit in Northampton, she spent the rest of the war in Washington, D.C., working in radio intelligence. After the war, she earned a Ph.D. at Harvard under the G.I. Bill, and later returned to Northampton with her husband Klemens von Klemperer.

volunteered one meatless day a week and were being advised concerning proper study, sleep, exercise and eating habits because of the nation's need for "well-trained and well-disciplined minds." Military drill by the WAVES was offered to "those students wishing to prepare themselves for Army or Navy service." A few students shoveled snow on campus that winter, and in April 150 volunteered to help area farmers with the tedious, back-breaking job of setting onions.

Now that the Soviet Union was also at war with Germany, 25 "campus leaders," together with members of the faculty and administrative staff, fired off a telegram to President Roosevelt demanding the "immediate opening of a second front in Europe."

A letter from one victim of an earlier front in Europe, a British POW in Germany, somehow reached the Gazette in November. Held in Hamsdorf, one Sgt. Mooney had acquired a brochure concerning the Connecticut Valley and requested that literature and maps about local farming be sent to him. German censors had written across the envelope that "prisoner of war" had to be printed in English, French and German on any material sent.

In December, the Northampton Women's Club heard Professor William Avirett of Deerfield Academy lecture with "an optimistic outlook on the war's progress." In Washington, Chairman Andrew May of the House Military Affairs Committee had already predicted a short war with no need for drafting teen-agers and family men. He was quoted as seeing an end of the fight by 1943. On December 7, 1942, the Gazette reported: "Northampton Has Two Dead on The Anniversary of The War: Zigmund Sieruta of 9 Spring Avenue and Neil Champoux of 20 Linden Street." Charles Kolodzinski was mentioned as a POW in Germany. This was only the beginning.

Casablanca Conference

President Roosevelt, seated left, and Prime Minister Winston Churchill, with their joint staffs at the legendary Casablanca Conference held January 14-24, 1943, in North Africa.

1943 — The End of the Beginning

By the beginning of 1943, the tide on the military front was finally turning in favor of the Allies. The German Wehrmacht was deep into Russia, but Gen. Friedrich von Paulus's 6th Army had been abandoned by Hitler and was succumbing to cold, hunger and disease; 110,000 men, including 20,000 wounded, surrendered at Stalingrad on January 31. The Japanese had been checked at Midway. More and more supply ships were safely reaching Britain despite German U-boats. In North Africa, Gen. Erwin Rommel had been beaten by the British at El Alamein, and British and American troops together had carried out the invasion of North Africa.

Between January 14 and 24, 1943, President Roosevelt and Prime Minister Churchill met in the North African city of Casablanca, Morocco, to plot the Allied strategy that they hoped would lead to ultimate victory. It was at the Casablanca Conference that Roosevelt first publicly introduced the concept of "unconditional surrender," surprising Churchill by announcing it at a press conference. Some historians believe that the demand for unconditional surrender may actually have prolonged the war by undermining opposition to Hitler and Mussolini in their own countries and by encouraging their nations' peoples to fight on literally to the death.

One of the first residents from Northampton to go off to war in 1943 was a dog named Blitz. "Dogs For Defense" was a government program designed to procure dogs to serve, with carefully trained soldier or Marine handlers, as guard dogs, as scouts, as message carriers and to locate the wounded. Blitz, a German Shepherd, was duly photographed and written up by the Gazette before he left for Boston on January 5. Before long his master, Richard Himmelsbach, would follow him into the military.

Dogs for Defense

Richard Himmelsbach's German Shepherd dog, Blitz, went to war under the "Dogs For Defense" program.

News of the deaths of Northampton servicemen began arriving early in February with that of Pvt. Edwin Malinowski, who had left Northampton with a group of 42 draftees on September 2, 1942. Only five months in the Army and assigned as a medical corpsman, it was Malinowski's fate to ship out on the doomed U.S.S. *Dorchester* the following January. With 524 soldiers aboard, the *Dorchester* left St. John's, Newfoundland, on the night of January 23 en route to Greenland and Britain. His family tried to get word to him that a daughter, Joy, was born on January 30, but they have always doubted that this information reached him.

In those dreaded waters, dubbed "Torpedo Junction," on the bitterly cold night of February 3, the *Dorchester* was hit; she listed sharply to starboard and began rapidly to sink. She was only 150 miles from Greenland. Panic ensued, and overcrowded lifeboats soon went down. Those stranded on the ship scrambled for life jackets. Four chaplains, Protestants George Fox and Clark Poling; Alexander Good, a Jew; and John Washington, a Catholic, tried to maintain order and calmly handed out life jackets until the supply ran out. They then removed their own and gave these away. The four were last seen, arms linked and praying, as the *Dorchester* went down. Of the 904 men aboard, 605 were lost.

The chaplains' heroism is commemorated in the Four Chaplains' Window of the main chapel at the Veterans' Hospital in Leeds, where a memorial service for them is held each February.

In this same period, a young man from Northampton survived the sinking of his ship. Twenty-year-old James Goodsell was a Seaman 1st Class on the U.S.S. *West Madiket*. As part of a convoy sailing through "Torpedo Junction," the *Madiket* was hit and went

Lost at Sea

Petty Officer 2nd Class Donald Ducharme, of Leeds, was reported missing and presumed dead when the submarine U.S.S. Amberjack and all its crew disappeared without a trace in the Pacific in 1943.

down within 10 minutes, 1,000 miles off St. John's, Newfoundland, the sole victim of a submarine attack. Goodsell rushed to his bunk to get the $200 he had stashed there before he sought a lifeboat. After nine hours on a makeshift raft, Goodsell and several others were picked up by a British corvette and carried to safety in St. John's. Goodsell managed to survive two more sinkings, both on the dreaded Murmansk Run, and would finally emerge from the service in August 1944, a well-seasoned sea veteran of 23.

Early in February the Ducharme family in Leeds received a telegram announcing that their son, Petty Officer 2nd Class Donald Ducharme, was missing aboard the submarine U.S.S. *Amberjack.* A year later, another wire arrived officially acknowledging the loss of the *Amberjack* and all who sailed in her. According to existing Navy records, she had been operating from an Australian base north of Japanese-held Rabaul in the New Britain Islands north of New Guinea. The record states: "The *Amberjack* made contact with the South Pacific naval command on February 14, 1943, and was next to report on March 10, 1943, but did not. The *Amberjack* was presumed lost. Japanese war records do not contain any reference to action against any submarine, on surface or submerged, in that region during that time."

Doris (Ducharme) Willard cherished this memory of her brother's last shore leave.

"We were seated on the porch of our home in Leeds. Our dog, an Airedale-collie named Luke, suddenly jumped up and ran off down the hill and out of sight. A few minutes later, obviously just off the bus, Donald came trudging up the hill with Luke trotting beside him. Somehow the dog had sensed that Donald was coming home and went to meet him. I can never forget this."

Also from the Pacific theater early in 1943 came the news that Lt. William "Pete" Jackimczyk, a navigator on a B-17, was officially listed as missing. His unopened Christmas gifts had already been returned to his family. Not until the spring of 1944 would they finally learn the manner of his death, when Cpl. Joe Hartman, the tail gunner of his plane, wrote to Jackimczyk's sister, Veronica.

"It all happened around 11:30 a.m., December 1, 1942. We had been sent up to Henderson Field on Guadalcanal ... to fly a series of photographic missions over Bougainville Island ... a 'hot spot.' "

The plane was attacked by six Japanese Zeroes, one of which they shot down. "Then," related Hartman, "a seventh Zero got above us, at that time unobserved, and dropped four phosphorous bombs on us. They all missed, so then he turned over and dove his plane into ours. Striking us about mid-ship, we were split in two. The front half exploded and burned as it fell."

As tail gunner, Hartman was in the fusilage, which was not in flames. Coming to, he bailed out "after about a 15,000-foot fall" and landed in the sea.

He swam to an island, which proved to be Choiseul, about 15 miles off the northwest tip of Bougainville. "Natives found me on the beach," the airman continued, "and I asked them to go out and search for my crew. They did, and four hours later came back with all that they found floating on the water — a camera case, books, first aid kit, etc. The whole island was searched without results. One of the men did wash ashore the next day, and we buried him there, close to where he came ashore. It wasn't Pete."

Hartman then went on to describe his two-month stay on Choiseul where he continued his search for his crew members or their remains. He found nothing.

"I know this is not what you have been hoping for," he wrote on April 9, 1944. Apologizing for not having had Veronica's address sooner, he wrote, "I know that you will go on feeling, as though by some miracle, he may still be there. I felt that same way for weeks and did not leave until I was sure."

Also in aerial combat in the Pacific was Capt. Edwin Olander of Northampton who, as a Marine fighter pilot, flew with the legendary Black Sheep Squadron that shot down 94 Japanese planes in 12 weeks of combat. Olander later flew with the Wake Island Avenger Squadron. A veteran of almost 100 missions, he won the coveted Marine pilot's label of "Ace" with his fifth downing of a Japanese Zero.

Like so many men of his generation, Olander had grown up filled with admiration for the aviation heroes of the 1920s and 1930s and had himself spent many boyhood hours at LaFleur Airport washing airplanes and sweeping out the hangars. A graduate of Amherst College, he was a newspaperman before he volunteered for the Marines in the summer of 1941.

"I was sure the war was coming, and I wanted to fly, so I went in as an old man of 24," he said. "I did what I wanted to do and became a fighter pilot and got into combat ... and I was lucky enough to come out of the war with no damage to body or mind."

Olander described the gull-winged F4U-1 Corsair that he flew as "a beautiful plane" with a rated speed of 415 mph at sea level that made it the fastest aircraft at that time in the Pacific theater. The primary achievement of Olander's squadron was their neutralization of Japanese air power over Bougainville and Rabaul.

A vastly different kind of aerial warfare was experienced by the men of the Army Air Corps who served in the European theater. Rather than tropical islands and coral atolls, they flew over great seaports, marshaling yards, oil fields and cities and towns all over occupied Europe where war materiel was cranked out for Hitler's armies. More than 90,000 Allied airmen died; 69,606 Britons and 25,000 Americans

When he had to bail out over France in October 1942, during one of the first big Allied air raids over Europe, Lt. Charles Kolodzinski was one of only three men in his crew to

Lt. William Jackimczyk

Jackimczyk was killed in the Pacific Theater. He posed for this picture in front of Budgar's Drug Store on his last home leave.

Capt. Edwin Olander

Olander became a Marine air ace with "Pappy" Boyington's "Black Sheep Squadron" in the Pacific theater.

survive. Unconscious when he hit the ground, he later remembered "coming to" with an injured leg, French hands stripping him of his bars and necktie, and two German soldiers appearing to take him into custody. He recalled receiving good care at a Wehrmacht hospital where, "like a good German soldier," he learned to sit at attention in bed when the doctor approached. After his recovery and routine interrogation, Kolodzinski became a prisoner of the Nazis for 31 months at Stalag Luft III near Sagan, not far from Berlin. In

Allied POWs

POWs, or "kriegies," both British and American, at Stalag Luft 3. All were airmen whose planes had been shot down. Lt. Charles Kolodzinski of Northampton is second from right, front row.

their camp, the Allied prisoners could both see and hear the bombers pounding Germany — British by night, the Americans by day.

Life in the POW compound was not the circus portrayed in the television sitcom "Hogan's Heroes," but the prisoners did have hidden radios for outside news, and they did dig tunnels, including the legendary one immortalized in *The Great Escape* by Paul Brickhill. Kolodzinski himself spent several weeks in a punishment cell when he was caught — as intended — working on a decoy tunnel to distract the German guards from the real one. *Tunnelbau* was the notation on his German POW personnel card, which he "liberated" from the camp headquarters when tank units of Patton's 3rd Army roared in and freed the prisoners in April 1945.

In a diary given him by the International YMCA in the early days of his imprisonment, Kolodzinski listed the names of all those who made it out in "the great escape." On Hitler's express orders, as they were captured they were shot, one by one, and their ashes returned in urns to the camp.

Kolodzinski also listed the contents of the International Red Cross food parcels from Britain, Canada and the U.S.A. that helped a little to relieve the prisoners' constant hunger. "It wasn't so bad at first, while the Germans were still on top," he recalled, "but as they went down so did our rations. Our stomachs shrank but still we were always hungry."

John Qua, the enlisted man at Camp Edwards who had just returned from maneuvers on December 7, 1941, applied for flight training and became Capt. Qua, pilot of a B-17 with the 8th Air Force 92nd Bomb Group flying out of England.

Arriving there in April 1943, Qua was on hand for the earliest and roughest daylight missions that the 8th Air Force undertook. With no fighter escorts, the 92nd lost 60 planes on their first raid on the Schweinfurt ball-bearing factory in August. "There were so many crash landings on our return — including us — that the actual figure was some 70-odd planes lost by the 8th Air Force on that one mission. Incidentally, my group went over to Britain with 13 crews, and only four made it back home with their missions completed. ... There were 40 to 50 Luftwaffe fighters coming at us on those missions in 1943, and they were really good. The gunners of my crew actually shot down 14 of those German fighters on our 25 missions. It was terrifying. ... I went back on the second big raid in October and at one point I said to myself, I'm not gonna make it. This is it! And then a feeling of calm came over me — very strange — and I was O.K. after that. I never got scratched.

"Eventually our navigator — a really nice guy — went mental. Just cracked up. Couldn't take any more. Those navigators were under a terrible strain trying to get us to our targets and then get us back. We came back from one mission, and our navigator went and sat on the edge of his bed and just stayed there. Never got up. Finally, we had to call the medics, and he was sent home. There were some suicides too, when people just couldn't go on."

Qua's saddest recollection was of his crew's bombardier, Sgt. Winston Toomey from South Dakota. " 'Pappy, I think I'm hit,' he called out to me in the middle of a mission. There was nothing I could do; you are on target and that's it. A whole stream of bullets had swept over us from the tail forward. Toomey held on long enough to toggle his bombs. We don't know how he did it. And then he died. One shell had gone right through him. He was awarded the Distinguished Service Cross, given for exceptional heroism in combat."

Qua kept the letter from Toomey's wife in Huron, South Dakota, dated October 25, 1943, apologizing for bothering the crew but wanting to know "how he was the last few days and if he suffered much." Then she asked that the Christmas gifts she had sent be given to "some boy who maybe didn't get so much."

Ken Beckman was a navigator, eventually lead navigator, with the 305th Bomb Group in England. In cool and measured tones, he later recounted the stark details of his two tours of duty, beginning with his arrival in England on October 27, 1943.

He was among those replacements sent in for crews lost in a disastrous October raid, the second, over the Schweinfurt ball-bearing plant, when 62 aircraft were shot down and more than a hundred airmen were killed. Out of the 305th Bomb Group only one plane survived. By November 23, Beckman had already chalked up 43 hours in combat and felt "hardened — and also lucky. Before long, however, out of a barracks that slept 18 of us navigators, there would be only three of us left. These losses were due primarily to the German fighter planes whose pilots were pretty darn good."

Beckman recalled, "as if it were yesterday," his first five missions over Berlin, with formations of over a thousand planes, temperatures of minus 60 degrees, and thick clouds. "The clouds seemed full of planes ... you'd perceive, almost touching you, the shape of another airplane's wing or spot a bomb bay or a tail. It was frightening. You fully expected to hit or be hit by another airplane. There were a couple of dozen disastrous collisions that were never reported to the American public as far as I know."

Other missions, some of them nine to 10 hours long, were made in an effort to knock out the German aircraft plants producing fighter planes and also to hit the submarine pens along the coast of Europe. As time went on, the number of Luftwaffe fighters that rose to meet the big B-17s diminished.

Surviving his first tour, and with some thought then of making a career in the Air

Sgt. Winston Toomey

Capt. John Qua's valiant young bombadier, who toggled his bombs on target, but was later found dead at his post.

Lt. Joseph Bonneau

Co-pilot on a B-24, Bonneau came from Maine to train at Westover Field.

Corps, Beckman volunteered for a second tour. "With fewer fighters to harass us, our greatest danger now was the flak sent up to cripple or destroy us. By now it seemed to me that all the flak in Germany had my name on it, and the German fighters still left in the air all knew which plane I was in."

From this point on, his account was a litany of direct hits by flak resulting in seriously damaged airplanes, of engines out of commission or on fire, of horrendous return flights running low on gas. "You can't imagine what you can tear out of a plane — even things bolted down — to lighten it and extend your range. One time we made it back with just a few minutes of fuel left.

"On one mission our bombadier missed an airfield near Brussels, and on a later mission we were glad it was still intact, and was in American hands. ... We were ready to bail out on hearing 'we're hit — we're hit — we're hit!' and seeing flames along the wing. Then the pilot called out 'Hold it! Everybody hold it! Fire's out!' We made it to the very same field we had missed on that earlier mission."

Twice Beckman came within a hair's breadth of being wounded; once when a piece of flak tore up the side of his boot but missed his leg and the second time when a three-foot tear ripped his sheepskin-lined trousers and chewed up the ammunition box he sat on. "There was sawdust all around me," he recalled, "but I was still intact." Three times he and his crew had to ditch — once in the English Channel and twice in the North Sea. "The British air-sea rescue teams were tremendous, fantastic, the way they'd get to us and pull us out of the water."

Debriefing

Lt. Kenneth Beckman, left, a B-17 navigator, after a mission with the rest of the plane's crew, pondering why they missed their target.

Beckman received six Air Medals, two Distinguished Flying Crosses, plus "a bunch of combat ribbons" and numerous other decorations and citations. He reached the rank of Major at age 22, the youngest, he was told, in the 8th Air Force, in the European Theater of Operations, and in the Army Air Corps.

A native of Biddeford, Maine, Joe Bonneau trained at Westover Field in Chicopee, and met and married Elaine Beliveau of Florence before he shipped out. In Britain, Lt. Bonneau was a copilot of a B-24 in the 44th Bomb Group. Their twenty-ninth mission, with a bombing altitude of only 8,500 feet, he believed to be the lowest mission on record in the 8th Air Force. Asked about how he handled fear, Bonneau said years later, "Scared? When wasn't I scared?" He was told by one of the enlisted crewmen that the crew's young waist gunner used to scream in the night as he slept.

Bonneau's closest call came when he volunteered to replace an ill pilot of another

On Alert

Lt. James Raymond geared up and, "waiting to go" on a mission.

"Nose Art"

Lt. Raymond admires the "Sky Goddess" on his B-17. Paintings on the fuselage of planes became an art form during World War II.

plane. At the last minute, the pilot appeared and insisted on flying the mission. They never returned.

Jim Raymond, a squadron leader with the 385th Bomb Group, recalled his training days and his flight to England via Iceland. He could reconstruct entire missions from his logbook. Losses were high for his group's first missions: 18 out of 36 on one and 14 out of 32 on another. He laughed later over that point in their early-morning briefing when the crews would be advised as to how many guns they could expect to direct flak at them at one time, i.e., "only" 2,500 over central Berlin.

"Sometimes the sky seemed as if it was paved with flak like an asphalt road. It would sound like pebbles on a tin roof as it hit, but what it left was jagged holes in the airplane. The flak looked like dark clouds of little exploding puffs, but it was shrapnel that hit you. A pilot friend of mine found a chunk in the seat under him, and when he looked more closely, spotted an ordnance number that was the same as his own serial number. A strange coincidence.

"The unsung heroes of the air were our ground crews," said Raymond. "They'd work all night ... to get all the parts and materials to repair all the damage we suffered or correct any flaws we discovered." As for fear, he said: "At 60 degrees below zero you can still sweat, really sweat, enough to have to wring your clothes out." He added, "I used to think of the guys down there below us in the mud for months on end. They had a different war from us. If we got back, we at least could sleep in a clean, warm bed."

His worst memory was of a crew that he had trained. When an incorrect order was given, their plane headed into flak and went down before his eyes. "All those tall, handsome young kids — some of them no more than 19. No parachute came out of that plane. I saw them go down in flames."

One of the most decorated enlisted airmen out of Northampton was Staff Sgt. Chester Borowski, who racked up 275 combat hours on 69 missions as a radio operator and tail gunner on a B-26. Borowski emerged, after four years in the service, with the Distinguished Flying Cross and the Air Medal with 11 Oak Leaf Clusters. One of four brothers — all of them in the service — he lived on Island Road which, in proportion to its number of families, is believed to have contributed more men to the military than any other street in the city of Northampton.

Staff Sgt. John Niemczyk flew 30 missions as a tail gunner with the 92nd Bomb Group

One of Northampton's Most Decorated

Staff Sgt. Chester Borowski, fourth from left, with his B-26 crew.

in Britain. After their sixth mission, Niemczyk's airplane became the lead ship, with all the danger and responsibility that that position entailed. Cold and alone back in the tail, he relied for luck on a small Sacred Heart Apostle of Prayer card, given him by a Protestant fighter-pilot friend. This card he carried in his wallet all his life. He had other mementoes: two pieces of flak, one that embedded itself near him in the tail of the airplane and the other that lodged in the helmet he was wearing. He remembered the embarrassing time when he attempted to protect himself in the tail with flak jackets. Their heavy weight affected the handling of the plane and earned him a chewing-out from the pilot.

His worst memories were of seeing other planes in the formation shot down. "It's a terrible thing to see a plane suddenly explode in a cloud of black smoke with 10 men inside it," he said.

Niemczyk named his son Bruce, after Bruce Baker, a 20-year-old ball-turret gunner who died when his parachute failed to open. "The name Bruce may not go with Niemczyk," he said, "but this is how I remembered my friend."

While this extensive aerial warfare was being carried out over Europe during 1943, the Allies took their first terra firma bite of the continent.

The invasion of Sicily began on July 10. Planned at the Casablanca Conference in January, and code-named Operation Husky, this invasion did not go smoothly. A great armada of more than 3,000 ships landed some 160,000 men and 600 tanks, but the initial

Staff Sgt. John Niemczyk

A typical B-17 crew. Niemczyk, second from left, front row, was tail gunner for the lead ship in his unit, the 92nd Bomb Group in Britain.

Pvt. Robert Gustavis

On the left, as an 82nd Airborne Paratrooper trainee. He would be "blooded" in the invasion of Sicily, the largest amphibious operation in history — including D-Day in Normandy.

Cpls. William and Harold McGrath

The McGrath brothers both served during World War II. William, right, went in with the 82nd Airborne at Sicily.

drop of the American 82nd and the British 1st Airborne divisions, totalling 4,600 men, had tragic consequences. Inexperienced pilots, heavy cloud cover and intense antiaircraft fire combined to scatter the paratroopers. Many became isolated far from their units, or were drowned in fields flooded by the Germans.

In the midst of this slaughter were three young men from Northampton in the 82nd Airborne: Staff Sgt. John Dickmyer, Sgt. Robert Gustavis and Cpl. William McGrath.

Not long afterward, in a letter home to his former employer at Peck and Peck on Green Street, McGrath described "all that I can write to have it pass the censor" about the invasion, including his lieutenant's orders concerning their jump. "'Stand up and hook up — check equipment — stand in the doors.' Then on came the green light and the command of 'Let's go!'" The corporal then describes the antiaircraft fire and aerial plane attacks on them while the men floated to earth, adding that "plenty of us had narrow escapes, for a few mistakes were made — but soon corrected. And so we started a job which turned out quite successful."

Within 11 days Sicily had been cut in two, and the Americans were rolling into Palermo on the northern coast.

A much franker and more detailed account of the Sicily landing was given after the war by Robert Gustavis. As the 82nd flew in, Gustavis recalled seeing what he thought were flares going up: instead these proved to be shells. "It was like a wall of fire. Our plane began to rock. The lieutenant called out, 'I'm hit! I'm hit!' He ordered me to push him out when it was time to jump, and I did so even though he was wounded. As I went

Sicily

The capture of Sicily in 1943 was considered the "end of the beginning" of Europe's liberation — but the human cost was high.

down all I could see or think of was the stuff coming at me. The plane exploded on landing. There were paratroopers dropping everywhere and screaming all around me. My whole squad died — some of them hanging in trees. Our 1st sergeant died in a tree. As day came on, some of us managed to join together. The fire we had come through was from our own ships plus ground fire from our 45th Division and the enemy."

The simple explanation later given for this debacle of "friendly fire" was that Italian and German planes had been flying hit-and-run attacks on the ships, and thus the American C-47s were fired on by our Navy before their identity was ascertained. Of the 144 C-47s that flew in, carrying 2,000 paratroopers of the 82nd Airborne, six were shot down even before the men could jump; 229 paratroopers ended up killed, wounded or missing; 23 of the planes were destroyed and 37 badly damaged. One plane that made it back to North Africa had more than 1,000 holes in it. Sgt. Gustavis survived to return to Fort Bragg to train other paratroopers, and there met a fellow survivor of that disaster in Sicily, the wounded officer he had been ordered to push out of their C-47.

Sgt. Dickmyer was captured during the Sicily landing — one of 237 survivors out of his unit of 800 — but was liberated only 36 hours later and went on to fight later at Casino, at Anzio, in the Netherlands and at the Battle of the Bulge.

Prime Minister Churchill would one day say of the eventually successful Sicilian campaign that, while it was "not the beginning of the end," it was indeed "the end of the beginning" of the liberation of Europe.

On November 20, 1943, the Pacific war moved in on the Gilberts, specifically the islands of Makin and Tarawa at the extreme end of Japan's defense perimeter. Makin fell quickly, but Tarawa taught U.S. forces a bloody and terrible lesson. The Japanese defenders themselves believed Tarawa could never be taken. Due to miscalculation concerning the water's depth offshore, the American landing craft got hung up on the coral reef in three feet of water. Thus the Marines had to wade, in waist-deep water, 700 yards in to shore under murderous fire, including shore batteries firing eight-inch naval guns that the Japanese had captured when Singapore fell on February 15, 1942. Only half of the Marines made it in, about 5,000 men, and by nightfall there were 500 dead and 1,000 wounded, with the survivors still pinned down on the beach.

In the four-day battle that followed on this atoll of less than three square miles, out of the garrison of 4,500 Japanese, only 17 would survive. One thousand twenty-six Marines died and 2,557 were wounded. The prize, however, was an airfield that opened up the way to the Carolines and the conquest of the Marshall Islands.

Water Tender 3rd Class William Gutowski of Northampton was at Tarawa aboard the U.S.S. *Independence*, one of the new class of light aircraft carriers that formed the cutting edge of the Navy in the Pacific. Having joined the ship when it was commissioned, Gutowski would serve on the *Independence* throughout his personal war of "three years, two months and 18 days." Six Gutowski brothers served in the Navy, and Tom, a Pharmacist's Mate 3rd Class, would be awarded the Navy Cross posthumously for heroism at Saipan.

Bill Gutowski's own worst experience was at Tarawa. The ordeal for the *Independence* began just before 6 on the night of November 20. "We were attacked by a whole flight of Jap torpedo bombers," he recalled. "There were at least two, and possibly three hits on our starboard side forward of the torpedo wing. There was a hole big enough to drive a bus through. We stopped dead in the water with three of our four screws out of commission. It was a night of terror. Everybody was scared. We thought sure we'd go down. Luckily, our casualties were light. We got temporary repairs from the repair ships in Vlithe Gulf and headed back to Pearl Harbor, burying our dead at sea on the way."

After "six wonderful months" with the *Independence* in drydock at San Francisco, Gutowski returned to action in the Pacific, at Okinawa and the Battle of Leyte Gulf off the Philippines. During its battle-scarred career the *Independence* accounted for 113 Japanese planes shot down and 11 ships sunk. Following the surrender of Japan in 1945, she and her crew would sail into Tokyo Bay itself.

Less lucky was the carrier *Liscombe Bay*. A half hour before dawn on November 24, while covering the occupation of Makin, she was hit amidships by a single torpedo and disintegrated in a thousand-foot sheet of flame. It was still dark when she sank 23 minutes later — with the second largest casualty list of any naval vessel in the war. Only 260 men survived out of a crew of about 1,000.

One of the survivors of the *Liscombe Bay* was her finance officer, Lt. Albert Strong of Northampton, who ended up in the sea with his shoes and clothing burned away, trying to hold up a young sailor who shortly died. Home on leave the following spring, Strong visited the family of John Campbell, an Aviation Radioman 3rd Class, of Easthampton, who was still listed as missing. Strong's sad task was to tell the Campbells that their son had been among those men standing by waiting to take off from the *Liscombe Bay* in their gasoline-and-bomb-laden planes when the torpedo struck. None of them, Strong was certain, could have survived the explosion.

Fighting on the ground at Tarawa were two Marines from Northampton: John Clifford, who would write home at battle's end that he was "well and uninjured," and Raymond "Buddy" Hibbard, who informed his relieved family that the only hurt he received at Tarawa was "a scratch from a bush." A crueler fate was awaiting Hibbard six months later at another awful island, called Saipan.

Water Tender 3rd Class William Gutowski

With crewmates on the carrier U.S.S. Independence, Gutowski is standing fifth from left, in the back row.

Center of the City

The Draper Hotel (1871-1958) on Main Street as it would look on October 12, 1946, the day veterans were welcomed home with a parade. On the right is the Western Union Office where telegrams arrived reporting the fates of young Northampton men. Standing in the doorway, center and right, are Marge and Ben Mysorski. They both worked at Western Union during the war.

1943 — We Hated to See Those Telegrams

In Northampton, the nerve center of the war would ultimately prove to be a simple storefront office at 163 Main Street next to the Draper Hotel. This was the Western Union telegraph office, presided over by manager John F. O'Brien, affectionately known as "Mr. Obie." To this message center, from war theaters all over the world, came the news of the capture, or wounding, or death of Northampton men.

Harold Shockro remembered his days as a telegrapher at Western Union during the war. "We hated to see those telegrams coming in from the Department of the Army or Navy. ... I remember that on Thanksgiving morning, 1944, the first telegram that came in was one stating that my own first cousin, Bernard Begin of Florence, had been seriously wounded in action." Begin was the soldier who had been at Fort Devens on December 7, 1941, en route to Company G headquarters for his discharge when the news came from Pearl Harbor.

"The whole family was getting together for Thanksgiving dinner," recalled Shockro. "I held the telegram until after dinner to give to his mother, so as not to spoil the dinner. Bernard, thank God, recovered and returned home safely."

Patrick O'Keefe, still in high school, worked part-time delivering those telegrams. He remembered the one that concerned Sgt. Mitchell Talenda, one of the four Northampton men serving in the Philippines when they fell to the Japanese in the spring of 1942.

"It was a pleasant warm evening in May, 1942 — shirtsleeve weather. ... Only two of us were in the office, Harold Shockro and myself. About 8 o'clock the teletype began to clack away ... I heard Mr. Shockro say out loud to himself, 'Mitchell Talenda?'... Then he cut and pasted the message on a Western Union form, sealed it in an envelope and stamped this with a red star. I thought to myself, someone's been killed in the war.

"I found the Talenda house down on Isabella Street and went to the door and knocked. All the way down I was thinking how awful this was — to be bringing grief to good people. A woman opened the door. She was tall and wearing a black dress. 'Telegram, Mrs. Talenda.' She stood there holding it in her hand unopened.

"Riding back, I thought, I do not want to have to deliver any more of these."

Four years later, O'Keefe — by this time himself a paratrooper veteran of the 101st Airborne — would be talking with his father, Sgt. Cornelius O'Keefe of the Northampton Police Department, about that telegram. No, his father told him, Talenda had not been killed. "He survived a Japanese prison camp, where a brutal guard, whose victims called him Cyclops, used to beat him with a baseball bat. I know it's true, because I had a beer with Mitchell at White Eagle Hall on my day off, and he told me about it."

Those telegrams, identified with two red stars signifying an emergency or death, had to be handed directly to the addressee. When possible, the Western Union office tried to locate a clergyman of the family's faith to accompany the delivery boy, Shockro recalled, "to help ease the blow."

Business continued to boom at the local draft board all through 1943. By October, Selective Service Board 117 was trying to reassure local residents that young fathers would not be drafted as there was "a sufficient log of 1-A men available." These comforting words were swept away only one month later, in November 1943, when the draft board announced that eight of 13 eligible men who had become fathers before Pearl Harbor would now be drafted. A month later, another 25 men who had become fathers

Western Union Deliveries

Victor Chabot in his Western Union delivery uniform before the war. During the war he would serve in the military.

News Via V-Mail

An Army nurse who served under fire at Anzio, Lt. Ramona Gilligan wrote frequent V-Mail letters home. Although in great personal danger, she did her best to allay her parents' fears concerning her safety.

German Prisoner

Even as recruiters geared up their enlistment efforts for the Army Air Corps, news reached Northampton of local youths killed, wounded, or taken as POWs, as in the case of Tech. Sgt. Robert Clark, who was taken prisoner by the Germans.

before our entry into the war were taken by the draft.

Edmund Cadieux's daughter Linda was 5 months old when he was drafted. His wife, Beulah, remembered the November day in 1944 — her daughter was not quite 2 — when she answered the door and was handed a yellow Western Union envelope. "I put it on the table in the hall and didn't open it. I knew somehow what was in it. Then I put Linda in her stroller and walked for three hours. I don't know why I did this — I just did. And then I came back home and opened that telegram to learn of my husband's death."

In the fall of 1943, a tremendous push began for future pilots: "Silver Wings Are Ready And Waiting For Local Youths" read a full-page Gazette ad. To interest men between 17 and 21 in aviation, an Air Show was staged at LaFleur Airport. Local Civil Air Patrol members were on hand to give rides in their planes. About 6,000 people attended this event, reported the Gazette, and 110 young men signed up for pilot training.

At this same time, Tech. Sgt. Robert Clark of Northampton was reported missing following a raid over Germany in a B-17 "Flying Fortress." Clark would spend the next two years as a POW in Germany.

One of the effects of so many young people being away in the war was a vast increase in transactions of all kinds at the city's post office. The year 1943 was the biggest year on record, with $17,000 more taken in than the previous year; this despite the new franking privilege allowed to all military personnel including the WAVES. A labor shortage at the post office had to be relieved by hiring, for the first time, 18 women for part-time work.

The Postal Service also imposed limits on what could be mailed. Air letters, for example, could weigh no more than two ounces, and no packages could be sent by air as the space was needed for strategic war materiel. Someone came up with a new method of transmitting letters, called "V-Mail." A one-page letter written on a special form could be filmed, reduced in size and sent by air. Each family was allowed three sheets per day.

Eleanor Roosevelt Visits Northampton

First Lady Eleanor Roosevelt, center, with her secretary Malvina Thompson and Capt. Herbert Underwood, who commanded the WWII training school for WAVES at Smith College, during her visit to Northampton on March 24, 1943.

One of the most popular mailings that went out on a regular basis was "The Florence News Letter," prepared and mailed by the Rev. Basil D. Hall of the Florence Congregational Church. "Helen Newell was married a short time ago to Leonard Deinlein of Hatfield," reported the newsletter of December 28, 1943, "and she had a while with him in Texas. Now he is overseas, and she is back in Northampton living with her sister Ruth." Cpl. Deinlein would be killed in Italy five months later on May 26, 1944.

A big event on March 24, 1943, was the appearance in Northampton of First Lady Eleanor Roosevelt, who came to visit the WAVES and also appear at a Smith College assembly. Apparently the local police were not given her precise schedule, and thus they found guard duty extremely difficult. Mrs. Roosevelt wrote up her day's adventures in her syndicated "My Day" column for March 25. She wrote of watching the WAVES at drill and also engaging in "some very strenuous setting-up exercises. As I looked down at them I could not help thinking how smart and keenly alive a large group of women all dressed alike look. The same thing had impressed me about the WACS. It must be that putting everything you have into your work brings about that look of alertness and vigor."

On March 27, at 4:30 a.m., State Rep. Ralph Lerche of Northampton was awakened by the telephone. The caller was an irate sailor from Northampton who had just returned to the United States after 18 months at sea. He had gone to a restaurant near Keesler Field, Miss., for a hamburger and was denied service unless he cared to take his meal out into the street. A local law apparently prevented eating establishments from feeding servicemen in uniform after midnight. Fresh out of combat, this sailor was fighting mad. Lerche had to explain that he himself could do little, but that he would refer the case to U.S. Rep. Charles Clason, who represented Northampton in Washington.

One of the films that played at the Academy of Music in 1943 was "Army Wives." "There are millions of 'em, and they all have the same yen," went the ad. "Here's the riotous lowdown on the gals who chase their G.I. guys from camp to camp to keep the home fires burning." The reality, though it often did have a comic element, was considerably more poignant.

One Army wife was Ethel (Cohen) Feldman. Pvt. Joe Feldman of Northampton had been courting her at her home in Springfield when the war broke out. Feldman was being trained as a Link trainer instructor at Ellington Field in Houston, Texas. For more than a year there were "letters every day that had to be written before you went to bed," she recalled. "I hate writing letters even today." Once engaged, their wedding hinged on his getting a furlough. He arrived home on a Sunday, and the ceremony took place the following Tuesday evening. After a five-day honeymoon on the Cape, Feldman returned to Texas. His new wife went down later by train: "Banana peels and garbage all over the aisles," she recalled. "Also screaming babies and poor soldiers trying to sleep." For a time, for $30 a week, they shared an apartment with a young woman whose husband was overseas. They were shown another so-called apartment, renting for $75 a month, that consisted of a crude, filthy former hen house in a family's backyard. "We don't want the service people in the house," they were told.

Newlyweds World War II Style

Joe and Ethel Feldman. She is wearing his overseas cap.

"You had to have a sense of humor," said Ethel.

Another new bridegroom was Dan Manning, the draftee who returned to Fort Devens the night of December 7 to discover Pearl Harbor had been attacked and that his discharge would be indefinitely delayed. Now an infantry officer, Manning was assigned to Camp McCoy in Wisconsin where his unit was trained to fight on skis — a skill he never did get to use. His wife Helen joined him at a little town called Sparta nine miles from the camp.

At first the Mannings lived in a single room heated only by a vent that brought warm air up from the first floor. "That room was so cold," he recalled, "that when I could be there on Sunday, we'd go to church and come back with the Sunday papers and then go to bed to read them just to keep warm."

Helen found a job at the courthouse and later was able to find better quarters: a single room divided by a plywood partition into a bedroom and living room. A kitchen and bathroom down the hall were shared.

"We were the envy of other couples," she said, "because we actually had a living room." When Manning shipped out to the European theater, Helen — five months pregnant — returned to Northampton.

Bending to the needs of the times, Northampton High School began to present diplomas in absentia to young men in the military. Some, like Robert Oborne, the Navy seaman who had been at Pearl Harbor, managed to get home for the event. New courses were also instituted at the high school, such as aeronautics and preparation for navigation training. "War Has Shifted Educational Trends To The Scientific," advised the Gazette.

Back in 1942, Alderman Edmund Lampron had proposed that an Honor Roll be erected listing the names of all city residents serving their country. Despite some opposition from those who claimed it would be too elaborate, too expensive or too unsightly, by June 1943 the Honor Roll was erected. The original structure cost $920 and contained

Wartime Romances

On the left, Lt. Manning and his wife Helen, outside their wartime "apartment" in Sparta, Wisconsin.

Below, Irene Wade O'Donnell and her new husband, Jim O'Donnell, during a brief honeymoon period following their "war wedding" in the south.

1,500 names. Soon wings had to be added to the white, black-lettered panels as more and more of the town's young people went off to the war. When it was dedicated on June 1, the Roll already bore nearly 2,000 names.

Besides serving as the host community for the WAVES, Northampton made another wartime contribution to the U.S. Navy through a pilot-training program conducted at LaFleur Airport. Chief Pilot Roger Atwood and an experienced crew taught more than 300 students in groups of about 50. The college-aged trainees were housed at Williston Academy in Easthampton, where they did their scholastic work. "Pilots were badly needed by the Navy, and this was one more way to get them," recalled Atwood. Donald Hood, a pilot who had taken many area children up for their first flights in the 1930s, was one of the instructors. Another was Elizabeth Dunn, a Smith College student, class of

Flight Instructor

During the war, Elizabeth Dunn served as a flight instructor for young Navy pilots at LaFleur Airport.

Youngest Commercial Pilot

At age 19, Roger Atwood was the youngest licensed commercial pilot in the U.S. During WWII he served as chief pilot for the U.S. Navy pilot-training program at LaFleur Airport.

1943. She recalled her amusement when she and one of her male students, flying cross-country, would land at a strange airport. "Everyone on the ground would assume that I was the student, and the man was the instructor," she said.

A fire of serious proportions broke out at LaFleur one winter night in 1943. On his way up Bridge Street to the Calvin Theater, Atwood himself spotted the first flames and personally hauled several planes to safety before the old hangar, a converted dairy barn, went up.

"They were standing on their noses to conserve space," he recalled, "and so much 'dope' and 'thinner' were used in those days that the last one I tried to save flamed up almost in my face as I tried to get hold of it."

For three days the airport was surrounded by armed Navy guards as investigators searched for signs of sabotage. The fire's origin was finally traced to a droplight left on in the repair shop while one of the mechanics went to the men's room. Damage was estimated at more than $25,000, and six planes were lost, but none belonged to the Navy and not a single flying hour was lost as a result of the fire.

From the very start of the war, the various ethnic groups that, by the 1940s, constituted the social fabric of Northampton, all strove mightily to demonstrate pride in being Americans. One way was through participation in the nation's various War Bond drives. In 1943, a "Bonds for Bombers" campaign under attorney Harry Jekanowski established a quota of $150,000 for Polish-American citizens of Hampshire County. In January they announced that they had raised their goal to $500,000, and they met it. Franco-American groups, the St. Joseph's Lithuanian Society, the Italian Trento and Trieste society and the local Hadassah chapter likewise established and met goals during this and subsequent campaigns. The 350 members of the German-American Citizens Association gave dances in their clubhouse to raise money for the American Red Cross.

The Forbes Library also went to war with a Victory Books Campaign under the direction of Librarian Joseph L. Harrison. This was part of a joint effort sponsored by the American Library Association, the American Red Cross and the United Service Organizations to supply more than 10 million books to every military service branch as well as to the U.S. Merchant Marine. The Forbes became the area distribution center for Fort Devens, Westover Field and Camp Edwards. By the start of 1943, 11,061 books had been donated. Citizens had to be reminded that soldiers wanted "good novels, entertaining nonfiction and up-to-date textbooks," not "shelf-cleanings of books on baby care, chicken farming or the Thirty Years' War." In some American communities — not in Northampton — more than half of the book donations would prove unfit: not "naughty" but rather "too nice."

Other drives for service people included the Lions Club's "Smokes For Soldiers" and one by the American Legion Auxiliary to collect old phonograph records to be sold as scrap and permit the purchase of new records for military camps and bases. The armed forces themselves made repeated requests for items in short supply. "Typewriter Week" in New England began late in May of 1943, with the goal of collecting "44,000 used machines for the Army and Navy from business firms, factories, schools and public offices," according to the Gazette. The Navy had already issued a plea for binoculars and radio-telephone equipment. Citizens were instructed how to pack, label and mail their patriotic contributions, for which they would receive a check for $1. The Navy promised that "all such instruments still on hand at war's end" would be returned to the owners, and boasted that out of 31,000 binoculars loaned during the First World War, all but one pair were returned.

There were also paper drives, and barrels for copper and brass stood outside the Calvin Theater and the Academy of Music, with free matinee passes for patrons contributing a half pound or more. At one point late in 1943, Northampton was being far surpassed at fat salvage by small communities such as Williamsburg, which met its quota by 129 percent to Northampton's 62 percent. The national average was only 50 percent. When the Office of Price Administration conceived the idea of free red ration points (for meat) in exchange for fat, local contributions doubled and tripled at some local meat markets.

The regional as well as national labor shortage was becoming ever more severe. The problem was so serious at the Northampton State Hospital that local clergymen and Smith College students donated time to work on the wards there. There was also a shortage of farm workers in Hampshire County. During the summer of 1943, 13 young women, including seven from Northampton, were recruited for what was called the "Smith Farm Unit at MSC" (Massachusetts State College).

Above all, it seemed, Smith students were on a marriage binge. There were 83 engagements in 1943, and 28 marriages, primarily to military men. Some married students left college, but 18 young married women were part of the student body, something previously unheard of.

Food rationing was still proving a headache for local housewives, and one answer turned out to be Victory Gardens. In fact, this interest served to replace the frenetic air

Fats for Explosives

As part of their wartime contribution, American housewives saved fats for use in the making of explosives and medicinal items.

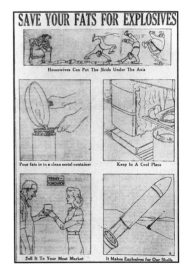

raid precaution activities of the war's first year. The Smith College faculty toiled on 45 plots of about 50 feet by 50 feet on land lent by the State Hospital. President Herbert Davis drew the first lot, and a $10 deposit was requested from him, as from all others, to be forfeited if the garden plots were not kept properly weeded and tended. The Hampshire County Extension Service offered classes in food production and preservation. The Northampton Girl Scouts made Victory Gardens a primary project during the war years.

Food rationing, mild as it was in this country compared with abroad, brought out the worst in some people. Hoarding was a constant temptation. The city's firemen laughed for a long time at the predicament of a prominent local citizen who had to summon the Northampton Fire Department to his residence. An accumulation of water in his basement, caused by efforts to put out the blaze upstairs, resulted in a veritable sea of food cans floating and bobbing on the surface with all the labels soaked off. At another home up on Round Hill, city garbage collectors found whole cartons of butter that had gone rancid and been discarded.

Gas rationing also proved too much to bear for certain local "feather merchants" (the term that those in military service applied to civilian gougers, profiteers and the like). In 1943, OPA investigators claimed that they were onto what "may be the tail of a big ring" of gas ration book counterfeiters. Sheets of fake A-6 coupons had been discovered in the possession of an Easthampton auto mechanic. They were so well copied that the use of "a special light owned by OPA officials" was needed to reveal them as bogus.

Meanwhile, the Gazette reported that some citizens were claiming that gasoline restrictions were discriminating unfairly against the east coast while other regions "live as usual," especially the middle west. Families, willing to give up vacation trips by automobile, were said to be demanding at least enough gasoline to reach local picnic areas. They resented, it was reported, "the Gestapo tactics of the OPA." On January 11, 1943, the Gazette reported "about 31 violators of the pleasure driving ban in this city over the weekend." Vehicles had been spotted parked "near places of amusement," according to

Future First Lady

As a Smith College senior in 1943, Nancy Davis — later to be Nancy Reagan — had the starring role in "Factory Follies," a cabaret program staged at area defense plants during employees' lunch-hour breaks. As "The Glamour Girl" who must be awakened to her wartime responsibilities, Davis receives a kick in the posterior from two fellow performers.

Police Chief Bernier, such as theaters, dance halls and golf clubs. The course of action was to be left to OPA authorities in Boston.

Throughout the war, Chief Bernier did his level best to control speeding in order to conserve gasoline supplies; he even proposed that offenders should have their ration books lifted. To alleviate the transportation problem, the Ration Board had approved many applications for bicycles, but few were available. People living less than two miles from their work were advised to walk.

The severe wartime housing shortage brought architects from the National Housing Agency to the city to find properties that could be converted into multiple units to house area war workers. Plans were made for about a dozen such conversions, including the Knights of Columbus home on Bridge Street, one of the city's finest Greek revival houses, built by the famed architect Isaac Damon in 1825 for his brother.

Already the city was anticipating an acute housing shortage when those in the military returned and wanted homes of their own. The Chamber of Commerce predicted that 212 new homes would be built in the city after the war, and that they would sell at an average price of $5,000 each.

The war continued to bring prosperity to Northampton. In 1942 city residents had spent $14,483,000, including: $3,633,000 on food; $1,286,000 on general retail items; $1,641,000 on apparel; and $451,000 in drug stores. Allotment checks to dependents of servicemen in the Army alone had brought in $262,000 to the city. The local Welfare agent, John Mahoney, reported that although his appropriation had been $47,000, expenses were only $30,000. The rest he returned to the city treasury.

Fur coats were being touted by McCallum's as "A Warm Investment For Years To Come." Dresses, suits and costume jewelry were offered together with "the dress-up hat — all ruffles and flirtatious." Ann August offered "Heavenly Gowns For Victory Dances" from $18.95 to $25. For Easter, Carlson's advertised military uniforms for little boys at prices from $2.95 to $4.95. "Dress him like big brother or Dad in the khaki of the Army or the blue of the Navy."

Various forms of recreation thrived. William J. Short, supervisor of music in the local schools, staged a "Victory Sing" in John M. Greene Hall on May 26, patterned after similar programs he had conducted during the First World War. This year the annual Elks Clambake served "non-rationed" foods. A crowd of more than 25,000 people jammed the Three County Fair on September 7 alone, most of them to wager a total of $102,266 on the horse races — "the first in this city in many years," the Gazette reported. A traffic jam of 5,000 cars reached the intersection of Main and Pleasant. The week's wagers totaled $413,278.

A block dance on Center Street in September, sponsored by the City Recreation Committee, drew a large crowd with many servicemen home on furlough in attendance. On stage at the Academy in October was Boris Karloff in "Arsenic and Old Lace," which made "murder merry and insanity irresistible." Invited to dine with the WAVES officers at Wiggins Tavern, the quiet and gentle Karloff (William Henry Pratt of real life) said he was "scared to death by all these young women in uniform."

Movies had degenerated in quality since 1939, the last year of "the golden age of films." Eager to supply entertainment for civilians with war-swollen pocketbooks, the film industry was turning out a fantastic mix of escapist movies and war-oriented junk with titles such as "Behind The Rising Sun" and "Hitler's Children." The former promised "the shocking truth about the Japs ... they force their daughters into gilded geisha palaces, manhandle captive women, wage war on babies, torture helpless prisoners and MORE!" Ads for "Hitler's Children" promised that "it BLASTS the Mask from Hitler's secret chamber of horrors ... sensational is too mild a word for it." Illustrations of uniformed men mistreating women filled these ads with sexual connotations.

With hindsight, the irony is that the actual treatment accorded to prisoners of the Japanese military, and to victims of the Nazi extermination camps, would prove to have been far worse that anything depicted in these two cheap, ugly films.

In June, Roger F. Clapp, the Boston area supervisor of the War Relocation Authority, mailed a statement from the Massachusetts Council of Churches to local pastors

In the Military Manner

Some American mothers whose small sons were safe from the effects of war (unlike other children around the world), chose to outfit their offspring in mock military uniforms.

Three County Fair Goes On

Civilians flush with war-produced prosperity flocked to the Three County Fair in 1943 to bet on the horses.

concerning the possible relocation of Japanese-Americans around the country. At this time the Authority was of the opinion that "those people whose loyalty is unquestioned should be assisted to resettle themselves in such other areas of the United States where they will eventually be assimilated and accepted by the community." The statement included a long list of reasons why this proposal was fair, just and even practical in light of the nation's labor shortage.

Reactions were immediate, both pro and con. Before the war, Northampton had long been the home of a Japanese merchant, Tadanori Ono, whose shop was a local favorite. When Ono died in 1931, friends in Northampton had helped his widow and children return to Japan.

Movie Propaganda

While American civilians watched movies depicting make-believe brutality by the Japanese, their sons, brothers and husbands, captured when the U.S. surrendered in the Philippines, were experiencing the real thing as POWs.

But now there was a war, and Japan was our enemy. A young Northampton Marine home on leave, Pvt. William Noble, wounded at Guadalcanal and suffering from 12 malaria attacks, urged resettling proponents to "go slow" in New England but expressed no hatred of the Japanese as a people: "It's my theory that no man should receive a kicking while he's down: but I don't think that just because he is down, I'd turn my back on him. I've seen only the military background of the Japanese." Noble also added, concerning the displaced Japanese-Americans, "I feel sure that we can make it up to them after the war."

Then Northampton suddenly attracted national media attention when Time magazine ran a story on September 20, 1943:

"Smith girls, drifting into pretty Northampton for college's opening last week, found the place in a town v. gown stew. A. Burns Chalmers, the college's pacifistic Quaker chaplain, is host to a 27-year-old mathematical physicist, Schuichi Kusaka, born in Japan, newly appointed to the Smith faculty. Kusaka was in Northampton with the approval of the FBI, but some townsmen had found his presence unfair 'to those who have died.'"

Kusaka had been "denounced," according to Time, by two prominent citizens of Northampton: Edward J. Gare, Jr., a jeweler, and John E. Boland, a dentist. Back on June 9, in a letter to the Gazette concerning the proposed relocation of Japanese Americans, Gare had written: "Let us wake up and put the Japanese back into concentration camps and when we win this war return every Japanese, alien, American-born, or naturalized, to the land he knows as home — Japan."

Upon his arrival in Northampton in September to join the Smith faculty, Kusaka was greeted with considerable hostility, much of it expressed in letters to the Gazette. "Threats had been made," according to Time, "to tar and feather Kusaka, and to dump him into Paradise Pond, traditional scene of campus spooning."

Instead, a small group of local protesters settled for hurling an artillery-barrage of tomatoes at the house at 76 Elm Street where, according to the Gazette, they believed Kusaka was living with Chaplain Chalmers' family. As it turned out, the Chalmerses had moved the previous year; thus it was the home of John Smith, a professor of French, that was left with broken windows and tomato-smeared furnishings and rugs.

Born in Osaka, Kusaka had left Japan at age 4 and grew up in Vancouver, B.C. He had had a brilliant career at the universities of British Columbia and California as well as at MIT and Princeton's Institute for Advanced Study. He was recommended to Smith by a Chinese physicist. In "perfect English," according to Time, "Kusaka declared his opposition to the Emperor of Japan, but, as shy as he was able, preferred not to enter the controversy."

One writer to the Gazette, James C. Hall, who had "buried a son last week," protested "against having to cuddle one Dr. Kusaka in our midst." As for his son, "the Japanese were responsible for his death." Julia B. Hopkins wrote that "Hirohito must be having a heluva good laugh for himself." But Ley William Dahmke, just about to enter military service himself, wrote a long, passionate letter in defense of Kusaka. Dahmke said he had recently been passed over as an applicant for the local police force even though he was "the second man on the eligible list." He was informed that this was because someone had referred to him as "un-American." This German-American told how his grandfather had died of his Civil War wounds and then backed up each of his arguments against

Japanese Professor Harassed

At left, Dr. Schuichi Kusaka, a Japanese-born physics professor hired to replace a member of the Smith faculty tapped for the war effort, met hostility and harassment at the hands of certain (not all) residents of Northampton.

Nazi Agent

Memories of Dr. Matthias Schmitz, a professor of German language and literature at Smith before WWII, who turned out to be a Nazi operative, may have fueled the wartime campaign against Kusaka.

intolerance with references to American history.

Two other letters in defense of Kusaka reached the Gazette: one from a young WAC, Cpl. Allison McCrillis; the other from an airman, Pvt. Robert Pease.

Northampton's Board of Aldermen, on the other hand, unanimously adopted a resolution voicing their "formal protest over the appointment of a Japanese alien to the faculty of Smith College as an ill-timed act, damaging to public morale on the home front." They felt the college should have given "more advance notice of its intentions" and also to have consulted "public opinion in Northampton." A copy of their resolution was forwarded to the president of Smith College.

At just about the time this nasty episode hit the national news, the pot apparently boiled over and finally put out the fire. Kusaka remained at Smith for two years, and then, having long since volunteered for the Army, left for basic training at Fort Devens in August 1945. He received his American citizenship shortly after and served with the Atomic Energy project at Aberdeen, Md. Discharged from the Army in 1946, he was awarded a Guggenheim fellowship that same year.

There were three obvious causes for the uproar over Dr. Kusaka: an element of traditional town vs. gown feeling; war hysteria; and, last but not least, the still-remembered presence in Northampton of Dr. Matthias Schmitz, a professor of German language and literature at Smith College from 1934 to 1939 — the year he had been exposed as an operative of the Nazi government.

Charming, suave and urbane, Schmitz had easily ingratiated himself with students and townspeople alike. His students enjoyed lively classes, long nature hikes and tall, handsome escorts from the German Embassy in Washington for their junior prom. For townspeople, particularly the Kiwanis Club of which he was a member, Schmitz proved a popular speaker concerning life in Hitler's Germany. With films at his disposal, he extolled aspects of German theater, art, architecture, road-building, physical culture, youth centers and labor camps for young German men. "The young people," declared Schmitz in one of his Kiwanis lectures, "support Hitler 100 percent."

In the summer of 1939 Schmitz left Smith to become director of research at the German Library of Information attached to the German consulate in New York City. Here, performing as a Nazi agent, Schmitz ran a propaganda mill and, it was believed, an espionage center. By that September he had attracted the attention of the House Un-American Activities Committee and the FBI. Charges against him were dismissed because of diplomatic immunity, the Gazette reported on September 20, 1940.

Schmitz remained in this country until taken into "protective custody" after Germany declared war on the United States on December 11, 1941. He was then returned to his country, together with other German nationals, in exchange for American diplomats.

In 1946, Nazi files discovered by the U.S. Army occupation forces disclosed that Schmitz had entered the Nazi party on December 1, 1936.

1944 — The Beginning of the End

For the Allies, 1944 would prove to be the most crucial and — in human terms — the most costly year of the war. During this year more than 50 Northampton men were wounded, some of them grievously, and some of them for the third or fourth time. Out of the city's final death toll of 112, 40 died during this one year.

The Battle of the Atlantic was not yet won in 1944, but the day of the deadly Nazi wolf pack was over. Single German submarines had to hunt as lone wolves. By war's end, the life expectancy of a German U-boat crew would be about three months.

In the Pacific, American forces would move in on the Marshall and Marianas islands, penetrating Japan's outer defense ring. In Europe, British and American air units continued bombing Germany night and day, while Stalin's armies kept driving Hitler's forces back toward the Polish border. The long-anticipated Allied invasion of France was being readied for June.

Early in the year, Allied military strategists decided on a landing in Italy at a place called Anzio, 33 miles below Rome. Operation Shingle, as it was called, was designed to draw German divisions away from the Eastern front as well as to distract the Nazis from the great invasion planned for the spring. Also, it was intended to assist the Allied troops bogged down south of Anzio and open the way to Rome.

The initial landing at Anzio was unexpected by the Germans and so proved relatively easy. Within 24 hours, on January 22, 1944, more than 36,000 Allied soldiers and 3,200 vehicles were landed, with only 13 men killed. The troops involved were the U.S. 3rd Division, together with detachments of Rangers and paratroopers, plus the British 1st Division and a British commando brigade. What they did not have, however, were the mechanized units necessary for a rapid advance off the beach once the troops were landed.

Hitler ordered the Wehrmacht to rush in reinforcements and hold the front line at all costs. The result was that the Allies were firmly pinned down on the Anzio beachhead, unable either to link up with the main Allied force stalled to their south or to head on north toward Rome. There they remained for four bloody months, until they broke out on May 25.

Among those from Northampton who were at Anzio, in various capacities, were Sgt. Paul Brown of the 1st Ranger Battalion, Lt. Ramona Gilligan of the Army Nurse Corps and Pfc. Origene Morin, a replacement assigned to the 45th Division, who served as an emergency courier on the beachhead.

Brown and his Rangers, who had survived action in Tunisia, Sicily and at Salerno, met disaster on their mission to take the town of Cisterna. In the dead of night the Rangers infiltrated the German lines by creeping through an irrigation ditch for a mile and a half, all the time believing they were unobserved. Suddenly, they were raked from all sides with deadly German rifle, machine gun, mortar and tank gun fire. Of the 767 Rangers who had started out to capture Cisterna, only six got back to the beachhead. Among those captured was Sgt. Brown.

As a POW at Hammerstein in Germany for 18 months, Brown endured a near-starvation diet that left him 42 pounds lighter when he was finally liberated on May 1 the following year.

Brown would die at the early age of 38 in April, 1959, and his obituary listed his

Lt. Charles Ksieniewicz

After his plane was shot down, Ksieniewicz spent three months hiding out with the help of the French Resistance before escaping to England. He was killed training young airmen in New Mexico, on July 24, 1945.

Homeless Wander Europe

Civilians driven out of their houses by military operations, like this Italian family adrift with nothing more than the clothes on their backs, became a common sight as the Germans and Allies fought in Italy.

Italian Campaign Proves Tougher Than Expected

The "soft underbelly of the Axis" was how Allied planners initially viewed Italy. With the occupying German troops determined to hold their ground, however, it proved to be anything but.

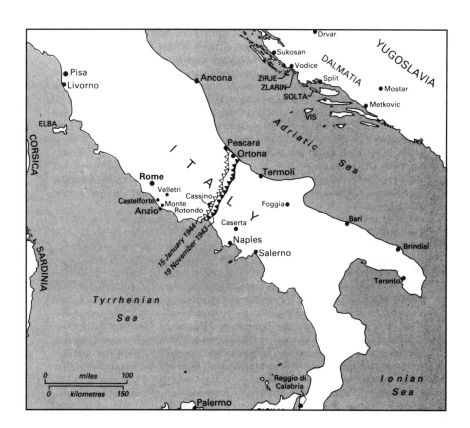

Trial by Fire

Pvt. Origene Morin, a message center clerk for the 45th Division, was among those pinned down on the beach at Anzio.

military exploits as a Ranger and mentioned his Bronze Star. He had, it said, been wounded three times during raids in Africa, Sicily and Italy.

Lt. Gilligan found herself dug in with the 94th Evacuation Hospital, half of it underground with a tent top, only six miles from the front. The nickname given this area by the troops was "Hell's Half Acre," and soldier patients said they had felt far safer back in their foxholes on the beach. After treatment, they were evacuated at night to hospital ships off shore. Gilligan recalled "four months of terrifying days and nights literally spent under fire. Sleep was next to impossible during the day when we were on night duty. We worked 12-hour shifts in teams of 20 doctors and 20 nurses on each shift. Day after day of rain and cold. ... Flak and shell fragments riddled our tents, but somehow out of the confusion and disorder of those tragic hours we did our job well."

Gilligan's assignment was with a 40-bed neurosurgical ward, and in one 24-hour period 138 operations were performed. During one heavy attack on the hospital area, 26 people were killed: three Army nurses, three medical officers, 14 enlisted men, and six patients. Sixty-four others were wounded.

In all, 17,000 military men and women died at Anzio. From January to May 1944, Gilligan and her 200 fellow nurses tended a total of 33,128 patients. At one point she and the other women refused to be evacuated. Six nurses died there, and four of them were the first women to win the Silver Star. Gilligan herself came out of WWII with five battle stars and would remain in the Army until her retirement as a major in 1962.

As a message center clerk pinned down on the beach, Pvt. Morin's memories of Anzio were also harrowing: "We came in on an LST along with trucks, ammunition and an antiaircraft gun," he recalled. "Getting off, we were shelled by the 'Anzio Express' — a giant gun the Germans moved about by railroad. There was so much shrapnel we had to live in holes. To move about was just to move from one hole to the next one already dug by somebody else. So many were killed or wounded there was a personnel shortage. Two men I knew survived getting wounded up front and then they both got killed back in the rear. I came in as a replacement, since there were so many men already lost by the 45th Division."

Morin's worst memory was the German antipersonnel bombs, "big bombs filled with small ones sort of like hand grenades. These would go off and they would sound like the rattling of huge anchor chains — a fearful sound."

Lt. Charles Ksieniewicz of the Army Air Corps — known as "Hooker" in Northampton, where he was the city's outstanding baseball pitcher — had a very different experience. His plane went down over Normandy on April 20, 1944, and in September his family received word only that he was "safe and well." Instead of being captured by German ground forces, Ksieniewicz had made contact with the French underground, who provided him with an all-important identity card. He became a *boulanger* (baker) by the name of Charles Moret.

Back home in the States a year later, and assigned as an instructor at Hobbs, N.M., Ksieniewicz began a written account of his adventures. When his plane went down, he wrote, he was conscious and thus able to get himself more than 10 miles away from the wreckage.

"I ran, ran and ran. You've seen Jab (a reference to a chum, Ralph Jabanowski, who served as a Chief Machinist's Mate in the Navy) steal second, third, and home, but believe me, he'd have been about halfway to second when I'd have been home the way I ran!" Ksieniewicz knew he had to avoid French collaborators and the Gestapo, but he had lost his kit with maps, first aid supplies and some French money, and he knew little or no French. Finally, he was discovered by a French farmer who gave him a tattered old coat and some food and hid him in his barn — which turned out to be only 150 yards from a German headquarters.

Soon turned out to fend for himself, dressed as a laborer, Ksieniewicz eventually met up with a farmer's wife who led him to a woman underground member. To himself he called her Mme. Defarge, from Charles Dickens' *Tale of Two Cities*.

"They had absolutely nothing to gain by helping me," Ksieniewicz's account continues. "If they were caught, all of them would have been tortured and shot. ... All they had to do was to turn me in, and their relatives in Germany (forced labor) would be returned — plus a 10,000 francs reward. ... When I got back to the States and heard people complaining about meat and butter cutbacks, I thought back to those French farmers giving most of their own clothing and meager food to help me out."

For many weeks, Ksieniewicz and several other downed Allied airmen moved in and out of underground hiding places in their effort to reach the Spanish border. Fear, stealth, cold and hunger entered his narrative here, but also relief on learning that all his crew except one had survived and that one of these, like himself, had escaped capture. The German occupation force was bracing for the expected Allied invasion and was on the lookout for agents and spies, so the escapees faced grave danger.

Ksieniewicz wrote of his joy at learning of the expected invasion, and then his narrative stops abruptly. The rest of the page is blank. Lt. Ksieniewicz had survived death in Europe only to meet it, as an instructor, back in the United States during a routine training flight on July 24, 1945. He left his wife Mary about to bear their twin sons, Charles and John, who entered the world one month before their young father had been scheduled to be discharged from the Army Air Corps.

By the early summer of 1944 England had begun to resemble a vast, crowded military encampment. Three million Allied soldiers, sailors and airmen had been assembled there. Tanks, trucks and jeeps sat in crowded rows in every park and field. Airfields were packed with bombers and fighters, and transport ships filled all the ports. This small island nation had become one gigantic airdrome for the RAF and the USAAC and a staging area preparing for the greatest military invasion in history, the Allied invasion of Europe.

On June 6, 1944, the American people would awaken to learn that the long-awaited invasion was already in progress.

Many of the men who were there that day, including Sgt. Ray Sakrison of Northampton, saved the wallet-sized scrap of paper that was handed out on the eve of D-Day, on which Gen. Eisenhower's prayer for victory was printed:

"Soldiers, sailors, and airmen of the Allied Expeditionary Forces! You are about to embark on the great crusade, toward which we have striven these many months. ... Let us

Sgt. Ray Sakrison

During off-duty hours in England, readying for D-Day, Sakrison tried to see something of the country.

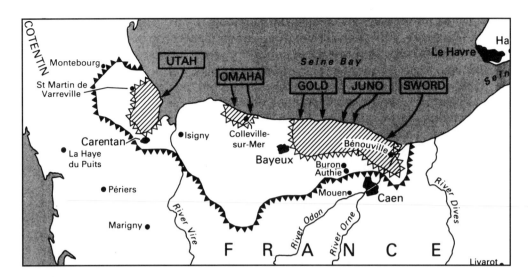

D-Day Targets

The five invasion beaches hit by Allied troops on D-Day, June 6, 1944.

beseech the blessings of Almighty God upon this great and noble undertaking."

Gen. Erwin Rommel, the man who had led Germany's renowned Afrika Korps until his defeat at El Alamein in October of 1942, had been charged with preparing the defenses of the French coast against the inevitable Allied invasion. "The war will be won or lost on the beaches," Rommel predicted. "We'll have only one chance to stop the enemy, and that's while he's in the water ... struggling to get ashore ... the first 24 hours will be decisive ... for the Allies, as well as Germany. It will be the longest day."

For six months, half a million men under Rommel's command had labored to construct massive pillboxes and deathtraps of every description to halt the Allied invaders. Coastal waters and beaches were mined; rear areas and possible landing fields were booby-trapped or flooded. All available guns, rockets and mortars were strategically placed.

For the Allies, the invasion itself involved 2,876,000 men, 5,300 ships, 20,111 vehicles, 1,500 tanks and 12,000 planes. On the evening of June 5, transport planes ferried 24,000 American and British airborne troops across the Channel to land behind the lines and seal off the five beachheads. The following morning, June 6, the British went in on Gold, Juno and Sword beaches; the Americans at Utah Beach and at Omaha Beach. Omaha proved to be the nastiest of them all.

Twenty-four-year-old Lt. Dan Manning of Northampton, executive officer of Company E, 23rd Infantry, 2nd Division, was among those who took part in the Normandy invasion. After eight months in Northern Ireland, the so-called Indian Head division had been moved to Wales. Originally not slated to take part in the invasion, the Indian Head men were designated as reserves at the last minute.

"For three days we sat aboard transport ships on the English coast," Manning recalled. "There we played cards, did calisthenics, jumped as the claxon horns periodically announced air raids and the like. On the morning of D-Day, June 6, we were right in line with the battle-wagons firing away. I was amazed — awestruck you might say — that a guy like me from Massachusetts was participating in one of the biggest events in the history of the United States. This will be written up in the history books, I thought, and I'm going to be part of it. Everybody was quiet ... most of the guys were only 21 or 22 years old. Nobody wanted to act scared, so they joked as if they were going off on a picnic. We were all frightened, but this was a job we had to do, and we were going to do it.

"That evening the word came: 'We're moving out in an hour.' Boy, that sure perked everybody up. Crossing the Channel to Omaha Beach, a cruiser hit a mine and blew up right in front of us."

There were dangers to face even before the company hit the beach, such as leaping from the transport onto the landing craft without dropping into the gap between the two crafts as the sea tossed to and fro.

"That's how we lost our first man," said Manning. "He went straight down. You think, gee, that's tough, and then you have to forget it and just go on. Then when the ramp of the LST went down on a sand bar, there was suddenly some deep water to traverse, and

D-Day Casualties

Huddled on Omaha Beach on D-Day, the "medics" attend to American wounded.

Pvt. Gomez, my runner, a little guy about 5-foot-3, suddenly went down. Somehow we managed to get hold of him and haul him out. Each of us, remember, was loaded down with about 60 pounds of equipment: our O.D. (olive drab woolen uniform) shirt and pants; our field jacket; and then another layer of clothing impregnated against gas. Then there was our rifle, helmet, gas mask and pack with our rations, extra socks and the like.

"When we got to the beach there were still bodies lying around, but what really got to me was a medical tent already full of wounded men lying there waiting to be sent back to England.

"There were shell holes everywhere. The beach master was doing his job, and mine sweepers were still trying to clear away the mines. When we reached the top of the cliffs we headed for our rendezvous five miles inland where we were told to dig in. The foxholes we dug that night were done on our first night under fire on enemy soil, and I can tell you, they were the deepest we ever dug during the whole war."

Some years later Manning would discover that two cousins of his, the sons of a WWI Canadian soldier and a British army nurse, had shared that day with him. Pat Manning of the 29th Division was killed during the landing, and his brother, Ibie, of the 4th Division, was destined to die a few weeks later in the *bocage*, or hedgerows, of Normandy.

Also a member of the 2nd Division that day, serving as a mine detector in the antitank corps of the 38th Infantry, was Pfc. Ellis Hover of Florence, who — like Manning — would have to slog on and fight his way through Europe. Hover, who would emerge with five battle stars, a Presidential Unit citation and the Bronze Star, wrote home that he had survived the invasion but could not describe it due to military censorship. He did indicate, however, that it seemed more like a week than a single day — an echo of Rommel's prediction.

Pvt. Raymond LeBeau

Having survived the invasion on D-Day, LeBeau, age 20, was killed two days later in Normandy, June 8, 1944.

On Leave in London

Sgt. Donald Simison with an English friend in the days before he took part in the Normandy invasion on D-Day plus one.

D-Day Survivor

Lt. Dan Manning after weeks of combat, with "I'm glad to be alive" written all over his face. Due to casualties he was now commanding officer of his company.

Sgts. Ray Sakrison and Donald Simison, who had left Northampton together in the draft back in May 1942, also ended up in the invasion, on D-Day plus one, as supply sergeants in the 29th Division. "I was lucky," said Simison, "and hardly even got my feet wet. But when we actually got onto Omaha Beach the thing that still sticks in my mind is the piles of bodies I saw. You couldn't believe it. Like cordwood."

Sakrison recalled stumbling over a body close to the beach as he waded in. "That sobers you up right away. I don't ever want to see anything like that beach again."

Chief Machinist's Mate Ralph "Jabber" Jabanowski made it through D-Day aboard a mine sweeper and would one day describe the scene to a Gazette reporter as "an inferno."

D-Day Participants

Left to right: Chief Machinist's Mate Ralph "Jabber" Jabanowski; Tech. Sgt. Stanislaw Sniezko; Cpl. Henry Kurzydlowski; Coast Guardsman Francis LeDuc; Seaman 1st Class John McCarthy; Lt. Connie Nanartonis.

Tech. Sgt. Stanislaw Sniezko, whose brother William was a POW in Japanese hands, was awarded the Silver Star "for gallantry in action in the vicinity of St. Laurent sur Mer ... on June 6, 1944." His citation reads: "Displaying outstanding courage in the face of heavy enemy fire, Sgt. Sniezko repeatedly left his position of comparative safety to rescue wounded comrades, administer first aid, and to reorganize and reassemble his section. Sgt. Sniezko's aggressive leadership contributed materially to the success of the landing operation."

The French government would award the *Croix de Guerre* to Cpl. Henry Kurzydlowski, of Northampton, a Polish immigrant and member of a chemical-combat unit that cleared mines on D-Day. A few days later they also charged into a burning ammunition dump with firefighting equipment to prevent it from blowing up.

Coast Guardsman Francis LeDuc of Leeds spent D-Day aboard one of a fleet of 63-foot cutters that saved more than 900 Allied soldiers during the invasion.

Eighteen-year-old Seaman 1st Class John McCarthy of Florence, who had enlisted the day after his 17th birthday the previous year, wrote home that as a member of an LST crew he was grateful to have survived that terrible day.

1st Lt. Connie Nanartonis, one of the two men from Northampton who had flown off to Canada in 1940 to join the RCAF, now a glider pilot in the 9th Air Force, was pressed into action during the invasion aboard one of the C-47s that flew supplies and ammunition into Normandy and then returned to England with the wounded. Nanartonis always remembered the stench of those planes because of the condition of the grievously wounded men, some of whom also suffered air sickness to add to their misery.

By nightfall on D-Day, more than 2,300 American, British and Canadian soldiers had died, but nearly 160,000 Allied troops were ashore and had secured some 80 square miles of France. Costly and fearful fighting lay ahead, but the long-planned landing in France was a reality at last.

Two Northampton men — Stanley Greenberg and Salvatore Polito — served as medical corpsmen in Normandy. Greenberg was attached to the 5th Infantry Division and Polito to the 30th or "Old Hickory" Division. Both men, not yet out of their teens, would survive some of the most savage fighting in Normandy. Traditionally known as "Doc" to their platoons of 40 men, the duty of these soldiers was to respond to the cry of "Medic!" from the wounded, usually at great personal risk to themselves. Unarmed, and supplied only with a small medical kit on their hip, their sole protection was the Red Cross insignia on their helmets and armbands plus, in their pockets, a card with their photo, fingerprints and the rules of the Geneva Convention.

"Our ministrations were pretty basic," recalled Greenberg. "We applied compress bandages, splints, sulfa powder and injected morphine for pain. Our job then was to get the wounded onto litters and back to the surgeons in the field hospital. Treating real wounds proved actually not as bad as some of our color training films. A medic plays a kind of passive role; you can't fight back."

A month after D-Day, when his unit went in at Utah Beach, Greenberg observed the still-lingering litter and filth of the invasion: smashed equipment, wrecked gliders, parachutes still hanging in the trees, the smell of gasoline and of dead animals. The apple trees were all in bloom and beautiful in contrast to what lay underneath them.

"Here I saw my first case of combat fatigue," Greenberg recalled, "a soldier shaking and crying. But this was nothing compared to the men of the 1st Division I saw as they came back from weeks in the line. Bearded and covered with dirt, their faces were vacant, eyes staring, and they shuffled along bent over like old men." After 10 days under fire himself near Caumont, he said that what ultimately bothered him most was the stench of dried blood on his own uniform. "You've been drenched in it; as a medic you feel and smell like a butcher."

At one point, Greenberg ran to assist some wounded lying in a tank trap about 10 feet deep and six across. "I had just bent over the first man," he recalled, "when I felt a blow to my back just as if I'd been struck with a hammer. I knew I'd been shot, and when I started spitting blood I also knew that it was a lung wound and that I'd die if I stayed down there. I got out a jackknife I had and cut holes in the dirt sides of the trap to climb out by. I was lucky. A Sherman tank came along, and some guys got out — under fire — and hauled me in and got me back. Then I recall lying on a litter next to a young German kid with his foot shot off, and I felt sorry for him. Later I would learn that one of the best chest surgeons in the U.S. had operated on me in that field hospital. I was also told that except for penicillin I wouldn't have made it. 'In the First World War,' a doctor told me, 'all these cases like yours died!'"

For Stanley Greenberg, many months of painful treament lay ahead, followed by a long convalescence. But for him at least the war was over.

Salvatore Polito went in on Omaha Beach on D-Day plus six. "The 1st and 28th Divisions had been decimated," he said. "They were no longer fighting divisions." His 30th Division would experience its own terrible fate. "There was a sergeant I can never forget," said Polito. "He sang hymns all the time, and as we went in on the beach he was singing 'When the Roll Is Called Up Yonder I'll Be There' — kind of a strange thing to sing under those particular conditions. A few days later he was killed.

"Near St. Lo, we learned that the Air Force was going to come in to help us blast our way out of that hedgerow country. Our positions were allegedly marked, and the sky was filled with American planes as far as you could see. With all this firepower we've got it made, we thought. Then suddenly the lead bombers began to unload on *us* ... we could hardly believe it. The other bombers of course followed this pattern. They murdered us — they knocked us out. Gen. Lesley McNair, a good general who stayed with his men, was killed. We were hit so badly we couldn't attack. From then on we never again trusted the American Air Force."

The bill for this blunder was 111 American soldiers killed and 490 severely wounded by bombing and the new killer, napalm.

Despite all his training, Pvt. Polito had never actually given a morphine injection until that day. "I just closed my eyes and plunged the needle in. One man was hit in the jugular vein. Nothing I could do would stop the terrible bleeding — it was like a fountain. I even tried to hold my hands over it. I couldn't help him. I had to sit there and watch him die."

Polito's unit would be among those troops who, during the Battle of the Bulge in December, discovered the massacre at Malmedy, where S.S. troops had mowed down American prisoners in a field. "They weren't just killing prisoners but also whole families of innocent civilians that we'd find dead."

On January 15, 1945, in Belgium, Pvt. Polito himself would become a casualty. "How we ever won the war is beyond me ... we had such stupid leaders," he said later. His unit was "ordered out into an open field ... trying hard to stay apart from each other and not bunch up. We expected to be captured at least ... I felt uneasy that day. Let's move up there a little bit, I said to the right guide, and then the next thing I knew I'm on the ground, and he's gone — completely obliterated. I'm conscious, but I can't get up. The litter bearers couldn't get to me, so my own guys made a makeshift litter and got me out."

Polito too had a long convalesence but, unlike Greenberg, recovered enough to be sent back to duty where he was put in charge of a V.D. clinic. Here he took a certain grim joy in backing officers into a corner for their penicillin shots. "I used to really plunge that needle into their posteriors," he admitted later with a smile.

Cpl. Stanley Greenberg

A medical corpsman in the 5th Infantry Division, he survived a near-fatal chest wound in the Normandy fighting.

Pvt. Salvatore Polito

A medical corpsman in the 30th Infantry Division, he was wounded during combat in Belgium. He received the Bronze Star for retrieving a wounded comrade under sniper fire.

War Buddies

Lt. Joanna Hathaway, Army Nurse Corps., and her husband-to-be Staff Sgt. John Grimes, surgical technician, both served in France with the 35th Evacuation Hospital.

Pfc. Joseph Okolo

Killed in Normandy on June 15, 1944.

Pfc. Joseph Okolo, who had left Northampton early in 1941 with the National Guard Company G, met his death on the Normandy beachhead on June 15. "He was killed immediately by enemy bullets," a friend wrote back to his sister, Caroline.

"My parents decided not to have his body brought back," she said. "Instead, he is buried in Le Havre, France. I have always remembered his serial number, 20108694."

Another Northampton veteran of the fighting in Normandy on the heels of the invasion was Joanna Hathaway, an Army nurse. Lt. Hathaway crossed the English Channel to Omaha Beach on D-Day plus 18. In her role as Operating Room Nurse 3443 with the 35th Evacuation Hospital, Hathaway was at first located at St. Saveur, only a quarter of a mile behind the front lines. With a field artillery unit nearby, the site was very noisy, and it was hard to sleep after their 12-hour shifts. At the end of one of her shifts she answered a call to find herself in "a sea of wounded Germans ... I went numb. This was my first contact with the enemy and all of them needing our help."

Thereafter, the 35th averaged about two weeks in each place as they followed the battle lines. One hospital unit would leapfrog over another, as the line moved forward, to keep a fully functioning unit always near the front. Hathaway's most dangerous moment was when their convoy was misdirected in the middle of the night, and only an alert M.P. saved them from heading straight into a combat zone.

"My worst experience involved a young soldier brought in with a live shell still embedded in his shoulder," she remembered, "but also terrible was another man who was still alive but minus most of his body parts. The gas gangrene among the patients at Helensburg in Germany was also terrible."

On May 18, 1945, Joanna Hathaway married Sgt. John Grimes, a surgical technician from Georgia, with a German wedding license, at Erlagen. They were separated immediately, since Army rules did not sanction marriage between officers and enlisted personnel in the same unit.

The first news to hit Northampton about a local man taking part in the Normandy invasion concerned Pvt. Charles McDonald, a paratrooper in Company D of the 501st Parachute Infantry Regiment, a unit of the 101st Airborne Division popularly called the "Screaming Eagles" because of their distinctive shoulder patch. McDonald was wounded in the left arm and shoulder, but he was able, late in June, to write to his parents

Normandy Invasion

Pvt. Charles "Caesar" McDonald and his fellow paratroopers of the 101st Airborne Division parachuted into Normandy on the evening of June 5 ahead of the invasion the following morning.

from an Army hospital in England that he "wouldn't have missed being in it (the invasion) for anything." In September his parents would receive the Purple Heart he had promised to send them as soon as he located "a piece of paper to wrap it in."

McDonald and the Screaming Eagles had gone across the English Channel on the evening of June 5, together with the American 82nd Airborne and the British 6th Airborne — 24,000 paratroopers in all — charged with sealing off the five beachheads just ahead of the invasion. The Britons were flown in by seasoned pilots and made a good drop; the Americans were not so lucky. Some drowned in the sea or in defensively flooded areas, while others were dropped miles from their objectives. Chaos reigned for a time. During those fateful hours, McDonald and other wounded men — Americans and Germans — holed up in a French farmhouse under fire from both sides. As men of both nations died, the chaplain of the 101st Airborne, Father Francis Sampson, gave absolution to Germans and Americans alike.

"How we survived that night I shall never know," Sampson would later write in his book, *Look Out Below!*, describing the ordeal, "except that the calm, fervent prayers of those wounded men didn't leave God any choice ... but to answer them."

At one point, McDonald is said to have charged a group of German paratroopers that he thought were harassing wounded American paratroopers. Some years after the war Father Sampson would tell Pat O'Keefe, another veteran from Northampton, that "Black Mac," (his own nickname for McDonald) was "the bravest man I ever met." Of Father Sampson, McDonald said: "You almost didn't want to run into him, because he went where things were the worst. You saw Father Sampson, and then you knew you were in a tough spot."

Also in France, not long after the invasion, was 1st Lt. Harold Bauver, communica-

101st Airborne Division

Gen. Dwight D. Eisenhower, center, chats with men of the 101st Airborne Division — the "Screaming Eagles" — as they prepare for D-Day landings.

Surviving the Blitz

Sgt. Mary Daley and members of her Women's Army Corps unit stationed in London narrowly escaped death when one of the German "rocket bombs" landed in the area where they were billeted. She is adjusting her cap before a mirror in a onetime drawing room now roofless and full of debris.

tions officer in the 4th Armored Division. One of his indelible memories was what he called "the red panel incident." Proceeding along a road in France, Bauver's tank column saw, following their progress, a flock of American B-26 bombers overhead with all their bomb bays open. A sergeant suggested that their column should display the two-foot-square red-plastic panels that identified American ground units to American airmen if necessary. This suggestion was brushed aside by the colonel. Then Lt. Bauver, who realized the danger they were in, gave the order himself.

Sometime later, wounded and in an English hospital, Bauver compared notes with a B-26 pilot in the next bed who had actually been aboard one of those planes. The pilot told him they had been about to bomb what had appeared to them to be German tanks below when the sudden display of the red panels, ordered by Bauver, had prevented the tank column's destruction.

One week after D-Day, on June 13, 1944, Hitler introduced a new concept in warfare, his *Vergeltungswaffen* or "vengeance weapons." The first was the jet-engined V-1 bomb, soon to be renamed the "buzz bomb" or "doodle bug" by Hitler's intended British victims. In three days, more than 250 British civilians were killed by V-1s. Valiant efforts were made to shoot them down, and Lt. Nanartonis remembered actually watching British fighter pilots "climb for altitude, since the bombs went faster than the Spitfires, and then dive on them to get their wing tip under the wing tip of the buzz bomb so as to turn it back on the source from which it came."

Despite these efforts, by the end of the summer of 1944 these devices had killed 6,000 people, wounded 40,000 and destroyed some 75,000 buildings in Britain. The great ports of Portsmouth and Southampton, so necessary to Allied supply lines, however, providentially went untouched while Londoners died.

On September 8 began the first V-2, or rocket bomb, attacks on Britain. These silent and sophisticated V-2 bombs, developed by Werner von Braun and Walter Dornberger (future space-program scientists in the U.S.), were launched from Peenemunde in the Netherlands. About 9,000 of these bombs, far more frightening than the buzz bombs, would kill 8,000 Britons between September 8, 1944, and March 29, 1945, when the rocket-launching site was captured by the Allies. Plans were discovered there, incidentally, for a future rocket bomb capable of spanning the Atlantic.

Sgt. Mary Daley of Northampton, a WAC attached to the Office of Strategic Services (OSS), was stationed in London during some of the heaviest bombing of the city, including both the V-1s and V-2s.

"At one point," Daley recalled, "the buzz bombs seemed to be coming over every 15 minutes for three whole days. You didn't have to worry as long as you could hear them. It was when the noise stopped that you tried to take cover — that's when they were going to hit." In the summer of 1944, American servicemen and women became victims right along with the Londoners.

"London will never be conquered, will never fail," roared Prime Minister Churchill. "Here we began the war, and here we will see it ended." Statistics would show that more Londoners were killed by these bombs than the number of Allied soldiers who died during the first two weeks of the invasion, and ultimately 60,595 British civilians died during the war.

Double Duty

Lt. Earl Tonet of the 2nd Marine Division survived combat on Saipan and would go in again on Okinawa.

***

As Allied troops fought to break out of Normandy in June 1944, other Americans out in the Pacific theater were struggling to take the Marianas Islands, including Saipan, Tinian and Guam. Only 1,200 miles from Tokyo — far closer to Japan than Hawaii is to California — Saipan and Tinian were destined to become the air bases from which the B-29s would eventually begin to bomb Japan. First, the islands had to be taken.

Operation Forager began on June 15 with 20,000 men landed on Saipan by nightfall; two-thirds of them were Marines from the 2nd and 4th divisions. By July 9, the island was considered secure, but the cost had been high, with more than 16,000 American casualties including 3,426 dead. There were an estimated 23,000 Japanese dead, however.

One of the most gruesome episodes in the Pacific war took place on Saipan when about 8,000 Japanese civilians, who had withdrawn to cliffs along the northern shore, chose suicide rather than to cast their lot with the victorious Americans. They had been taught that the soldiers would torture, rape and kill them. Whole families either killed themselves with grenades provided by their own soldiers or jumped from the cliffs to the sea below, some stabbing or throwing their babies off first.

One American who helplessly watched this horror unfold was Lt. Earl Tonet of Northampton, who headed a 37mm antitank gun unit of the 2nd Marine Division. For him an indelible image of this tragedy was of one young woman in a red dress that billowed about her as she fell to the rocks below.

On July 7, Tonet also experienced the largest *banzai* charge in the Pacific; 3,000 Japanese soldiers and sailors all bent on suicide. "It was like a cattle stampede — unbelievable. They came on screaming and yelling — waving every weapon you can think of — rifles, sabers, machine guns, grenades, even 'idiot sticks' that were just sticks with bayonets fixed to them. They penetrated the lines — actually jumping on our men in foxholes with hand-to-hand combat even by cooks and clerks. It was our artillery that finally stopped them, with the guns lowered to point-blank range of 20 yards."

Combat Losses – All Marines

Left to right: Pfc. Raymond Hibbard and his platoon sergeant, Sgt. Alvin Sinclair, both from Northampton, survived combat on Tarawa, but died together on Saipan. Sgt. Mitchell Rutkowski was killed on Tinian.

Tonet's one day as burial detail officer remained strong in his memory. "The stench has never left me to this day. It was a sickening experience — bodies swollen and rotting in the hot sun — dismembered and smashed — full of maggots." Tonet would fight again on Tinian and Okinawa.

Sgt. Robert Lyons of Northampton, also a Marine, won the Bronze Star at Saipan when "without thought of his personal safety he rushed to a flaming pit" where an 81mm mortar shell exploding in a mortar tube had killed one person, seriously injured another, and then set on fire several rounds of ammunition. Lyons removed the wounded and fought the fire until it was extinguished. His citation was signed by Gen. Holland M. Smith, or "Howlin' Mad" as his Marines called him.

Two men from Northampton had survived action at Tarawa only to die together at Saipan: Pfc. Raymond Hibbard and his platoon sergeant, Alvin Sinclair. Hibbard never even got home after his boot training. He was shipped directly to the Pacific, and was killed in action on June 28, 1944.

Sinclair had never before written his parents just prior to going into combat, but he did write two days before the invasion of Saipan: "I'm writing this one just in case something happens." Two days before he went into battle, he had met his brother, Lt. Richard Sinclair — also a Marine — whom he had not seen in two years.

After the fall of Saipan, the Japanese warlord Gen. Hideki Tojo resigned as Prime Minister, indicating how important to Japan's survival this island had been considered. Indeed, its capture is said to have opened the final phase of the war in the Pacific by providing the closest base yet from which to bomb the Japanese home islands. Bombing began on November 24, when 111 B-29s took off to attack the Musashi aero-engine plant near Tokyo.

Radioman 3rd Class Sam Lococo was also in the Pacific in June 1944, serving aboard the destroyer U.S.S. *Healy*. "We were providing escort service for the aircraft carrier U.S.S. *San Jacinto*," said Lococo. "This, I now know, was the ship off which a hot young Navy pilot named George Bush flew his missions — including the one where he was shot down. One of my own most memorable experiences as part of the *Healy*'s crew was the day we rescued — much against their will — a couple of Imperial Japanese Navy pilots. It was June 23, 1944. Hit by antiaircraft fire, their plane crashed in the sea near us. We immediately launched a whaleboat to pick them up. One man was badly injured; he died and was buried at sea. The other, with only a leg injury, tried to keep us from picking him up. The Japanese had been taught that the Americans were savages, so probably he was afraid of us. He kept saying in English, 'You are going to kill me. You are going to kill me.' We pulled him from the sea, dressed his wounds in the sick bay on the *Healy* and then transferred him to the U.S.S. *Lexington*. We treated that pilot like a king."

On July 24 came the assault on another island in the Marianas, Tinian, which was taken at a cost of 1,771 wounded and 327 dead. One of the dead was Northampton Marine

Sgt. Mitchell Rutkowski, one of five brothers all in the service. Not long before his death, Rutkowski saw his brother Bruno, a photographer's mate 1st class, for the first time in three years. The Japanese dead on Tinian numbered 6,050.

Tech. Sgt. Michael Shebak, engine specialist for one of the big new B-29s flying bombing missions over Japan, would arrive on Tinian in the spring of 1945. Shebak was a survivor of 36 missions in the China-Burma-India theater, including 15 trips over "the Hump" — a 14,000-foot-high mountain chain between India and China — and six crash landings, in three of which the plane was totaled. Now, watching a film one night in the mud and muck on Tinian, he heard a man near him say, "Boy, I wish I was back in Northampton." There followed a reunion with "the two Powers brothers, Hank Organ — a journalist — and Steve Murphy — part of the ground crew of the *Enola Gay* that would deliver the atomic bomb to Hiroshima."

On August 6, 1945, the atomic bomb itself would be flown from Tinian, headed for Hiroshima. "All those islands we fought for," said Earl Tonet, "were, in effect, stationary aircraft carriers. The Japanese had developed them — fine runways on Tinian, for example — to use against us, and now we were reversing things to use them against the Japanese."

By August 10, the island of Guam — an American island territory for 40 years that had fallen to the Japanese on December 10, 1941 — was back under American control at a cost of 7,000 casualties including 2,124 dead. Of the Japanese garrison, 18,500 defenders died. One survivor, an army sergeant named Shoichi Yokoi, would be discovered hiding in the jungle 28 years later.

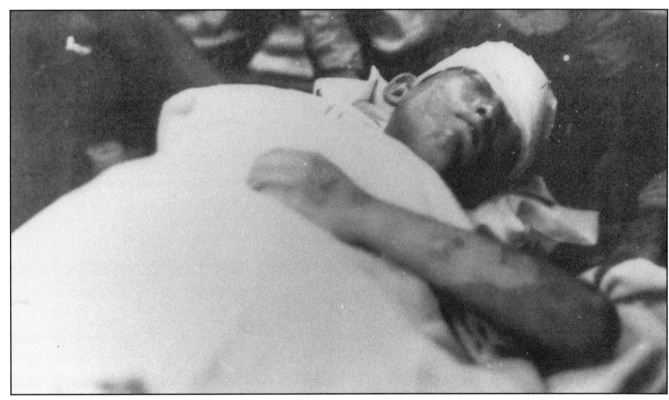

Japanese Pilot Saved

Rescued from the sea by the crew of the U.S.S. Healy *after his plane was shot down, this young Japanese pilot received first-aid treatment for a leg wound and burns before being transferred to the U.S.S.* Lexington *for further medical care.*

Sgt. Julian Bubrowski

Posing here with two Italian waifs, one of whom is wearing his overseas cap, Bubrowski survived a serious wound in North Africa only to be killed in Italy on October 20, 1944.

1944 — Some Couldn't Even Remember Their Names

Back in the European theater during the summer of 1944, the campaign in Italy ground on. The Allied effort to drive the Germans out of Italy, once dubbed "the soft underbelly of the Axis," had proved a bitter thing. According to some historians, the whole Italian campaign of 1944-45 was a serious strategic error requiring Allied forces to battle their way up the narrow mountainous peninsula, the geography of which greatly favored the dug-in German defenders. After the near disaster at Anzio, the sacrifice of the 36th Infantry Division by Gen. Mark Clark at the Rapido River, and the siege of the monastery at Monte Cassino, keystone of Germany's Gustav Line, that in the end was destroyed in a raid by 230 bombers, the 5th Army finally entered Rome on June 4, 1944, only two days before the Normandy invasion.

Lt. Ramona Gilligan's 94th Evacuation Hospital followed the fighting up through Italy. "We were always as close to the fighting as our commanding officer could get us, and we were the first hospital unit to move into Rome behind the infantry and in front of the field artillery. We were not even supposed to be in that position. Our C.O. had moved us too soon, and I heard he was called on the carpet for it later. We set up our hospital in tents around a monastery that had been used by the Germans."

The Italian campaign had already taken the life of one Northampton man. On August 22, 1943, the B-26 on which Staff Sgt. Alfred Conz served as a gunner and radio operator had gone down on a mission over Naples. He left behind his widow, Lola; they had been married only three months.

It was in the summer and fall of 1944, however, that the bill for the campaign in Italy really began to mount. In Northampton on June 21 the parents of Pvt. Bernard Finn and Pvt. Adolph Butor, both men wounded in earlier engagements, received more bitter news. Finn had again been seriously wounded, and Butor had been killed — both of them apparently in the battle for Rome. Three months later, Pvt. Roy Tebbutt of Florence was also reported seriously wounded. Sgt. Julian Bubrowski, who had survived serious wounds received in North Africa the previous year, was killed in Italy on October 20.

In March 1945, Pfc. Frank Cimini would receive the Silver Star posthumously for an exploit in 1944. Two stories on Cimini had reached the Gazette, one from Italy from an Army public relations writer on April 3, 1944, and another by an AP war correspondent, Sid Feder, on May 15. As a scout observer for his company, in the 88th Infantry Division of the 5th Army, Cimini had survived three days alone, under fire by both the German and American artillery, and had managed to escape a carefully staged ambush as well. Hungry, dehydrated and suffering from concussion, he survived to rejoin his company. "I was sure glad to see I Company this morning," he was quoted as saying. "I thought I was finished." Cimini was killed in action in Italy on July 24, 1944.

A happier fate in the land of his ancestors awaited Sgt. Anthony Labato of Northampton. An ordnance clerk with the 15th Air Force, he was stationed about 50 miles from the town of Turi in southern Italy. Knowing that his parents had emigrated from Turi in 1913, Sgt. Labato made his way there in the spring of 1944.

"The area had been occupied by the Germans," Labato said, "and so the townspeople were very careful. I walked around for some time and spoke to people and asked them questions. Before long, people who turned out to be relatives of mine began coming forward. They showed me family photographs and asked me to identify them, which I was

Army Nurse at Anzio

Lt. Ramona Gilligan emerging from a tent. The 94th Evacuation Hospital, after participating in the break-out at Anzio, headed north toward Rome.

Killed In Action

Left to right: Staff Sgt. Alfred Conz and Pvt. Frank Cimini, who lost their lives in Italy, and Pvt. Lawrence Cave, killed in France.

able to do. I could also talk with them since I knew their regional dialect through my parents. I even met my grandfather on my mother's side, a man in his 90s, and my uncle on my father's side of the family. And there were lots of cousins. Other people in the town wanted to know about relatives as far from Northampton as Chicago."

After the invasion of Normandy in June, the European theater of operations became a deadly war of attrition, with the objective of destroying the German army on all fronts and finally crossing the Rhine and moving on into Germany itself. But the struggle to break out of the *Bocage* region of Normandy proved uniquely horrible and difficult. These hedgerows, or field boundaries, some of them created by Celtic farmers 2,000 years earlier, had earthen banks as thick as 10 feet that were impenetrable even to tanks and big guns. At intervals of 100 to 200 yards they served as defense lines for the Germans, who were dug in and determined to make the Allies pay dearly for every inch of ground.

"None of us had really anticipated how difficult they would be," Gen. James Gavin of the 82nd Airborne later admitted. Americans suffered and died among those hedgerows all through July. Pvt. Lawrence Cave of Florence was seen to go down before a German machine-gun nest in one of these hedgerows on July 9, according to a letter written to Cave's parents by his officer.

Capt. Dan Manning of the 2nd Infantry Division was among those who fought their way out of Normandy in the action called Operation Cobra. It was this breakthrough that finally smashed German strength in the hedgerow country. "It was one of our toughest times in fighting," said Manning. "The thing that saved us was the invention of those two-foot so-called 'dragon's teeth' on the front of the Sherman tanks that could smash openings in the hedgerows."

The 2nd Division's next challenge was the capture of the vital seaport of Brest. "All through Europe we were used as a kind of spearhead division," said Manning. "We'd go into a place and knock out the defenses, and then some other unit would come in and take all the credit, it seemed." He added with a smile, "People would come up to me after the war and say they'd never heard of us doing very much."

After that, for the men of the 2nd Division it was on into Belgium, the Ardennes, the Rhineland and even into Czechoslovakia where they would enter Pilsen on May 7, 1945. Manning believed he missed death by inches at least twice — once when a shell just missed his elbow and another when a map case was shot off its strap on his shoulder.

By the autumn of 1944, France and Belgium had been largely liberated, great European ports were now open to the Allies, supply lines were well established and the once-mighty German Wehrmacht was weakening.

Operation Market Garden began on September 17, with the objective of securing a bridge over the Rhine at Arnhem in Holland. With the first daytime drop of paratroopers in the war, and also the largest airborne operation in history, Operation Market Garden was intended to open up the shortest route to Berlin and thus end the war in 1944.

Involved were 16,500 paratroopers of the British 1st Airborne and the American 101st and 82nd Airborne divisions, plus 3,500 glider troops, who were dropped behind

Wartime Tourist

Sgt. Anthony Labato spent his off-duty hours sightseeing in Rome.

Pvt. Edmund Cadieux

A radioman in the 28th "Bloody Bucket" Division, he was killed in the Huertgen Forest, called "The Death Factory" by American soldiers sent in there.

German lines at Nijmegen, Eindhoven and Arnhem. Due to bad weather, faulty intelligence work, the sudden appearance of a German Panzer unit and plain bad luck, however, the operation largely failed. It resulted in heavy losses, especially for the British 1st Airborne, with 7,000 out of 9,000 men killed, wounded or captured.

The one item not in short supply in the operation was the human courage of the men who fought there, one of whom was Lt. Nanartonis, who had become flight leader for a 25 glider group.

"We ran into a lot of flak outside of Nijmegen. Very heavy," Nanartonis recalled. "Stretched out over a 50-mile area, we were only about 800 to 1,000 feet over German antiaircraft guns. By now we knew what was in store for us. One ground officer had asked me, 'what kind of a pilot are you?' 'Time will tell,' I answered him. 'If we're not shot up, I think you'll be happy.' We managed to land, however, with me dodging a cow at the last minute. We hooked up with some Allied troops and then learned that we were encircled some 50 miles behind the German lines. We ended up only about six miles from the bridge at Arnhem, which is remembered today, in the book and film about this tragic episode, as *A Bridge Too Far*."

Posthumous Award

Beulah Murch Cadieux, Edmund's widow, with their little girl, Linda, beside her, accepting her husband's Bronze Star.

Ordered to turn back and try to get themselves to Brussels, Nanartonis and other men from his unit flung themselves down in a woods to sleep off their exhaustion. In the morning they discovered deep tank tracks on a road so close to them that they realized German tanks had missed them by only a few feet during the night. By commandeering civilian vehicles of the Dutch, who did not protest, they made it back to Brussels.

Nanartonis went on to fight as a volunteer flying in supplies to American troops caught in the Battle of the Bulge near the end of the year.

Someone wise in the ways of the U.S. Army during the Second World War has remarked that if you were an accountant or bookkeeper in civilian life you were destined to end up in the infantry, which is precisely what happened to Northampton's Edmund Cadieux. A bookkeeper for Armour and Company on Market Street, married, and the father of a 5-month-old baby girl, Cadieux had been drafted in November 1943. His one-year military career as a radio man in the doomed 28th Division would end in the *Huertgenwald*, or Huertgen Forest, in Germany, 50 square miles of woods bounded by the cities of Aachen, Duren and Mondschau.

"A battle that should not have been fought" is how Gen. Gavin later referred to the slaughter that went on there. Americans who fought in the Huertgenwald simply called it The Death Factory. For six months, between September 1944 and February 1945, the American generals in command (including, ultimately, Eisenhower) sent more than a half million soldiers into this hellish forest that instead should have been sealed off and isolated. The 28th Division, to which Cadieux was assigned as a replacement, was also known as the Bloody Bucket Division because of its distinctive red shoulder patch. Based on the fate of the 28th in the Huertgenwald, the nickname proved appropriate. Some 30,000 American soldiers died or were wounded there, while countless others ended up with combat fatigue.

Cadieux was a member of Company L, 109th Infantry Regiment, one of the hardest hit units of the Bloody Bucket during the death of their division in the Huertgenwald. The citation conferring the Bronze Star medal after his death relates that "Pvt. Cadieux exposed himself to heavy enemy mortar fire, in order to provide his company with the necessary radio communication during an attack on the Germans. When he reached high ground with his radio, an enemy mortar shell fell between his legs and seriously wounded him. Although Pvt. Cadieux was in severe pain and could not move, he remained at his radio for more than two hours, without aid of any kind, transmitting vital information concerning his company and enemy positions. He later used his radio to direct aid men to his position and that of a wounded officer struck by fragments of the same shell. ... Later that day Pvt. Cadieux died of his injuries."

Cadieux's body was brought back to the United States after the war was over. It arrived at Northampton's Union Station on the exact date he had left as a draftee four years

After the Battle

This is how exhausted "warriors" looked after experiencing combat in the Huertgen Forest. An American is at the left, a German at the right.

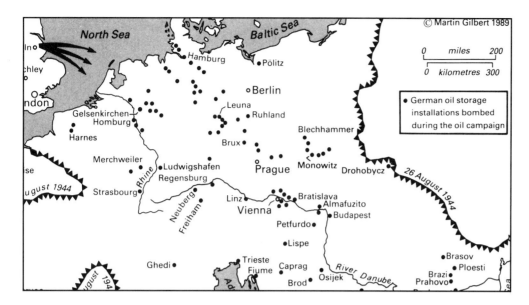

The Ploesti Oil Fields

This map shows German installations in the Ploesti oil fields of Romania — Hitler's source of supply.

Bomber Pilot

Lt. Jim Coyle, pilot of "Big Idjit," one of the 15th Air Force B-24 bombers whose task was to knock out Hitler's oil supply in Romania.

earlier: November 14.

Capt. Manning, who survived The Death Factory, recalled the fighting there as so utterly confused that, in the cold and snow and fog one day, "We passed a company of Germans trudging in the opposite direction before we even realized they were the enemy. Neither of us did a thing; we both just kept moving."

While the 8th and 9th Air Forces flew out of England, other young Americans were stationed in Italy with the 15th Air Force. These men were entrusted with the unenviable task of trying to destroy Hitler's source of oil in the Ploesti oil fields of Romania, said to be the most highly defended target in Europe. Many of them still feel, and perhaps rightly, that some of the glory that went to the 8th Air Force in Britain belonged to them, and figures today show that the 15th indeed suffered notably higher losses than their Britain-based colleagues. The raids over Ploesti, beginning in August of 1943, were kept up until oil production ceased.

The 15th members sang a little dirge to the tune of "As Time Goes By" from the pre-war film "Casablanca:"

"It's still the same old story, the 8th gets all the glory,
while we go out to die...
the fundamental things apply, as flak goes by."

At age 22, Jim Coyle, who later made his home in Northampton, was the pilot and oldest crew member of a B-24 named the "Big Idjit" that flew 51 missions between February 1944 and June 1945. Their first mission was over Albania, and their last a 1,000-plane mission over Vienna to distract the Luftwaffe from the Normandy invasion. The B-24, known to its crews as "the pregnant bitch" because of its shape, lacked the dash of the B-17. "It also took a lot more tending than the B-17, which could practically fly itself," said Coyle. "But we could fly longer missions and carry more bombs."

Coyle's plane was assigned the most exposed and dangerous tail position. "The colonel didn't like me and probably wanted to get me killed," he recalled with a laugh. There would be five missions to the Ploesti oil fields for "Big Idjit"; once they barely made it back alive, flying only about 500 feet off the ground with two engines out. Coyle's "extraordinary achievement" in getting his crew back from that raid was recognized in an official citation praising his "professional skill, courage and devotion to duty," but also in an accolade from one of his crew: "Owing to the competence of the pilot ... that's you Jim ... and the man upstairs we were able to make it back. Fred Kalinka."

"I was a hot pilot," Coyle said, "but we also prayed a lot." He carried the same crucifix his father had carried through WWI.

Another Ploesti "graduate" was Tech. Sgt. Lucien Fugere of Northampton, who was an aerial photographer aboard a B-24. Forced to bail out over Romania, only seconds

Tech. Sgt. Lucien Fugere

An aerial photographer, Fugere spent five months as a POW after his plane was shot down over the Ploesti oil fields.

On the Road to Bastogne

The road sign points to the town of Bastogne and the Battle of the Bulge.

Battle of the Bulge

This map shows why Hitler's last-gasp break through the Allied lines in December of 1944 came to be known as the "Battle of the Bulge." Shown is the Allied line "bulging" around Bastogne in the Ardennes.

before their plane blew up, the crew of 11 survived — five of them wounded, including Fugere — to endure five months as POWs of the Romanian government. Despite bad food, vermin-infested beds, and wounds left open to heal by themselves, Fugere survived. In the spring of 1946 he would be in the Pacific to photograph the atomic bomb test at Bikini Atoll in the Marshall Islands.

For the Allied military in the European theater, the year 1944 ended tragically, with a massive last-ditch surprise attack by the Germans, who intended to break through the Allied lines in the Ardennes Forest, split the American and British forces and retake Europe's largest port of Antwerp. Launched at 5:30 a.m. on December 16, this offensive would ultimately involve more than a million soldiers. The final bill for this Battle of the Bulge, as the Allies named it, was high. For the Americans it meant 8,497 killed, 46,000 wounded and 21,000 missing or taken as prisoners of war. For the Germans it cost 12,652 dead, 57,000 wounded and 50,000 prisoners. Besides battle wounds, men on both sides suffered from hunger, combat fatigue, trench foot, frostbite and pneumonia.

In the end, the action actually slowed down the Allied drive into Germany for only about six weeks.

Cecil Clark of the U.S. Merchant Marine, whose ship came into Antwerp at this time, remembered "the long lines of G.I.s returning from the front. Wild-eyed, worn-out kids. Some couldn't even remember their names. I know, because one of them was Jack Byrne from home. He was dazed and confused when I first saw him in the line, although when I met him later in the Red Cross canteen, he was fine."

Hitler had managed to put together 24 divisions, 10 of them armored, to go against a thin American line in the Ardennes. This line, composed of five American divisions numbering 75,000 to 80,000 men, was a dangerous combination of battle-hardened and inexperienced troops. On December 16, 14 German divisions broke through weak American positions on a 75-mile front that made the dent, or "bulge," in the Allied line.

It was also during the Battle of the Bulge that the *Greif*, a German unit made up of English-speaking troops wearing American uniforms and with American weapons and vehicles, appeared. They penetrated American lines and caused havoc.

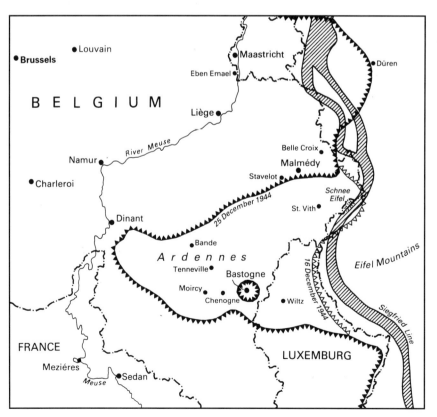

Pvt. McDonald, who had survived action with the 101st Airborne during the Normandy invasion and again during Operation Market Garden, now found his unit, the 501st Regiment of the Screaming Eagles, alerted in mid-December concerning "some sort of breakthrough" near Bastogne. "We were trucked in," recalled McDonald, "to a site where we were ordered to dig in just as it started to snow. The ceiling was zero — no planes able to fly in or out with equipment or supplies. Troops were straggling back in just pieces of their units. At 2 a.m. our outpost phone ceased contact, and I was ordered to go out and trace the line, an order that I protested. I was told to do it or be court-martialed, so I got another guy to go with me. We found the line cut, and both guys at the outpost were dead.

"There were penetrations in our area by English-speaking German troops. A dozen of them showed up at an American company near us and soon started firing at us. Their weapons were not frozen, but ours were. They even had the password of the day. We started calling ourselves the Battered Bastards of Bastogne.

"I recall Christmas especially. We were surrounded, and the Germans had big amplifiers aimed at us and played all the Christmas carols plus 'White Christmas' and 'I'll Be Home For Christmas.' In perfect English they promised us a fine Christmas dinner including 'apple pie just like Mom used to make.' I thought it was funny when they suggested that we bring our own mess kits with us as they themselves were 'a little short of utensils.' We didn't surrender, and everybody knows now that Gen. Anthony McAuliffe sent a reply of 'nuts' to the Germans when they suggested this to him.

Hitler's Final Assault

One of the young German soldiers thrown by Hitler into his last-ditch attempt to achieve a victory over the Allies. Three German armies attacked on a 50-mile front in eastern Belgium and Luxembourg.

"Close to the end of December," McDonald recalled, "the skies finally started to clear, and our planes could drop food and ammo and we were ordered to attack. The Germans had built great foxholes, some big enough for two or three men, and some even had stoves. In one we found a big chunk of beef. On January 3 I was cooking this beef on one of those stoves — first time I ever volunteered for anything. Two officers were there with me when a shell came in. One of the officers was killed, and the other — a cartoonist in civilian life — lost his right arm. The concussion blew me eight to 10 feet away, and pretty soon I knew I'd taken shrapnel in my right leg from the calf up to my hip. For some reason a bottle I had in my pocket didn't get broken. I was lying in the snow, bleeding, but the snow probably slowed that until the medics got to me. I ended up on a hospital train en route to Cherbourg. One of its staff was that blonde English movie actress, Madeleine Carroll, serving as a volunteer nurse.

"One of my great memories of this period," said McDonald, "is of another paratrooper named Sullivan from New Jersey ... a little guy, good-looking, and very high strung. He had some kind of a sixth sense where danger was concerned. After seeing him dive out of an area just before a shell came in, one that nobody else had heard, I decided to keep an eye on Sullivan. Two or three times, by my following right after him, he saved my life. The last time was on a road near Bastogne. All of a sudden Sullivan dove off the road into the underbrush. Before long a German plane came down the road strafing everyone and everything in sight. I was OK, because I'd learned to move when Sullivan moved, and I'd been right on his tail."

The skies began to clear on December 23, and with support from the air, the "dogfaces" of the U.S. Army began their counteroffensive in the Ardennes. By January 9, it was all over for the Germans, and by March all that would stand in the way of Allied penetration into Germany would be the Rhine itself.

The clearing skies that brought needed air cover for beleaguered Allied forces on the ground brought death to Lt. Robert Kinney in the sky. Only two years earlier Kinney had been sharing a room with Jack FitzGerald while they both worked at the Watertown Arsenal.

Both FitzGerald and Kinney had volunteered as Aviation Cadets and ended up as navigators in the 9th Air Force in Europe. During training they were soon separated, but FitzGerald long recalled the day in December 1944, in France, when he came back from the officers' mess and there sitting on the end of his bunk was his friend. Kinney had time for a two-hour visit with his former roommate — the last man from his hometown that he would ever see.

Lt. Bob Kinney

A lead navigator with the 9th Air Force, Kinney was killed on December 23, 1944, just before he was to be sent home after flying more than 60 missions, on one of which he was wounded.

    The lead navigator with the 9th Air Force's "Bridge Busting" marauder group, Kinney had already won the Silver Star for safely bringing his group back from a mission despite being wounded by flak. "We talked about that mission," recalled FitzGerald, "and it's sad to think about. He had already flown 61 missions and had four more to go in order to get rotated back to the States. He said he was all done with flying. I also remember him saying, 'May all my boys be girls.' He didn't want his children to have to fight in a war, and he was very happy about his little 3-month-old baby girl he had never seen. ... I asked him to visit my folks and tell them how I was, and how I looked, and he said he would. I walked out to the flight line with him, and that was the last I ever saw of him.

    "My folks got a letter from me saying that Bob would be home soon, but before it arrived everyone in 'Hamp already knew that he was missing even though I didn't."

    Lt. Robert Kinney's plane went down on December 23, 1944. The following July he was officially declared dead.

    In 1918, the Yankee Division's 104th Regiment had been the first unit to be decorated

Lt. Jack FitzGerald, U.S. Army Air Corps Navigator

Three generations of Jack FitzGerald's family served in four wars: his father as a sailor in WWI; he himself in WWII and Korea; and his son, a West Point graduate, in Vietnam. All three bore the same name: John FitzGerald.

by a foreign power when the French government awarded it the *Croix de Guerre*. That honor was again awarded the 104th in World War II. And Company G, 104th Infantry of the 26th Yankee Division, which still included many men from the Northampton area, was praised by its division commander for its performance during the Battle of the Bulge. Major Gen. W.S. Paul gave the following commendation to all enlisted men and officers in the division:

"When you initially attacked for seven days and nights without halting for rest, you met and defeated more than twice your own number. Your advance required the enemy to turn fresh divisions against you, and you in turn hacked them to pieces as you ruthlessly cut your way deep into the flank of the 'Bulge.' Your feats of daring and endurance in the subfreezing weather and snow-clad mountains and gorges of Luxembourg are legion; your contribution to the relief of Bastogne was immeasurable. It was particularly fitting that the elimination of the 'Bulge' should find the Yankee Division seizing and holding firmly on the same line held by our own forces prior to the breakthrough. I am proud of this feat by you as well as those you performed earlier. We shall advance on

Pfc. George Nolan

Killed in action on October 26, 1944. His buddy, Bob Novotny, wrote: "George and I were just like brothers. ... He will go to heaven alright. He had gone to confession and communion shortly before (his death)."

Company G in France

Staff Sgt. Bernard Begin, left, and 1st Sgt. John Daley of Company G, 104th Infantry, 26th "Yankee" Division. As their troopship landed in France, Sgt. Daley confided to his friend, "I know I'm not coming back." He was killed on November 11, 1944.

Berlin together."

Among the dead of Company G were: Pfc. Joseph Okolo, killed in Normandy shortly after D-Day on June 15; Pfc. Robert Loudfoot, killed in France on July 11; Tech. Sgt. Willard Straw, killed in France on October 30; and 1st Sgt. John Daley, killed on Armistice Day, who was awarded the Silver Star posthumously for crawling forward under heavy artillery and small-arms fire with orders from the battalion commander to withdraw the company. "He remained with the company," according to his citation, "and helped direct the withdrawal until mortally wounded."

Among the wounded of Company G were Staff Sgt. Bernard Begin, wounded on Armistice Day, who learned of Daley's death even as he himself endured a painful ambulance trip with a bullet wound in his right hip and frozen feet that would require eight months of treatment; also Tech. Sgts. Edward Poudrier, John Bombard and Robert Streeter, all destined for further wounds in Germany early in 1945. Pvt. William Feeney, who had transferred to the 101st Airborne and who had gone in on D-Day, also would be wounded in Germany.

Among those decorated in Company G, besides Sgt. Daley, were Pvt. Melvin Cross

and Tech. Sgt. Robert Streeter. Cross, an automatic rifleman, was promoted to sergeant for single-handedly covering the right flank of his platoon under fire as they withdrew temporarily from a position which they later took. Streeter would receive the Silver Star for a similar action in which he was said to offer himself as a target and was the last man of his unit to crawl to safety.

One news story sent back to the Gazette concerned Northampton's Pvt. Stephen Pilat, of the 45th Division, during these last days of 1944 in Europe. In some small and unnamed French town, Pilat's unit was being harassed by a German sniper whose position could not be determined. Aware that his wife Josephine was momentarily expecting a baby, Pvt. Pilat responded to a call from headquarters. A telegram had arrived for him, and even as he reached for it, the elusive German sniper spotted him and fired, giving away his own position. Two men prepared to fire on the house when suddenly a white flag emerged from an upstairs window and the sniper appeared. "Then Pilat opened the wire that had caught a sniper," concluded the story. "'It's a girl,' Pilat announced with a grin."

Four months later, in Germany, Pvt. John Lord, also of Northampton, sought out his fellow townsman, Pilat, now a sergeant, to compliment him on winning the Silver Star for gallantry in action as acting platoon sergeant. Pilat would before long add an Oak Leaf Cluster to his Star following a rifle duel with a team of seven German snipers. He killed two and captured the remaining five.

Meanwhile, out in the Pacific during the autumn of 1944, the struggle for the island of Peleliu produced the highest fatality rate of any amphibious assault: 9,171 American and 13,600 Japanese dead. Action then zeroed in on the Philippines, where the American invasion began when Gen. Walter Krueger's 6th Army landed on Leyte on October 20.

Pvt. Stanislaw Lojko's name had appeared in a story in the Gazette the previous spring as a member of a field artillery unit that had captured Momote Airdrome on Los Negros Island in March. Lojko died on Leyte on October 26.

The campaign for the Philippines was costly for both sides: some 350,000 Japanese, who garrisoned the islands, and 62,000 American casualties including 14,000 dead. Once again the Japanese Imperial Navy made a bid — their last — to wipe out the U.S. Fleet. What is now called the Battle of Leyte Gulf constituted, in terms of the number of ships involved, the greatest naval battle in the Pacific. Some call it the greatest naval battle of all time. Lasting only from October 23 to 25, it resulted in the destruction of the Imperial Japanese Navy as a fighting force. They lost three battleships, four carriers, 10 cruisers, and nine destroyers — more than 300,000 tons of combat ships compared to 37,000 tons for the Americans.

It was here too that the *kamikaze*, or suicide pilots, made their final futile sacrifices of their own lives to the Emperor by diving directly onto the decks of American ships.

Japanese navy planes flying out of Luzon also claimed many victims, one of which was the carrier U.S.S. *Princeton*. A Japanese "Judy" bomber hit the flight deck with a 550-pound bomb that tore through the hanger and finally reached the bomb magazines and blew off her stern. More than 500 American seamen died in that inferno on October 24.

Edward Wong of Northampton, a member of the crew, had already met death, in July, off Saipan. His sister Violet, about 7 years old at the time, remembered the moment that the telegram came with the news of his death. As usual, Mrs. Wong was at work in the kitchen of their Main Street restaurant, the Pagoda. Unable to read English, she had to have the wire read to her. "And then," remembered Violet, "the kitchen suddenly became very quiet."

Machinist's Mate Edward Wong

Oldest son of the Wong family, who operated the Pagoda restaurant on Main Street, and brother of little Helen and Violet Wong (seen in the earlier Hawley Grammar School scrap-drive photo on page 57). He died on the U.S.S. Princeton, in July, 1944, off Saipan.

War Work

While Sgt. Mitchell Talenda suffered for more than three years as a slave laborer for the Japanese, his mother, Emelia, toiled as a machine operator at International Silver Company — also known as "the bomb shop" — in Florence.

1944 — People Here Haven't Seen a Thing

Throughout 1944 the draft continued its relentless call. "Family Men Must Make Up Much of Military Shortage," announced a Gazette headline on February 28. On that same day, the newspaper reported that nearly 100 local men had reported to Springfield for their pre-induction physicals. These included an alderman, a councilman, a Smith College professor and a member of the police department. Draft boards were being urged to draft more fathers, to reduce deferments and to seek out men "needlessly exempted for industry and agriculture." Muriel Andre, daughter of attorney (and former mayor) Jesse Andre, who served on the draft board, discovered that any new young man she dated was soon snatched by the Selective Service system.

On March 25 sad news came out of Tennessee for two Northampton families, those of 1st Sgt. Bernard Jackimczyk and Pfc. John Netto. These two men were among 20 soldiers who were killed in a training accident crossing the Cumberland River while on maneuvers. Stories drifted back to Northampton of a swollen river, of heavily laden troops, and of an officer who ordered the river crossing against the advice of certain "non-coms" present. 1st Sgt. Jackimczyk's body was not recovered, but Pvt. Netto's remains were eventually returned to his family in Northampton for a military funeral.

Local salvage drives continued to meet or surpass their goals. The Gazette reported the shipment of 36 tons of tin cans on January 17, but warned "The Need of Tin is Still Great." Civilians no longer had to turn in an empty toothpaste tube in order to buy a new one, however, because new tubes were being made with so little tin they were not worth salvaging. Constantly urged to keep up their salvage of fats for munitions and medicines, Northampton households produced 146 percent of their quota for January, with 6,232 pounds of fat, and in February they did better still, with 161 percent. The practice of awarding extra meat-ration stamps for fat boosted donations considerably.

A new salvage item made its appearance in September: milkweed pods. The Gazette explained that the floss was used to make lifejackets buoyant, replacing Javanese *kapok*, a tree fiber that was no longer available. Bill Ames, then 13, later remembered being taught how to gather it. "I also remember that we had to dry it on the fence around the Vernon Street School," he said.

Homeowners were encouraged to convert from oil to coal for heating purposes, as did the Hampshire County courthouse at a cost of $680. Kimball and Cary Fuel Company urged their customers to buy "Bee-Hive Reclaimed Coke — the only unrationed fuel available" to mix with other fuel. When neighbor Michael Garvey learned that Alice Hickey of Crescent Street was cutting her fuel use to the point where her house was damp and cold "for the war effort," for fear of exceeding her oil ration, without her knowledge he intervened with the ration board to get her some extra gallons of oil.

In January, the local Protestant churches banded together for "union church services," a practice initiated the previous year to conserve fuel. On the other hand, while Christmas lighting on Main Street had been eliminated early in the war, in 1944 it was reintroduced with provisions made for the lights to be extinguished "immediately in case of an emergency."

Despite the focus on war-related problems, traditional local nuisances still claimed their share of attention. Mosquitoes made headlines in the spring, when the City Council voted $2,000 for their control. DDT would make its appearance in Northampton at the

Tennessee Maneuvers

Pfc. John Netto, left, with a friend, Seaman Bruno Kenderski. Netto and 1st Sgt. Bernard Jackimczyk, below, were among the 20 soldiers who drowned in the ill-fated crossing of the Cumberland River during the Tennessee Maneuvers of March, 1944.

war's end, but in 1944 the approach involved spreading oil on wet areas where the mosquitoes hatched in the spring. Local physician Justus Hanson informed the public that while malaria was not yet a threat, it likely would be when servicemen returned from all parts of the world.

Other natural disasters threatened Northampton during the summer of 1944. A gypsy moth invasion was so severe that the Gazette warned that 500 acres of trees in the city might soon be bare. Dutch Elm Disease, which for several years had been "spreading into this section from a beachhead near New York City," the Gazette reported, was well established by the summer of 1944 and being studied by professors at Massachusetts State College in Amherst. Boy and Girl Scouts were drafted as vigilantes to spot diseased specimens for Tree Warden Wallace Howes.

Northampton continued to mark the national holidays. On Memorial Day, local women held a service on the Coolidge Bridge and dropped flowers and wreaths into the Connecticut River for Northampton men lost at sea. Armistice Day was celebrated with the customary tree-planting ceremony in Childs Park, although the parade was omitted in 1944.

It seemed that every Northampton serviceman who could visit his hometown's sister city, Northampton, England, did so, including former newsman Lt. Francis Sheehey, who sent home copies of the English newspaper, the Chronicle & Echo. They contained stories that closely paralleled Gazette stories on subjects such as Victory gardening, rationing woes, soldiers' weddings, Red Cross work and salvage drives. One rather different story involved an English villager "fined two pounds for trying to catch a rabbit."

The Victory Gardens planted all over Northampton earlier in the war were now bearing fruit — and vegetables — to the point where food preservation assumed an important role in community life. Maybell Andre's notebook, preserved by her daughter Muriel (Andre) Adams, listed the various methods taught by the Hampshire County Extension Service: canning, dehydrating, freezing, salting, fermenting and storing. "Canning and freezing are the most popular," noted Mrs. Andre. Canning centers were located at the Unitarian and Florence Congregational Churches, Smith's Agricultural School and the Northampton School for Girls. Twenty-five "canning clubs" operated around the city, and demonstrations were given by Ella Heyne, home service director for the Northampton Gas and Electric Company. Courses on "wartime feeding," with attention to point rationing, as well as recipes and preparation, were offered at Smith's Agricultural School.

An ad appeared in November for the Northampton Cold Storage Company at 29

Sub-Normal

A cartoon in the Gazette of September 3, 1943, alluded to the impending scarcity of coal for the winter of 1944.

Destined for the Dinner Table

Young John Skibiski's wartime contribution was raising and tending his family's flock of chickens.

Hawley Street. "Save Perishable Foods By Storing In Your Own Private Locker." A new post-war business was launched.

The hard news in Northampton in 1944 involved production of war materiel. Hundreds of local citizens continued to commute daily, by carpool or train, to the U.S. Armory, American Bosch, Indian Motocycle, and Perkins Machine and Gear in Springfield; to Worthington Pump and Machinery in Holyoke; to Stevens Arms in Chicopee Falls; to Pratt and Whitney in East Longmeadow; to Greenfield Tap and Die; to the Mayhew Tool Company in Shelburne Falls; and to the Sperry Company in Easthampton, which made bomb sights. Nearly 1,700 citizens performed "war work" in Northampton itself at the Prophylactic Brush Company, the Rowe Foundry and International Silver Company in Florence. Dan Ruddy, who served as procurement officer of the Springfield Ordnance Procurement District, which supplied war materiel to all the armed forces, recalled the whole area of western Massachusetts and Connecticut as one gigantic beehive of industry. "Incredible, just unbelievable what was cranked out in this one district of ours ... over one billion dollars worth in western Massachusetts alone."

Much of the production dealt with guns and bombs, but Prophylactic turned out 34 million toothbrushes for the government plus helmet liners, bayonet scabbards, camouflage ponchos, canteens, medical kits, gears and bearings, and plastic components for radio proximity fuses — used to detonate missiles within a predetermined distance of a target — which at war's end were labeled "the number two secret weapon of the war." The number of Prophylactic employees more than doubled between 1941 and 1945.

At the height of the war one small Northampton firm, Dinsmore and Jager on Walnut Street, had 15 to 20 people working around the clock turning out 1 1/4-inch flash tubes that were vital components of the fuses that went into bombs. They were the only plant

Dan Ruddy

Procurement officer for the Springfield Ordnance Procurement District during WWII.

International Silver Company

The International Silver complex in Florence as civilians saw it during WWII. The structures to the left have since been demolished.

in the whole country producing this particular item, according to Ruddy.

Factory F of the International Silver Company in Florence also played a major role in war production. Beginning in December 1943, it worked solely for the military and produced more than 31 million knives including table, paring and mess kit knives. A major contribution, however, and that which led their own employees to call it "the bomb shop," was the production of more than six million magnesium incendiary bombs. One newspaper account referred to these as making "a ring of fire around Berlin" when as many as 350,000 were dropped in a single raid in 1944. One of these bombs was displayed in the window of McCallum's department store. Workers at International Silver met every quota, and by the end of 1944 were in line for the Army-Navy E Award for excellence in surpassing production and shipping goals, bestowed on them in March of 1945. These

On the Line

Above left, the young women, including Elsa Boudah Cox, on the line in "the bomb shop" where they did finishing work on the magnesium bomb-casings for incendiary bombs. Above right, the same workers are dressed in their best for the Army-Navy E Award bestowed at a ceremony on March 23, 1945. Front row, l. to r.: Doris Hnojowy, Elsa Cox, Thelma Young, Katherine Diemand, Stacia Buinickus, Margaret Nehring. Back row, l. to r.: Jane Massey, Frances Sadoski, Lillian Kisielewski, Ann Guyott, Elizabeth Kowaleski, Catherine Donovan.

Sweat Shop

The casting room at International Silver where men, working in terribly hot temperatures in the summer months, poured the magnesium casings for the incendiary bombs that incinerated Berlin, Tokyo and other cities.

awards were presented at special ceremonies, and the big "E" flags were flown along with the American flag, by those defense plants that won them.

With so many city residents working around-the-clock shifts in area war plants, the Gazette ran a plea for more consideration for those trying to sleep during the day. Parents of small children were asked to instruct them to play away from the houses of defense workers. There was even a popular song, "Milkman Keep Those Bottles Quiet."

The labor shortage continued, and women who had never before worked outside their homes took jobs in defense plants. With so many women now employed, a new phenomenon appeared in the city: problems concerning children and their care. This had already become prominent in reports of the Society for the Prevention of Cruelty to Children (SPCC), directed by Carrie Gauthier. "The employment of mothers results in inadequate supervision of children," she had reported in October 1942, after there had been 250 cases that September alone. Teen-age girls were noticed out on the city's streets late at night, while younger children were discovered "left for long hours ... while their parents worked in war plants, often into the late evening, expecting children to plan their own meals and recreation," the Gazette reported. Gauthier warned that "increased income does not always mean fewer neglected children. Money does not compensate for lack of parental care and supervision." In 1944 she had 451 cases on her agenda, with five children taken to Juvenile Court. The fathers of many were in the armed forces.

The problem was even reflected in a motion picture at the Academy entitled "Where Are Your Children?" — "The frank story of rampaging youth ... speeding to the screen in the form of headlines."

In May of 1944 a new Recreation Commission was formed in Northampton with the purpose of opening supervised playgrounds. Seven of these were operating by the summer of 1944. Camp Nonotuck of the YMCA extended its summer season "for the benefit of working mothers," and results of a survey by the Sociology Club of Smith College showed "sufficient need for some sort of nursery school to provide adequate care for working mothers' children." The local Kiwanis Club staged an essay contest for ages 10 to 18, for their suggestions on how to "combat juvenile delinquency through local activities."

The FBI was predicting a big crime wave at the end of the war, according to a Boston representative of the bureau who spoke to the local Rotary Club. The perpetrators, warned Agent Norman Valentine, would be returning "civilian criminals now in the service" and the "present crop of juveniles" already involved in "delinquency."

One example of wartime "crime" in Northampton involved a man whose wife was in Florida and a woman whose husband was overseas. Police broke into the apartment, according to a newspaper account, and "found the two together." They were each given a six-month sentence for "lewd and lascivious cohabitation."

By the autumn of 1944 the labor shortage on area farms was acute. Workers brought in from Newfoundland provided some relief as did student volunteers from Smith College, 45 of whom, for example, helped to harvest apples and potatoes that fall. A proposal to bring in German prisoners of war as a source of labor, however, was met with protest by Edward J. Gare Jr., the same merchant who had been so opposed to Dr. Kusaka's presence the previous year. He considered them enemies "whether they come in with a hoe or a rifle." Nevertheless, on October 9 more than 60 of the POWs brought into Bradley and Westover airfields from Fort Devens began work on farms in Hampshire County and soon demonstrated their capacity for hard labor. From among the nearly 400,000 German prisoners brought to this country, some 4,500 Nazi idealogues and troublemakers had been sorted out and confined at a special camp near Alva, Oklahoma, according to historian Allen V. Koop. Some of the men at Fort Devens, as a matter of fact, were survivors of the 999th Wehrmacht division, a punishment unit composed of anti-Nazi political prisoners such as Social Democrats and Communists, and including men who had fought against fascism in the Spanish Civil War during the 1930s. The behavior of German POWs in this country as emergency labor proved, for the most part, exemplary.

Land Corps Volunteer

A Smith College student at work on a local dairy farm. The Volunteer Land Corps was designed to relieve a shortage of agricultural workers in the Valley.

POWs Go To Work

Carefully selected German prisoners of war, recruited to relieve the local shortage of agricultural workers, proved a boon to farmers in the Valley.

Joanna Devine, who was a child in 1944, remembered two of these POWs, clad in gray-blue denim, who were let off the truck from Westover each morning to work on a farm on land today occupied by Northampton's industrial park. If there was an armed guard with them, she did not recall ever seeing him. During their lunch break these two Germans would shop at Holden's neighborhood store, near the corner of North and Woodbine streets, and at Joanna's mother's Bates Street store. Other POWs worked at farms in Hadley and Hatfield. These workers would reappear the following autumn, and one German youth of 22 died in the Connecticut River, apparently of heart failure, while enjoying a swim after a day of work in a potato field.

Wartime prosperity in Northampton soared to new heights in 1944. "With the vast arsenals of Connecticut and Massachusetts pointing the way," the Associated Press reported in May, "New England industries have received nearly one-tenth of the $183

Wartime Prosperity

WWII Gazette advertisements suggest that American civilians were living a great deal better than in pre-war Great Depression days.

billion spent by the government on war contracts since the fall of France in 1940." Massachusetts alone was "the nation's 11th biggest war producer in the three-and-one-half years, with $5,541,617,000 in contracts." Of this total, $133,219,000 went to Hampshire County.

By the end of 1944, the average wage for factory workers in local war plants was $43.35, close to the $44.43 average for 2,107 factories in 44 American cities and towns. Higher average wages could be earned out of town: $47.52 in Greenfield and $58.09 in West Springfield. Northampton's prosperity showed in the rapid expansion of its total retail business, which had risen from $11,346,000 in 1939 to $15,420,000 in 1943, a gain of 36 percent, despite wartime shortages. Thus did Northampton account for .024 percent of the nation's business with only .019 percent of its population.

A study of advertisements in the Gazette reveals how some of this discretionary income was being spent. Huge ads by McCallum's, Herman Miller and the Lynch Shop trumpeted the virtues of "luxurious fur coats," and women were even invited to "trade in your old fur coat with a liberal allowance toward a new one." Furs offered included "fisher-dyed raccoon," "black-dyed cross Persian," "South American weasel," and "grey-dyed Bombay lamb." Plain muskrat could be had for $450; Persian lamb for $543; a silver fox "greatcoat" for $650; or beaver for $995. Women were also paying up to $8.50 a bottle for colognes such as Arden's Blue Grass or Coty's Muguet de Bois. Ads for a new product called Endo Creme asked, "Who Says You Can't Look Younger Again?"

A wire service story in the Gazette disclosed a nationwide problem for civilian women: the poor quality of girdles made from synthetic rubber, which reportedly had little elasticity and not much resistance to body heat and perspiration. This crisis was alleviated in April of 1944 by a shipment of garter belts to the local department store. "Yes," announced a McCallum's ad, "they are NYLON!"

World War II saw the advent of the supermarket in Northampton when the A&P invited customers in April 1944 to "try this new method of food shopping" at their innovative installation at 137 King Street. The store boasted specific sections for rationed items requiring "points," and other sections for non-rationed items.

The city's new prosperity was also reflected in people's leisure-time activities. Women of the Northampton Country Club opened their social and sports season on April 26, 1944 with a tea for their 90 members. A series of luncheons and dinner dances was already scheduled. Dining and dancing were available for the general public at White

Eagle Hall and Carnegie Hall in Northampton, Toto's at Smith's Ferry, The Rapids in Huntington and at Valley Arena Gardens and Roseland's in Holyoke.

The Academy of Music also benefited from wartime prosperity. In addition to regular films, live theater productions before sellout audiences brought to town such stars as Ethel Barrymore in "The Corn is Green" and Eva LeGallienne in "The Cherry Orchard." Barrymore showed up with her own portable dressing room.

Other hits of this 1944-45 season were "Kiss and Tell" and "Life With Father." John Carradine appeared with his "Shakespearian repertoire," as did Pilar Lopez and his Company of Spanish Dancers in a version of Bizet's "Carmen." At the Calvin Theater in June "The Hitler Gang" played, and the leading actors — Martin Kosteck as Goebbels, Robert Watsa as Hitler and Alexander Pope as Hermann Goering — came to town to promote it.

Some of Northampton's discretionary spending went into the buying of bonds during the various War Loan or Victory drives. Local campaigns grew in sophistication as the war ground on, beginning with the display of a captured Japanese two-man midget submarine near the county courthouse in 1943 and continuing later with the appearance of a captured German Mark 4 tank. In January 1944, the fourth War Loan drive took the form of an experimental book-and-author rally held in John M. Greene Hall to raise money for the purchase of an ambulance plane to be named "The Northampton." Northampton

Guest of Honor

Sgt. Michael Florio, who lost a leg at Guadalcanal, was an honored guest at the big fourth War Loan rally in 1944.

Captured Japanese Submarine Goes on Display

The highlight of the War Loan drive in 1943 had been the captured Japanese midget submarine displayed in front of the Hotel Northampton on King Street.

was the first small city to try out this book-and-author approach, and its success or failure was to determine whether the treasury department would try it in other similar cities. Author Mark van Doren was the master of ceremonies. The band from Westover Field provided music, and authors appearing included Esther Forbes and Mary Ellen Chase. The goal was $250,000; $402,625 was raised. Sgt. Michael Florio, who had lost a leg at Guadalcanal, was "accorded the greatest ovation of the evening," the Gazette reported.

The Hampshire County Red Cross made a major contribution to the local war effort through its blood-donor program, surgical-dressing units, nurses' aide training classes, first-aid classes, the "Grey Ladies" who visited the state and veterans' hospitals, and particularly through the Home Service program conducted by Executive Secretary Nancy Trow. She worked with more than 20 cases a month trying to solve problems related to illness in soldiers' or sailors' families, information about wounded or dead servicemen, arrangements for essential furloughs, disability-discharge problems and hospitalization of veterans. Sgt. Mike O'Connor, for example, was enabled by her efforts to have his furlough extended so that he could spend a few days with his brother William, a sailor whose armed civilian oil ship, the U.S.S. *Esso Harrisburg*, had been torpedoed between Haiti and Puerto Rico.

Red Cross Director

Nancy Trow, executive secretary of the Hampshire County Red Cross during the war years, in a pre-war photo. On the back she wrote: "Isn't this a perfect picture of an Old Maid Social Worker?"

Westover Field in 1941

An early Westover Field shot showing barracks still under construction.

Records kept by Trow, still on file at Red Cross headquarters, disclose the extent of her operations. She lists the 974 pints of blood collected between October 1943 and February 1944 by the Hartford Mobile Unit, which came to Northampton regularly. The U.S. Navy Bulletin named it "the most efficient of the 35 blood donor centers in the country" in October 1944. Also listed are the 14,000 hours contributed in 1944 by the Nurses' Aide Corps that alleviated the Cooley Dickinson Hospital nursing shortage. Sarah McConnell was the first to chalk up 50 hours of volunteer service. More than a million surgical dressings were turned out by groups of volunteers in 1944, including those by a detachment of students at the Clarke School for the Deaf.

Added to the regular list of requests made by the Red Cross for hand-knitted items, such as sweaters, gloves and scarves, were requests for knitted "stump socks" as amputees grew in number in military hospitals.

A special type of Home Service case involved pregnant girls as young as 17. Nancy Trow tried to locate the fathers of the babies in order to determine the feasibility of marriage. Other problems were arising out of hasty war marriages that were already dissolving.

Westover Field, the Army air base located south of Northampton in Chicopee, played a significant role in Northampton life during the war years. Local dances were considerably enlivened by the presence of the airmen. The Westover band also played periodically at war bond rallies and other fetes. Two escaped prisoners, at first thought to be German POWs, turned out instead to be American Air Corps "garrison prisoners" who had escaped a Westover work detail. They were apprehended at the farm of Roger Owens on Route 9, two miles east of Amherst.

In one incident, a mammoth silver B-17 bomber circled three times over the treetops near Hopkins House, a residence for Smith College students. Then a tiny parachute, made out of a handkerchief, appeared carrying a candy bar and a note attached to "Miss Jean Little, Hopkins B, Smith College." The note read: "Pilot sends love. Co-pilot sends candy. Nine men on board send their love to nine sweet, good-looking Smith girls. The tenth man sends his love to 'Phipsie' (the president of Hopkins House). Hi! darling. See you again some day. All my love."

Not all of the Westover stories reported during this period were this charming, for most of them involved news of accidents, close escapes or disasters. In February 1944 a B-17 caught fire in the air, and the crew were ordered to bail out by the pilot, who nevertheless managed to land safely. On another occasion, a bronze-powder sea marker opened up a five-inch hole in the roof of Mrs. P.J. Murphy on 23 South Main Street in Haydenville, where it "rolled to the lawn, exploded and flared into a bright yellow flame which spread a yellow stain across a portion of the lawn."

There were other more tragic incidents. A blinding snowstorm on December 1, 1942, had caused the deaths of two young pilots in separate accidents — one in Westhampton and the other in Cummington. In April 1943, another fighter pilot had died in a crash near the farm of Claude Seymour in Westhampton. Two more Westover men had died later that same month over Apponang, R.I. Two planes crashed over Holyoke in May. One pilot was killed and the other parachuted to safety, landing in a tree from which neighborhood women heard him calling, "Help me! Get me down out of here!" The crashed aircraft caused damage to several houses but killed no one.

Three men had died when their bomber crashed on the Loftus farm in Belchertown that autumn, while six others parachuted to safety. A crew of 10 died when another bomber crashed only a quarter of a mile from Westover Field as it came in for a landing. Near Uxbridge, civilians on the ground watched horror struck as a bomber from Westover appeared to disintegrate over their heads. Only a few parachutes were seen, and one of those men died on landing. On May Day in 1945, a B-24 bomber would go down two miles east of the center of Williamsburg with two men killed and seven seriously injured.

On May 27, 1944, another B-24 crashed into the side of Mt. Holyoke. Ten young airmen died. Frank Tencza, born in 1944, would discover scraps of blackened metal while hiking as a boy in 1958. Aided in his detective work by the Air Force in Washington, Tencza would be able to recreate the disaster. On May 28, 1989, a granite monument would be dedicated to the memory of the 10 who died. "Those men were casualties of the war like those who were killed in combat," said Tencza, a Vietnam veteran. "They should not be forgotten."

A memorial book dedicated to all members of the 471st Bomb Group who died while training at Westover Field between 1943 and 1945 is on permanent display at the 439th Military Airlift Wing headquarters of what is today called Westover Air Force Base.

Plane Crash on Mt. Tom

One of the many crashes in the Westover Field vicinity occurred just after the end of World War II, on the night of July 10, 1946. Bound from Gander, Newfoundland, to Westover Field were 25 returning servicemen, all of whom were killed when their plane crashed against the 1,200-foot-high Mt. Tom.

With the war still very much in progress in 1944, the citizens of Northampton were already looking ahead to the post-war era. In June 1944, the Chamber of Commerce organized a Post-War Planning Committee with Harold Y. Beastall, assistant treasurer of the Northampton Co-operative Bank, as chairman. This committee prepared a questionnaire to be mailed out to every service man and woman from the city — even those, apparently, in combat theaters in Europe and the Pacific. Their hope was to learn plans so that they could estimate how many jobs would be needed at the war's end. By January 1945, 510 questionnaires (about one sixth of the total number of men and women in service) had come back with the following information: 214 wanted their old jobs back; 62 planned further education; 17 who had never had employment hoped for civilian occupations; 64 planned to seek jobs based on training received in the military; 54 wanted jobs different from their pre-war ones; and 98 were simply "undecided."

Of special interest to many of those on the committee were the provisions of the GI Bill that enabled banks to offer low-cost loans to veterans for home purchase or construction. A Gazette reporter noted that "every banking house in this city was represented at the session and 75 percent of the real estate agents in Northampton." These same planners also eagerly predicted a post-war $6 billion tourist boom in the Pioneer Valley. Even so, many of them opposed a proposed new "superhighway" to Montreal to replace Route 5.

On January 10, 1944, a new "wonder drug" — penicillin — was administered to a local youth at the Cooley Dickinson Hospital, after U.S. Army officials in Boston granted permission due to the severity of the case. In May the hospital was designated as the penicillin supply depot for the area, including Holyoke.

Also in 1944, the Gazette reported the advent of jet planes. "The Allies and Nazis both have them in operation ... great dogfights may occur between them ... their use in peacetime seems likely."

On Monday, September 11, 1944, a dispatch from London out of Nazi Berlin reported: "7 Sentenced To Die After Hitler Plot." The list was headed by Dr. Karl Goerdeler, former mayor of Leipzig, whom the Nazi government claimed "formed the bridge between the militarist traitors and political conspirators ... and worked out the plans of treason." Perceived by many today as political martyrs, these men — young army officers and government officials — plotted to kill Hitler and end both the Nazi tyranny and the war.

Efforts they had made to reach Roosevelt and Churchill had been rebuffed. They had little chance of success, and they knew this, but put their lives on the line anyway. Their "show trials" as traitors were filmed after their torture. These seven men died very slowly hanging from piano wire at Plotzensee Prison in Berlin, where a memorial would be dedicated to them after the war.

In June of 1944, the Gazette reported that 12,000 employees (out of 35,000) had walked off their jobs at an aircraft plant in Ohio to protest the mixing of white and black workers. The growing racial tension nationally was reflected locally that summer when some Hatfield citizens objected to the introduction of workers from Jamaica to alleviate the agricultural labor shortage. This same year, Roy Wilkins, secretary of the National Association for the Advancement of Colored People, appeared at a forum sponsored by the Inter-race Commission of Smith College, where his topic was "Racial Tension and the War." In November 1944, the WAVES accepted their first black officer candidates for training. Jane Freeman of Roxbury, age 22, was "the first colored woman to join the Reserve" with two others from New York due to arrive soon afterward.

A flap over the new novel, *Strange Fruit*, acclaimed in the Saturday Review of Literature and elsewhere, also reflected the growing awareness in Northampton of racial tension. On March 31, the Gazette noted: "Book Banned In Some Cities Now Is On Sale Here." *Strange Fruit* dealt with an interracial love affair and the institution of lynching. Threatened with possible legal action, the proprietress of the Hampshire Book Shop, Marion E. Dodd, wrote the Gazette: "We believe that the mature buyers of books are entitled to use their own judgement as to what they wish to read. Censorship in this state has had a checkered career, and this bookshop was influential ... years ago in getting the clause in the Massachusetts law changed ... (now) the intent and meaning of the book must be obscene in order to have a complainant bring a case against it. ... *Strange Fruit* deals constructively with one of the most pressing problems at the present moment." The controversy continued for some time, but the book remained on her shelves.

The end of 1944 saw the closing down of the Navy Midshipmen's School in

Former First Lady Helps Out

Marion E. Dodd, left, owner of the Hampshire Book Shop, with Grace Coolidge, handing out gifts to departing draftees —one of whom stares soberly in the background.

Northampton, and the departure of the 28th and last class of WAVES on December 27. Officials in Washington were already anticipating the war's end, although long hard combat still lay ahead for the military. A joint assembly of Smith College and Navy personnel acknowledged their accomplishment of providing — over a two-year period — 9,600 women officers to serve in the U.S. Navy. The First Church reported donations of $1,269.39 by the WAVES upon their departure. Lewis Wiggins, whose Hotel Northampton had billeted those trainees not quartered on the Smith campus, and fed them all, and whose Wiggins Tavern had served as a Naval officers' mess, announced rooms would be available to the public again after January 1.

On the third anniversary of the Pearl Harbor attack the Gazette once more reported the human cost of the war for Northampton. With some 2,900 men and women in service, 49 men had died — 38 of them in action and 11 in training accidents. Fifty-eight men had been wounded, some for the second or third time, and eight had died in non-combat situations. From one to two dozen men were reported missing in action or lost at sea, while about a dozen were prisoners of war. The same Gazette reported on 11 new draftees due to leave on December 19, and gave an account of the local funeral of Flight Officer Robert Knight, recently killed in a training crash near Merced, California.

One perception of Northampton in 1944 was provided in the Gazette by 1st Class Petty Officer Theodore "Bud" Jerome, who was home on a two-week rehabilitation leave after 14 months in action aboard a destroyer during the invasions of North Africa, Sicily and in Italy at the Anzio beachhead. Under fire during 132 German air attacks, Jerome was on one occasion the only man on the bridge, he said, to escape death. Another time, his ship was only 400 yards off the bow of a tanker that blew up under enemy fire. At times, Jerome said, their ship had been under fire for 34 hours at a stretch.

The local sailor was stunned that "things seem so normal back here" with all the usual comforts available. He was more accustomed, he said, to "people in devastated countries ... ferociously grabbing food and clothing cast off by our fighting forces." Jerome concluded, "people here in the States haven't seen a thing."

Draftees Pose at the Railroad Station

Among the most poignant images of World War II were the photos of young draftees lined up at the railroad station just before they left for military service. This particular group left Northampton's Union Station on September 21, 1942. Two of the men, John O'Brien and Edwin Malinowski, died while on active duty overseas.

First row, left to right: Michael J. Piepiora, Edward J. Snape, Henry R. Pontbriand, Thomas J. Powers, James F. Lucey, Francis E. Barnes, Leonard Alberts, Chester S. Anisowicz, James L. Allen, Leroy F. Barnes, Lawrence J. LeBeau.

Second Row: William J. Waldron, Charles P. Powers, John P. Clifford, Patrick J. Powers, Stanley S. Szarkowski, Thomas J. Henchey, Wesley J. Sarrasin, Tallis Ruskowski, Maurice J. McKelligott, Abner L. Adams, Henry Tessier.

Third row: Ambrose E. Bailly, Henry A. Lafoe, Edwin Malinowski, William F. Gwiazda, John M. Crabbe, Raymond F. Barrett, Jr., William F. Kirby, Daniel F. Fenton.

Top row: Howard R. Patch, Jr., acting corporal, Richard W. Keefe, Norman J. Menegat, Joseph A. Feldman, John M. Adams, William F. Kathericus, Jr., Charles S. Talenda, Joseph C. Adamski, John F. Osga, John O'Brien, George W. Stone and Rene P. Lajoie.

Hugh Crane

Hugh "Hymie" Crane, 6th Division U.S. Marine Corps, spent 82 days in combat and wrapping-up operations on Okinawa, plus 30 days of combat on Guam. Describing the battle on Okinawa, when he got to Sugar Loaf hill where the Japanese were dug in and trying to hold, he paused and quietly said: "That's where we broke 'em, but boy that was a tough go."

1945 — A Long, Dirty, Bloody Business

By the time 1945 rolled around, the American people had long since forgotten President Roosevelt's hope, expressed back in 1943, that victory might come in 1944. They were learning the full meaning of Assistant Secretary of State Adolph Berle's prediction just after the attack on Pearl Harbor: "It is going to be a long, dirty, painful, bloody business."

In January, American troops were still trapped at Bastogne, and the deadly German "rocket bombs" were wreaking havoc on troops and civilians alike in Europe and Britain. The Red Army was grinding its way through eastern Europe and was about to penetrate Nazi Germany. Out in the Pacific, American forces were fighting in the Philippines where, on January 30, 65 miles behind Japanese lines, they managed to free more than 500 American POWs who had been held for three years at Cabanatuan.

Still ahead for the American forces in the Pacific were the operations to take the islands of Iwo Jima and Okinawa on the doorstep of Japan. The war of attrition still had a long way to go.

The first of the remaining obstacles in the Pacific was Iwo Jima — an ugly eight-square-mile island covered with brown volcanic ash. About 760 miles south of the Japanese home islands, and part of the prefecture of Tokyo, Iwo was considered a primary military objective for two reasons. First, the Japanese were using it as a radar warning station and as a base for fighters intercepting the B-29s flying out of recently captured Saipan on bombing missions to Japan. Second, the Allies wanted another air base, closer to Japan, for those B-29s.

Heavily gunned and garrisoned, and honeycombed with caves and tunnels, Iwo Jima had been ordered held at all costs. This the 21,000 Japanese troops stationed there did — but they died almost to a man.

The U.S. would pay dearly for the island in return, with 6,821 men killed in action and more than 20,000 wounded. Four out of every five Marines who went in at Iwo were killed or wounded.

D-Day for Iwo Jima was February 19, 1945. The struggle that followed was later termed "the bloodiest, fiercest fight in the Marine Corps' 168-year history" by Marine Corps historians. The island was secured on March 16.

Store Keeper 1st Class William "Bumps" McDonald of the U.S. Coast Guard observed the Iwo Jima invasion from his ship, which was landing Marines and supplies. Many weeks later his written account would reach his parents in Northampton:

"I just can't put into words what it was like, but the Marines who landed & fought there said it was the toughest and most heavily guarded island they have yet landed upon. We were there on D-Day along with all kinds of naval support, and I don't think I have ever seen so many ships in one place. They fired & fired upon that island, but when the Marines landed, all hell broke loose & I guess I was on my knees praying along with everyone else. We could see the mortar shells flying all around the ship ... when we beached to take our cargo off, we got a chance to get on shore ... I don't see how the Marines landed ... the place is just covered with cinders from the volcano & all the vehicles that made the shore were stuck in them ... it rained & was very cold ... the sights were really awful ... dead bodies lying all around. The place itself was like an underground subway with tracks & elevators running around inside of it. It is something that I won't forget in a hurry."

Flag-Raising

Lt. William O'Donnell, 5th Marine Division, observed the original flag-raising on Mt. Suribachi. Only 54 by 28 inches and attached to an iron pipe, this flag was raised by the 40-man patrol sent to secure the summit. The more familiar flag-raising photo, above, taken by Joe Rosenthal was of a larger flag raised later on the same spot.

William McDonald, Store Keeper, U.S. Coast Guard

From his ship involved in landing the 3rd, 4th and 5th Marine Divisions on Iwo Jima on February 19, 1945, McDonald witnessed horrors that he later disclosed in a letter home to his parents.

Iwo Jima Landing

For U.S. Marines, their worst landing experience in the Pacific is thought to have been that at Iwo Jima. Heavily gunned and garrisoned, its Japanese defenders were secure in a network of caves and tunnels. Over the island's basalt bedrock lay a deep blanket of volcanic ash in which heavy equipment foundered, trenches collapsed and wounded lay exposed to further injuries and often death.

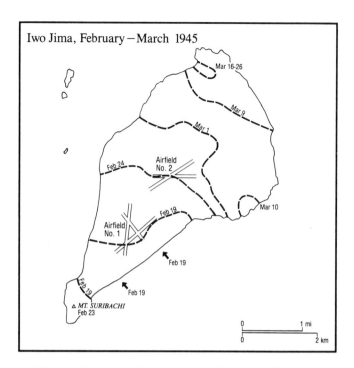

Witness of War

Forty-seven years later, Pfc. Thomas Hogan found it harrowing to put into words what he witnessed and personally experienced as a 19-year old Marine with the 3rd Division on Iwo Jima.

Thomas Hogan, who had worried back on December 7, 1941, that the war would be over before he could be part of it, left that fear behind forever during the 18 days that he and his 9th Regiment of the 3rd Marine Division fought at Iwo Jima.

Hogan celebrated his 19th birthday en route from Guam to Iwo, where he would face the combat that would almost end his life. His well-worn copy of the 9th Regiment's history, with many personal notations, is a testament to what this group of men endured there. In his 2nd Platoon roster are listed 43 names, and after each name (except two that are listed as "Non Eff" for Non Effective) are either the initials KIA (killed in action) or WIA (wounded in action). The final toll was nine dead, 32 wounded.

Throughout the regimental list are Hogan's notes, such as the following, after names of men he knew:

Horvat, Anthony D. Cpl. "Fond of giving Hitler-like salutes and shouting 'Sieg Heil! In case we lose.' Always good for a laugh. Killed at Iwo."

Harrington, Llewellyn. Pfc. "Good friend & tent-mate to Markham & myself. In next foxhole to me when I was wounded. Exposed self to mortar fire to assist me. Later rec'd gunshot wound in shoulder."

Gulledge, Charles. Pvt. "Killed by burst of machine-gun fire while making lone attack on pillbox above second airstrip. Good friend ... went overseas together."

Huntoon, Richard Pfc. "From Boston. Great singer. Rec'd slight wound on Iwo ... wound dressed. Returned to line. Killed."

American air attacks had proved unable to blast the Japanese from their entrenched positions, some of which were in more than 1,500 caves. Mortar, artillery and rocket fire zeroed in on anything that moved, including tanks and ambulances. Thus did the burden of battle fall on riflemen, machine gunners and mortar men. Inch by inch, Iwo would be won by men on their bellies or behind a tank, fighting their way from pillbox to pillbox with rifles and flame throwers.

For three days of carnage, the 9th Regiment fought for possession of Motoyama Airfield No. 2. They then pushed on to the north and east end of the island until organized resistance ceased.

"I served as runner and radioman for Lt. Hayden Scott all the while I was with the 9th Regiment," recalled Hogan. "I remember his right arm was shattered while he was directing tank fire at an enemy emplacement, and later had to be amputated."

At Motoyama Airfield No. 2, Hogan remembered, "On the first attack we were practically decimated. The survivors came back and we attacked again. I saw the most horrible sights of my life — it just got worse and worse. ... The Japanese positions were so hidden that we never even saw them. They poured mortars into us non-stop ... within three days I was a casualty myself.

"We were point platoon for our battalion. My lieutenant dragged a wounded man back and ordered me to dig a hole for the three of us. I got started but took time to toss my jacket up on the parapet. Within seconds mortar rounds began to 'whop' on us. After the second one I remember thinking, 'Holy Jesus, the third one is going to come in on me!' And it did. I remember a terrific explosion and then nothing more until I came to three days later.

"Casualties were 100 percent for my platoon within three weeks and 85 percent for the company. This is what happened to every line company on Iwo and some went even higher than 85 percent. The two hospital ships in the harbor filled up on the first day and so troopships had to become hospital ships ... practically everyone I knew became a casualty. At reunions today I see very few people I know."

Robert Sherrod, Far East correspondent for Time-Life Publications, said that on Iwo he witnessed the most savage combat that he saw in WWII. "Nowhere in the Pacific have I seen such badly mangled bodies. Many were cut squarely in half. Arms and legs lay 50 feet away from any body."

Lt. William O'Donnell of Northampton wrote home about the battle for Iwo Jima, detailing the ordeal of his men in the 5th Division and describing what was to become a remarkable moment in history: the raising of the American flag on Mt. Suribachi, the highest point of the island, on February 23. Firmly entrenched in holes and caves on this mountain, the Japanese had to be blasted out yard by yard. This took from February 19 to 23. Fighting on Iwo did not cease until the end of March, but a photo of the raising of the flag on Suribachi became the symbol of ultimate victory in the Pacific.

"I have just seen the men from my regiment raise the Stars and Stripes on the highest rim of Suribachi," wrote O'Donnell. "About one hour ago I stood beside Col. Harry Liversedge, the commanding officer of the 28th Marines, watching a four-man patrol pick its way up the face of the mountainous crater. We watched the figures wave, move over the rim and disappear. An hour later, Sgt. Weaver checked his watch with mine as a 40-man reconnaisance force from our 2nd battalion climbed to the crest, raised a makeshift pole and quickly ran the flag to its height. It was 10:30 in the morning, 97 hours since we hit the beach."

Among the souvenirs picked up on Iwo Jima by Sgt. Thomas Coogan of Northampton was a document, printed in Japanese characters, that he found lying beside a dead Japanese soldier. For 45 years Coogan wondered about its contents. Was it perhaps a letter from the dead soldier's family? When he had it translated years later, the paper proved to be a piece of music composed for the *shakuhachi*, or classical bamboo flute. The title is *Harukasane*, meaning "Aspects of Spring."

Once the Americans finally held Iwo Jima, the rock-solid airfield that 7,000 Seabees immediately constructed permitted P-51 Mustangs to serve as fighter-escorts for the B-29s. Also, by the end of the war, 2,400 B-29s and the lives of their crewmen had been saved by being able to land there. Sgt. Russell Bishop of Northampton served there as an armorer.

One wounded Marine who had survived Iwo Jima would be remembered saying, "I hope to God that we don't have to go on any more of those screwy islands." But one more island was waiting: Okinawa. And after that the home islands of Japan itself.

Only 350 miles southwest of Japan, Okinawa was the site of the last great amphibious assault of WWII. This 80-mile-long island of some 700 square miles resembles a banana in shape. It was scheduled to be the base for the invasion of Japan, and the Japanese were determined to defend it against American forces as long as their troops were able.

Five American Army divisions and three Marine divisions were tapped for the assault. The Army would lose 4,000 dead, the Marines 2,938. Some 5,000 American sailors died aboard their ships, primarily through mass *kamikaze* suicide attacks, and 5,000 more were wounded. Approximately 70,000 Japanese troops and 80,000 civilian Okinawans also died before the struggle was over.

Died on Iwo Jima

Five days after the landing, death caught up with Pfc. Edward Mazuch of the 5th Marine Division. He was killed in action on February 24, 1945.

Preview of What was Still to Come

The carnage that took place on Okinawa was a preview of what the invasion of Japan held in store: 12,000 American dead plus 36,000 wounded; 70,000 Japanese soldiers dead. At least 80,000 Okinawa civilians also died.

Pfc. Lucien Vanasse, 6th Marine Division

With his "war dog" King 310. King survived combat on Okinawa and came back to live in Northampton where he would one day be killed by a motorist on Bridge Street.

Operation Iceberg, as the invasion of Okinawa was called, began on April Fool's Day, 1945. It happened that year also to be Easter Sunday, and one Marine, Pfc. Joseph Benoit, recalled going over the side of his troopship and onto the landing craft to the tune of "Easter Parade" from the ship's loudspeaker.

More than 180,000 soldiers and Marines from 1,300 ships were landed on Okinawa. At first they met with little resistance. The Japanese plan was to permit the Americans to invade their mountainous stronghold, criss-crossed with heavily fortified underground caves and bunkers, and then make them pay dearly for every inch of ground. And this the American forces did. As Marines battled their way into the island's interior, naval vessels off shore were savaged by waves of *kamikaze* planes for 10 long weeks.

Pharmacist's Mate 1st Class Chester Wilusz wrote home of his experience aboard a minesweeper. "The Japs could not return to Japan. They had a one-way ticket, so they used it by diving their planes onto our ships ... in a short while I counted over 30 Jap planes shot down ... we shot down two that came at us while we were in the water picking up survivors from another ship. All needed medical attention ... I worked all night dressing the men's wounds and transferring them to a casualty evacuation ship."

In the end, it was tank infantry teams that carried the day against the dug-in enemy. Japanese resistance endured until June 21.

"It took us 82 days on Okinawa," remembered Hugh "Hymie" Crane of Northampton, who fought there as a lieutenant with the 6th Marine Division. "I did various jobs; once I was even intelligence officer. But mainly I was leader of a rifle platoon." Twice Crane would end up as company commander because of casualties. "I was lucky — never got a scratch — just wasn't my turn. My only war souvenir is my dog tags ... you come back with two of 'em, and this means you survived."

In the spring of 1945 a story by a Marine Corps combat correspondent, reprinted in the Gazette, related how "1st Lt. Hugh Crane of Northampton, Mass., a company commander for the second time," had led his men during the battle for Sugar Loaf hill on Okinawa. The history of the 6th Marine Division refers to Sugar Loaf as the place on Okinawa where "the most bitter, costly — and decisive — action" took place. The battle for the hill was fought between May 12 and 20, 1945, and before its capture 2,662 Marines were killed or wounded.

"Sugar Loaf," said Crane, "that's where we broke 'em, but boy that was a tough go."

Also in the 6th Marine Division during the battle for Okinawa was Pfc. Lucien "Joe" Vanasse from Northampton, whose partner in combat was "King 310." A sleek Dobermann pinscher, King was one of a platoon of 36 "Devil Dogs" that served as sentries, attack dogs, scouts, messengers, pack dogs, sledge dogs and wire layers. They were also used to locate wounded Marines. Seven of these dogs were killed in action.

King and his Marine handler shared a foxhole on Okinawa from April to early July. King's accomplishments included locating a Japanese officer who had hidden out in the brush when others of his group were captured. After Vanasse returned home, he secured his canine comrade's release and brought him to Northampton.

Once Okinawa was in American hands it served as a base for the B-29s on their bombing runs to Japan. The 20th Air Force was now seeking to destroy finally the war-making capacity of the home islands of Japan before the planned Allied invasion.

Meanwhile, in Europe, the war of attrition against Germany ground on. Young men from Northampton were paying their share of the price.

Pfc. George Senuta, a medic who had survived the Battle of the Bulge, was killed by a mine on February 5.

Pvt. William "Vinnie" Karparis, who had found that "the Krauts are pretty tough, but

Faces of War

Left to right: Pharmacist's Mate Chester Wilusz, U.S. Navy; Sgt. Russell Bishop, U.S. Army Air Corps; Pvt. William Karparis, U.S. Army; Lt. Francis Sheehey, U.S. Army Air Corps; Tech. Sgt. John Bombard, U.S. Army

we are tougher," was killed on March 17. He had just sent his address to the Gazette, asking for people to write him.

On April 5, Pvt. Frederick Bailey died of his wounds.

In mid-April, Lt. Francis Sheehey, who had flown 50 missions and then volunteered for a second tour, nearly became another casualty on his final raid over Dresden. With one motor out of commission, his B-17 barely "managed to make it back to friendly territory," according to a story in the Gazette.

Also in April, the Gazette received word that Pfc. Felix Albino had been awarded the Bronze Star for heroism during the 95th Division's drive across the Saar. "Without regard for his own safety, he braved a fearful barrage of enemy fire to restore essential wire communications" between his platoon and the regimental command post, the newspaper reported.

Tech. Sgt. John Bombard of Company G — who earlier in the war had escaped a serious leg injury when a Boy Scout knife sent him by his father had deflected a German bullet — was wounded again on May 6. When he regained consciousness two days later he found that the war in Europe had ended.

As spring came on, the ring around Hitler's Third Reich began finally to close. The Battle of the Bulge, costly as it was for the Allies, proved to be the German Wehrmacht's last stand. The Soviets took Vienna on April 13; by April 21 they arrived at the outskirts of Berlin. Patton's forces had reached the outskirts of Czechoslovakia but were suddenly halted on orders from Washington, setting the stage for the "Iron Curtain" that grew up between western Europe and the Soviet-dominated Communist nations to the east. Other Allied troops meanwhile knocked out one German unit after another as they secured the Ruhr that had been Hitler's great arsenal. Berlin itself fell to the Soviets on May 2, and while Field Marshal Alfred Jodl surrendered initially to Allied representatives of Gen. Eisenhower at Rheims on May 7, the Soviets required a repeat performance at Berlin on May 8 — the day now known as Victory in Europe, or V-E, Day.

When news of the surrender reached Britain, Staff Sgt. Leonard "Pat" Allen, who served with the 359th Fighter Group of the 8th Air Force stationed at East Wretham, was

Pvt. Rudolph Arel

"Buddy" Arel (who appears in the Northampton High School basketball team photo at the end of chapter one) at the wheel of one of the U.S. Army's "deuce-and-a-half" (2½ ton) trucks much admired by the Germans for their capacity to move troops and war materiel. "Things get a bit rough with us at times," he wrote his sister Ruth on November 28, 1944. "I'm taking lessons on how to whistle from the shells going overhead. Should be pretty good by the time I get home." He was killed in Germany on April 13, 1945, one day after President Roosevelt's death.

Victory in Europe

Staff Sgt. Leonard "Pat" Allen of the 8th Air Force experienced the jubilation of V-E (Victory in Europe) Day in London — "a holiday that will never be forgotten."

on a two-day holiday in London — where so much suffering and death had taken place at the hands of German bombers.

"Today," he wrote home to the Gazette, "London is the scene of the most enthusiastic and spontaneous jubilation and glee I have ever witnessed. Snake dances, conga lines, street gambling, band playing, noise making, flag waving, cheering ... the Union Jack of Great Britain, the Stars and Stripes, and the Sickle and Hammer of the Soviet Union are dangling from every window, wire and flagpole. London, which for years has lived in utter darkness, is tonight lighted up, blazing with lights and neon signs. Sleep is forgotten; skyrockets, salutes, torpedoes, Roman candles, searchlights fill the air. There is no fear in hearts and minds as there was during the blitz and the flying-bomb days and nights. It's a holiday that will never be forgotten by anyone, including myself. Winston Spencer Churchill's Blood, Sweat and Tears prayer has finally been answered. The war is over."

From the German POW camps now emerged thousands of American soldiers and airmen, among them men from Northampton. Some of them, such as Pfc. Joseph Gesiorek, captured in North Africa, and Lt. Charles Kolodzinski, shot down over France, had been held for nearly three years. Some, such as Cpls. Joseph Camposeo and John Balise, captured during Germany's last great push in December 1944, were ravaged by malnutrition. In the end the Germans had nothing left: no troops, no armaments, no food for themselves or their captives.

Pfc. George Berube, just freed from Stalag 9B, wrote home on April 5: "It seems so good to be a free man again. There isn't any news except that I am free and can come home again."

Once home, Cpl. Balise, 50 pounds lighter than when captured, described his prison ration: one cup of ersatz coffee for breakfast; a thin soup made of potatoes, turnips and beet tops for dinner; and for supper a single loaf of sour bread to be divided among seven men. Once, when given a dead, frozen horse, Balise said, "It didn't last long.

"The Germans said they had no supplies," Balise said. "We'd lie in our bunks ... food was the chief topic. ... Nearly all the men said they would start restaurants ... and spend the rest of their lives eating."

And then came the fearsome accounts of the opening of the Nazi concentration camps.

"May God forbid that this ever happen again," wrote Pfc. Ludovic Hebert of Northampton, a member of an antiaircraft battalion of the 5th Infantry Division. He described discovering railroad cars where 4,500 penned-up prisoners had either died of starvation or had been shot en route between Buchenwald and Dachau.

Lt. Robert Rochelau, also from Northampton, was among the first American troops to enter Buchenwald. The young officer wrote a graphic description of the stench, the dying victims, the torture cells. "It makes me mentally as well as physically sick. Never in my life do I want to see anything like that again," he wrote.

Despite the surrender of the Germans on May 8, for many American troops in Europe there was little sense of relief. It appeared likely that a good number of them would soon be shipped to the Pacific Theater to bring about the defeat of the other great enemy, Japan. The code name chosen for the invasion of Japan was Operation Downfall.

Based on previous combat experience in the Pacific, it was predicted that more than a million American lives would be sacrificed during that invasion. The target date was November 1. Those military units to participate were already selected, and on July 15 a first shipload of disgruntled veterans of the European Theater of Operations left Naples,

Sgt. Michael O'Connor, 965th Field Artillery Battalion

Mike O'Connor, right, and an unidentified friend, on leave in Paris, standing in front of Les Invalides — the famous French "Old Soldiers" home. Not long before, German soldiers were posing on the same spot.

It's Over!

Sgt. Anthony Labato, who served with the U.S. Army Air Corps in Italy, celebrated the Allied victory in Europe by posing with a copy of the U.S. Army newspaper, Stars and Stripes.

Italy, headed for the Pacific. Other American servicemen, like Sgts. Art Pope and Ed Kelley, who had been almost three years in the Pacific — and had begun to believe themselves forgotten men — now realized that death might be awaiting them in the assault on Japan.

One unit being eyed as likely candidates for occupation duty in a conquered Japan was the 95th Division. They had already spent 11 months overseas in Europe, with nine of these in combat. A field artillery radio operator in this division, attorney Frank Tuit of Northampton, recipient of a Purple Heart and three battle stars, protested this proposal for his division.

"The majority of men in the 95th Division," argued Cpl. Tuit in a public relations release to the Gazette, "have 2 1/2 years service in the Army, 11 months overseas, of which nine months were spent in combat or in hospitals, and have two or three battle stars ... I know that all the men in the 95th feel they have done their overseas duty well ... I am

Grateful to be Alive

From German POW camps in April, 1945, emerged thousands of Americans including Pfc. George Berube and Cpl. John Balise, first and second from left, — both half starved but grateful to be alive and free.

Cpl. Frank Tuit, 95th Division

A Northampton attorney in civilian life, Tuit, third from left, protested his division's planned shipment to the Pacific on the grounds that the men had just completed a long tour of combat duty in the European theater.

Cmdr. Stanley Lipski

Lipksi, on right in the far right photo with an unidentified officer, died a tragic death on July 30, 1945. As his ship, the U.S.S. Indianapolis *was going down, he gave away his life jacket and went into the sea virtually blind and with his hands badly burned. At some point, he said to those around him in the water, "I'm going now," and slipped out of sight under the waves.*

a lawyer ... and I think I have earned the right at my age of 35 to finish my Army service in the States until men with 60 points like myself are ready for discharge."

Frank Tuit was one of some 20 local attorneys, or about one-third of the Hampshire County Bar Association, who served in the military during WWII. The fate of Cpl. Tuit and that of millions of other American fighting men would be decided very suddenly by an event set in motion when the U.S.S. *Indianapolis* left San Francisco at 8 a.m. on July 16. Aboard her was a secret cargo: the vital components of the atom bomb that would be dropped at Hiroshima on August 6.

The *Indy*, as she was called, under her commanding officer, Capt. Charles McVay, made it to Tinian in a record 10 days, delivered her mysterious cargo and then set out — as ordered — for the Philippine Islands, where they were to train for the invasion of Japan. At 12:02 a.m., on July 30, 1945, midway between Guam and Leyte, the U.S.S. *Indianapolis* was hit by two torpedoes, delivered by the Japanese submarine I-58. She sank in about 12 minutes.

About 400 of the *Indy*'s crew of 1,196 died immediately on impact; the others — more than 800 men — ended up in the sea. Five days and four nights later, 316 survivors were rescued. The others had drowned or had died of their wounds and burns or of thirst or exhaustion. Not only the dead but also many of the living were devoured by sharks.

Aboard the doomed *Indy* as its gunnery officer was 34-year-old Cmdr. Stanley Lipski, born and raised in Northampton and a graduate of the U.S. Naval Academy in 1935. A genial and respected officer, assigned to naval intelligence, Lipski had wanted sea duty in WWII and had persevered until he got it. His sister Stacia Dialessi recalled him saying in 1940: "This is going to be quite a war. If I have to die, I want it to be at sea and to die a hero."

The official notification of Lipski's death was harsh. For some reason the telegram was not delivered to his family's home on Island Road. Instead, his father had to drive into town to pick it up, Stacia recalled.

Lt. Cmdr. Lewis Haynes, the *Indy's* chief physician, was with Lipski in the sea after they were hit. He told the Lipski family how their son had died. It was a hard death. Lipski went into the sea blind and badly burned, especially his hands. Throughout the first day in the sea, a sailor, Aviation Machinist 1st Class Anthony Maday, held the dying officer's head and hands above the oil-covered salt water. Finally Lipski murmered to Haynes: "I'm going now, Lew. Please tell my wife that I love her and that she should marry again."

The failure of the *Indianapolis* to show up in the Philippines had never been reported. Had it been, search-and-rescue teams might have been able to save hundreds of her crew. Instead, the survivors were finally discovered — quite by accident — by the crew of a bomber flying overhead.

One man from Northampton who by a stroke of fate just missed sailing aboard the *Indy* on her last voyage was Pharmacist's Mate Russell Morey. Recently married, Morey had asked for a transfer so as to have some time ashore with his bride. It came through one day before the *Indy* left San Francisco for Tinian.

Pharmacist's Mate Russell Morey

His U.S. Navy liberty I.D. card. Morey missed sailing aboard the doomed Indianapolis *by a single day when a transfer came through.*

Morey recalled the day he discovered Cmdr. Lipski's name and place of birth on a list on shipboard. "I got on the ship's phone and identified myself to him, and even though I was just an ordinary sailor he arranged for us to meet. We talked for quite a while together, and he was very nice to me."

Operation Downfall was to involve 11 U.S. Army and three Marine divisions, some 650,000 ground troops, slated to go in on Kyushu on November 1. A second landing of 16 more divisions was to invade Honshu the following March.

Following the Allied conference at Potsdam, a broadcast was made to Japan on July 26 announcing that the United States, Britain and the Soviet Union had agreed that Japan must surrender unconditionally or suffer "complete and utter destruction." But on July 30, it was reported that Premier Kantaro Suzuki had declared that his government would

Atomic Power Unleashed

This cartoon in the Daily Hampshire Gazette *depicted the dilemma unleashed upon the world through the development of atomic power. Would it be used for war or peace?*

Quitting the Business of War

YANK magazine, "by and for enlisted men," published a special V-J Day edition on August 24, 1945. The war had ended with the destruction of Hiroshima and Nagasaki on August 6 and 8 respectively. This cover photo shows ground crew men of the U.S. Army Air Corps "decorating" the nose of a bomber whose days of missions over Japan are done.

Army Medic

Lt. Col. Edward Manwell spent three years in the Pacific theater as a U.S. Army medical doctor. He believed WWII to be "perhaps the last just war."

ignore the Potsdam ultimatum. On August 4, 720,000 leaflets were dropped on Hiroshima, warning that it was going to be destroyed. Onlookers reported later that Japanese civilians were afraid even to be seen picking these up. They had been conditioned to commit a kind of mass *hara-kiri*, as expressed in a popular song of the time in that country, "One Hundred Million Souls For The Emperor."

That same summer of 1945, Field Marshal Hisaichi Terauchi issued the order that when the Allies began their invasion of the main islands, all Allied prisoners of war were to be killed.

On August 6, the Americans dropped the uranium 235 atomic bomb on Hiroshima. Eighty thousand people died. On August 9, a second bomb was dropped on Nagasaki. The death toll there was 40,000.

Suddenly, the war was over.

President Harry Truman later declared, "I regarded the bomb as a military weapon. I did it to shorten the agony of young Americans."

American servicemen who had fought or were stationed in the Pacific theater today remember their sense of relief on learning of the Japanese surrender after the bombings. At last they could go home. The killing and suffering were over.

"We thought it was wonderful," recalled Dr. Edward Manwell, who served three years as a medical officer in the Pacific. "There had been a great evil abroad in the world. We believed ours to be a just cause, and perhaps it was ... maybe the last just war."

On September 2, 1945, the Japanese officially surrendered at a ceremony aboard the U.S.S. *Missouri* in Tokyo Bay. Seaman 1st Class Robert Ouimet of Northampton was aboard the nearby U.S.S. *Chester*. Also present was Navy Lt. John Blanchard, who wrote home:

"There were thousands of planes of all types; I counted over 500 in one group alone. They were flying like swallows, this way and that. Then came B-29s all in formation. All the battleships were on one side. Airplane carriers, destroyers, every kind of craft you could think of ... we came in single file. The length of the line of ships was over 18 miles. We (the U.S.S. *Missoula*) were fourth in line. It was 7 a.m. The Stars and Stripes were

After the Surrender: American Troops Land at Wakayama, August, 1945

The symbol on the back of this man's coat means "culture" and/or "civilization." He sat on the shore of his country, devastated by the war that it started, watching the Yankee barbarians land to commence the occupation.

Sgt. Kenneth Pattrell

A clarinetist in the band of the First Cavalry Division, Pattrell, at right, also served as a medical corpsman in combat in the Philippines. The "First Cav" was the only such unit in which musicians doubled as medics. As Gen. McArthur's favorite division, it was also the first American unit to enter Tokyo following the Japanese surrender.

flying from the big hill, along the side of a lighthouse. The city itself is all burned out as far as you can see. On one big building that was completely gutted, someone had painted in big white letters, 'Three Cheers For the U.S. Navy.'"

The censor stamp on Lt. Blanchard's letter read: "Original Landing, V-J Day, Tokyo area, 9-2-45."

Lt. Earl Tonet of the 2nd Marine Division, who had fought on Saipan, Tinian and Okinawa, and who had fully expected to participate in the invasion on November 1, was instead sent into the ruined city of Nagasaki only a few weeks after its destruction. He later remembered very clearly the desolation and the suffering of the sick and dying people, particularly the children.

The danger from radiation was not much emphasized, and Tonet recalled with wonder how Army personnel said they had been instructed not to wash their vehicles in the water but that nothing had been said about not using it to wash themselves.

In recent years, surviving members of the 2nd Marine Division Association, Tonet among them, have been contacted by the Nuclear Defense Agency of the U.S. government, which was looking for veterans who might qualify for Department of Veterans' Affairs benefits as a result of "participation in a radiation risk activity" during the occupation of Hiroshima or Nagasaki.

Tech. Sgt. William Sniezko

Survived three-and-a-half years as a POW slave laborer in the hands of the Japanese.

Another man from Northampton was one of the first squad of 70 Marines to enter Nagasaki, in his case to take out ill and starving Allied POWs. This was Pfc. John Connell, aboard the U.S.S. *Wichita*, which was accompanied by four other destroyers and the hospital ship U.S.S. *Haven*.

"The majority of the prisoners, who had been in Japanese custody for more than three years," wrote Connell to his father, "were British, Dutch and Javanese. ... Those needing medical attention were taken aboard the U.S.S. *Haven* where they have been taking care of 500 a day. ... The atomic bomb was dropped about two miles from where we are. Where it did drop is unbelieveable. There is very little left of anything. It is all pretty level. Where we are, every house is pretty well wrecked."

Before long, Allied troops would be entering Japan in quite a different manner, as would young Pvt. Donald Hood of Northampton, first trumpeter in the "newly organized Army Air Forces band" sent in 1946 to entertain occupation troops.

It was during these same autumn months of 1945 that the Danforth, Miller, Sniezko and Talenda families of Northampton would finally learn the savage treatment their sons and brothers had suffered as prisoners of the Japanese for the three-and-a-half years since the surrender of the Philippines.

As the war had progressed, the Japanese had begun moving Allied POWs to the home islands by packing them aboard what came to be called "hell ships." Prisoners died of thirst, hunger, suffocation and disease — or were simply machine-gunned as they tried to escape when some of these unmarked Japanese ships were attacked from the air. More than 4,000 American POWs who had survived up to the autumn of 1944 died in this manner, among them Sgts. Vernon Danforth and Joseph Miller. Both were on a ship sunk by submarine action in the South China Sea on October 24, 1944. Out of 1,775 American POWs on that ship, there were only nine survivors. Of the 20,000 soldiers, sailors, airmen and Marines captured upon the surrender of the Philippines, less than 60 percent survived and returned home at the war's end.

Fifty years later, former Tech. Sgt. William Sniezko related his own experience as a prisoner of the Japanese. Along with some 76,000 other American and Filipino soldiers, his ordeal began on the seven-day "Bataan Death March" in April of 1942. Already weakened by disease and starvation, these men made the 65-mile forced march between Mariveles Airfield and San Fernando in Pampanga province. More than 600 American

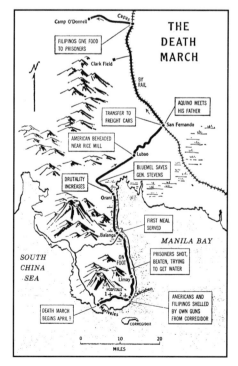

Bataan Death March

This map of what came to be called the Bataan Death March was kept by Tech. Sgt. William Sniezko, who survived the ordeal only through the whim of a Japanese officer.

soldiers and between 5,000 and 10,000 Filipino soldiers died of thirst, hunger and exhaustion or torture en route.

"When a man could no longer walk," recalled Sniezko, "they'd haul him off the road and sometimes bury him alive." He himself narrowly escaped crucifixion at the hands of a Japanese officer who ordered him to fall out and follow him into the woods. "Three times he asked me if I was a Catholic, and I was scared and said I wasn't. Then I got really mad and stretched out my arms and told him that I was a Catholic and that I wasn't afraid to die and to go ahead and do it. The officer looked surprised and then laughed and walked away, but before he left he said he'd have crucified me if I hadn't admitted I was a Catholic."

The march was followed by an eight-hour journey packed into box cars on the way to Camp O'Donnell, a former Philippine army post near Manila, during which some men died of suffocation.

The Japanese told the prisoners that Japan was not a signatory of the Geneva Convention and that their American prisoners would be treated not as POWs but as criminals. No medical treatment was provided, and very little food. Prisoners were soon eating grass, leaves, stray dogs and rats. One of Sniezko's first jobs was digging shallow graves at Camp O'Donnell for prisoners who were dying like flies, some 16,000 in the first few weeks alone.

He was then moved to a camp at Cabanatuan, in the province of Luzon, where conditions were somewhat better but where he was struck with dysentery. "Sgt. Joe Miller of Northampton saved my life here," he recalled. "He had been a crash-boat pilot in Manila, but I never even knew this. Now, as a prisoner, he worked in a Japanese mess hall. Every night he would steal gallons of tea and bring it to me and make me drink it. Besides preventing dehydration, there seemed to be some property in the tea that cured me."

Miller then got Sniezko a job in the same mess hall, where they persuaded the Japanese to set aside their garbage for the American prisoners instead of occasionally tossing it at them, "to watch them fight for it like starving dogs," Sniezko said.

"Joe Miller saved my life," said Sniezko, "and when I learned how he died (as one of the victims of the American blockade of Japan) I was very angry."

The comparative idyll in the Japanese mess at Cabanatuan ended after three months, when Sniezko was assigned to work as a stevedore on the docks at Manila, loading and unloading Japanese ships. Here the prisoners added to their meager rations by stealing, and they also committed sabotage on war materiel. Their ranking officer, a Lt. Cmdr. G.G. Harrison, would be held and tortured for 48 days in a Fort Santiago dungeon in an effort by the Japanese to trace the sabotage committed by American prisoners. According to Sniezko, Harrison never betrayed anyone.

After 23 months on the Manila docks, Sniezko was himself one of 1,600 men crammed aboard one of the "hell ships" carrying American prisoners to forced labor in Japan. Under attack at one point, he heard screams from other prisoner-laden vessels as they went down.

"We were packed down in the hold with machine guns aimed at the hatches if we tried to get to the decks. Only praying kept us from panicking and trying to reach the deck. We said the Rosary."

After 23 days the survivors were landed on an island off Yokohama to work with English and Canadian prisoners in an open pit nickel mine. There, during what proved to be the final week of the war, Sniezko was caught stealing vegetables from a nearby garden and subjected to terrible beatings and long hours of a torture that consisted of kneeling on bamboo rods while holding a heavy bucket of water over his head. Any spill resulted in further beatings.

Then, on August 15, the prisoners were informed that the Japanese had surrendered and the war was over. B-29s began dropping food from the air, and with silk from one of the parachutes the prisoners fashioned an American flag that they raised on September 2.

Sniezko's ordeal ended with a year of care at Lovell General Hospital at Fort Devens, Massachusetts.

Instead of being subjected to the Bataan Death March, Sgt. Mitchell Talenda was

Tech. Sgt. Joseph Miller

Risking his own life to save that of a fellow prisoner from Northampton — Tech. Sgt. William Sniezko, — Miller later died aboard one of the "hell ships" in which the Japanese transported American POWs to Japan near the end of the war.

While Joseph Miller suffered as a POW, Blanche and Bernard Miller served in the U.S. Army. She said she volunteered because of her brother's fate.

Former POWs

Upon release from Japanese captivity, these Massachusetts men resided at Fort Devens Lowell General Hospital for a year. Here they received medical treatment for their years of near starvation and brutal treatment. Northampton's Tech. Sgt. William Sniezko is third from the right in the back row.

Slave Labor Survivor

After three years as a slave laborer in a copper mine owned by the Mitsubishi company in Japan, American POW Staff Sgt. Mitchell Talenda emerged blind from the starvation and beatings he had endured.

transported to the horrors of Camp O'Donnell in a truck.

Talenda described his closest call with death, when he and a group of others were selected for forced labor in Japan. As they were marched to railroad cars that were to carry them to a ship, those American prisoners left behind were doused with gasoline and burned alive.

Talenda's fate was to end up in one of the Osarizawa copper mines, the oldest in Japan, having been in operation for 1,300 years. Located near Hanawa in Honshu, these mines were owned by Mitsubishi Mines Works, Inc. The inhuman treatment of the American prisoners there was taken up at the war crimes trials held in Tokyo during 1946 and 1947.

Various Japanese involved went on trial, including the commanding officer of the camp, Lt. Toshiori Asaka. An officer in the Japanese Imperial Army, he was fluent in English and had been an accountant in Tokyo before the war. Also put on trial were a Cpl. Tetsuro Yoshio, known to the prisoners as "Cyclops," and the mine foreman, Hichiro Tsuchiya, known as "Patches."

Every sort of cruelty to the prisoners was charged: brutal beatings, starvation diet, inadequate clothing, hazardous work assignments and collective punishment involving such things as standing at attention, in straw sandals, in snow and ice for 10 to 12 hours at a stretch. There was virtually no heat in the prisoners' vermin-infested barracks, and medical treatment was denied to the sick. Red Cross supplies were withheld or stolen. Prisoners — including Mitchell Talenda — were beaten with clubs, pick handles, a sledgehammer. At war's end the prisoners themselves arrested Asaka and delivered him to the military authorities in Yokohama. In April of 1947 Asaka would be sentenced to 12 years imprisonment at hard labor.

Informed of the sentencing on September 12, 1947, of the mine foreman, Tsuchiya, who was given 15 years in prison, Talenda was interviewed in Northampton by the Gazette. "Still suffering from back injuries, and virtually blind from his treatment as a Jap prisoner, Talenda, a former staff sergeant in the 60th Coast Artillery AA, asserted yesterday that Tsuchiya 'should be hanged.'"

On September 27, 1945, there appeared in the Gazette a letter from Sgt. Dennis McKenna of Northampton, a member of the 98th Evacuation Hospital in Yokohama. One of his assignments at the war's end was to help attend to "Patient No. 10,694.

Sgt. Dennis McKenna

McKenna, center, of the 98th Evacuation Hospital, was stationed with the U.S. Army in Japan at war's end. One of his assignments was to watch over "Patient No. 10,694," who was none other than the one-time warlord, Premier Hideki Tojo. He had attempted suicide.

Diagnosis: Gunshot wounds, attempted suicide." Sgt. McKenna's patient was none other than Ex-Premier Hideki Tojo, the Japanese leader who had plunged Japan into war back in 1941.

"He is short, bald and wears a funny-looking handlebar mustache," wrote McKenna. "He speaks very little English but was able to thank us ... when we changed him from a cot to a hospital bed ... it's pretty important that we ... get him well quickly to stand trial for his crimes. Tonight (September 13) he is resting quietly while I type this letter only two doors away from his private room."

Gen. Tojo indeed was tried for war crimes and sentenced to death. He was hanged on November 23, 1948.

McKenna went on to describe the black market operating by this time in Tokyo — "with soldiers selling cigarettes at 70 yen a pack; and sailors and Marines, like sidewalk vendors, sell anything from chocolate bars to cans of sugar. There are very few M.P.s here just yet, and that perhaps accounts for quick millionaire merchants in business."

The young American sergeant closed thus: "Though everything here is interesting, I think I'll find more interest in walking up Elm Street to Franklin in a couple of months. I certainly miss the old home town."

Sgt. McKenna's Record Book

This handwritten list of the patients on his ward lists the name of former Premier Tojo.

V-J Day

Although citizens of Northampton staged a wild, spontaneous V-J Day celebration on Main Street on the night of August 14, many also attended the city's official recognition of the war's end the following evening. This involved a parade down Main Street to the fairgrounds "for a program of speaking and prayer."

1945 — Welcome Home

On the homefront, the year 1945 opened with an incident marking the one time that the city of Northampton was probably in any real physical danger during the Second World War: the great runaway-horse caper of Saturday, January 13.

The event was reported in the Gazette the following Monday between photos and stories announcing the fates of Seaman 1st Class Christopher Cahill, whose ship, the U.S.S. *Spence,* had gone down in a typhoon in the Pacific, and Staff Sgt. William Ciekalowski, missing in action in the European theater since Christmas day (and later declared dead).

By the 1940s, the horse and rubber-tired wagon was long since an oddity on Northampton streets, but during World War II one such rig was still used for small hauling jobs. Its owner was Ferdinand Ice of the Mt. Tom Road area. On January 13 he parked it in front of the Growers Outlet on Pleasant Street. What panicked the animal was never determined, but once in a state of total fright it raced up Pleasant and onto Main Street, onto the sidewalk in front of the courthouse, where the wildly careening wagon hit the iron fence and several lampposts and parked cars. Tearing on up Main Street, the body of the wagon fell away, leaving the terrified animal attached only to two wheels and an axle. This strange equipage caught the attention of Thomas Scarborough of Amherst, who gave chase in his car. At Main and South he was joined by Joseph Punska of Hatfield in his car. They all continued up South Street until somewhere near Fort Street, where the horse was finally cornered and quieted down. Citizens discussed Northampton's jangled nerves and damaged fenders for days.

All through 1945 the work of the local draft board ground on, but the groups of men being drafted were much smaller. On January 10, a single draftee, Louis M. Carrier, was given a send-off at the railroad station. Carrier had volunteered for immediate induction on passing his physical exam three weeks earlier. On his solitary departure he was presented the usual going-away gifts by the Northampton Citizens' Committee. After this, groups as large as 19 left the station, but they were more likely to be just six to eight.

Citizens' Committee members were commended by the Kiwanis Club in February for their faithful farewells, and Grace Coolidge, Elizabeth Finn and Marion Dodd were especially singled out for their service.

The Gazette reported in May that the draft board had operated for five years, with four of the five original members still serving: Fred Paulson had resigned and been replaced by Gailon Hinds. The board had inducted 2,077 Northampton men up to this time while many other men had enlisted. Members of the board, who served without compensation, had attended an average of three meetings a week during their first three years and an average of two during their last two years.

Salvage drives also continued in Northampton through September of 1945, with a special plea for paper "because the goods of war going to the Pacific have to travel thousands of miles under conditions incomparable to those in Europe ... Considerably more paper is needed." Housewives were urged to continue turning in fat to their butchers as late as August. In September the final collection of tin cans was held.

In May the Red Cross Blood Donor Service of Hampshire County announced that it had completed its mission. Since the blood donor service began on November 28, 1942, the mobile unit had appeared in Northampton 19 times and received 3,831 pints of blood from residents of Hampshire County, with 2,519 of those pints given by residents of

Two Local Men Lose Their Lives

The deaths of Seaman Christopher Cahill and Sgt. William Ciekalowski hit the front page of the Gazette on the same day: January 15, 1945.

First Black Faculty Member

Adelaide Cromwell Hill's appointment was announced in February of 1945. She was the first black person to be appointed to the Smith College faculty.

Curbing Civilians

This cartoon in the Gazette lampoons the government's effort to curb train travel by civilians — thus opening up more space for service men and women. Wartime trains were always overcrowded.

Northampton.

Also in May, the local British War Relief Society halted its work. Between 1940 and 1943 it had raised $30,000, according to its report, and over the five years of its existence had shipped out more than six tons of clothing, plus 10,000 knitted garments.

Already planning to return to its traditional 34-week schedule by the fall of 1945, Smith College had exhibited other symptoms of an early conversion to peacetime with its Charity Ball in January for 800 couples. Besides the appearance of the star of the West Point football team, a general's son, there was to be "a large contingent from Harvard Medical School, Yale University and various midshipmen's schools," according to a college spokesman. "No corsages will be worn because of wartime restrictions," it was added. No new dresses were to be purchased for "Ivy Day" in the spring, "in order to spare the small reserve of dress goods in the country," the Gazette reported in March.

Due to the labor shortage, students were still having to perform college housework, but nevertheless the tuition of $1,000 was going to be raised in 1946 to $1,250 "to meet increased costs of living and the increase in wages and salaries."

The first black member of the Smith College faculty was announced in February with the appearance of Adelaide Cromwell Hill as an instructor in sociology. That same month the college eliminated the usual spring vacation "to relieve strains on transportation," but SCAN — the campus newspaper — reported that Smith students were actually making more trips than ever away from the college.

On May 31, a Victory ship, one of a series of cargo ships named after American colleges and universities, was launched as the S.S. *Smith Victory*. These ships, one of the

triumphs of American wartime shipbuilding, were made in sections that were brought together assembly-line fashion with a construction time of only six weeks. In the officers' mess of the *Smith Victory* hung a picture of College Hall, a map of the campus, and a photo of Elizabeth Cutter Morrow (a trustee of the college), who had dedicated the ship. The college presented the S.S. *Smith's* library with a gift of 50 books.

That same spring a controversy raged on campus concerning the wearing of dungarees. "Slovenly dungarees are not particularly attractive to men," opined Professor Jere Abbott of the music department. On the other hand, William Christian of the department of religion recommended leaving the choice of garb to the students "who are here to work and not to dress up." Professor Dan Aaron of the English department went further and

Elizabeth Cutter Morrow

A trustee of Smith College from 1920-1950, chairman of the board of trustees from 1948-1950, and acting president of the college from 1939-1940, she was chosen to dedicate the S.S. Smith Victory *in 1945.*

Beauty Contest Winner

A member of the Class of 1945, Marcella May Harrington won a "beauty contest" at Smith College, an event intended to make fun of such contests staged in co-educational state colleges and universities. One contender was a male sophomore from Amherst College.

Former B-17 Pilot First Male Student at Smith

In the autumn of 1945, Meredith Stiles, a former B-17 pilot now a student at Amherst College, was accepted into a language class at Smith and thus became the first male student at this women's college.

actually endorsed dungarees as "a democratic way to dress."

Inaugurated by SCAN, the phenomenon of the beauty contest surfaced at Smith College during 1945. "This is purely a battle of form and feature," declared SCAN. "Intellect will carry no weight in the decision." On the night of March 16, contestants chosen from each college residence were to parade across the stage of Sage Hall. "These razzle-dazzlers," warned SCAN, "must wear heels and dresses." The winner was Marcella Harrington, Class of '45, from Fort Lauderdale, Florida. That the affair was at least in part a satirization of other beauty contests is seen in the fact that one Harry Webster of Amherst College, clothed as one of the "razzle-dazzlers," "came near to walking off with the honors," according to SCAN.

In May, Magistrate Anna Kross, a New York City judge, delivered a more serious message to the students, advising them to examine their role and position in post-war America. Seventeen million women had helped to win the war, she pointed out, both in military service and in factory work. "With the return of peace, we hear that woman's place is in the home," she said. "Women have a part in the home, but it was not established to enshrine and to isolate them."

The really big news at Smith in 1945, however, was the appearance on campus of a war veteran named Meredith Stiles, the first male student at the college in 74 years. Recently discharged from the U.S. Army Air Corps, Stiles had served as a B-17 pilot with the 401st Bomb Group in England. He came to Smith because he needed an advanced Spanish course not available at Amherst College, where he was a student. A story about him appeared in the Army's overseas newspaper, The Stars and Stripes, in October. That same month the Academy of Music featured a Universal newsreel: "Today's American Hero: The Only Male Student At Smith College." In Smith's Rally Day Show the following spring there would be a prologue delivered by a mythical student named "Myles Steredith."

There continued to be problems with juveniles in Northampton throughout 1945. "The principle offenders," declared Carrie Gauthier of the Society for the Prevention of Cruelty to Children, "are the parents who work long hours in war-production factories and make no adequate provision for their youngsters' care." The hiring of teen-age girls to sit with babies "while parents work or seek recreation" was also raising problems, she maintained. In March, there were 221 children under the care of the SPCC.

Police Chief Bernier attributed an increase in cases of vandalism to lack of "proper supervision from parents." One theft from The Music Shop at 143 Main Street involved a youth who stole a "Magnavox recording machine" plus a large number of records including the popular wartime song, "Don't Fence Me In."

In the autumn of 1945 there arose a great flap over an alleged secret society at Northampton High School. According to the Gazette, this organization, called "The Syndicate," boasted between 90 and 150 members who had signed a pledge "to work to overcome the police of this city and to start a new era of vandalism which will terrorize the people of Northampton." Police believed that the idea for The Syndicate came from the "Dead End Kids" films of the period. While some citizens viewed the whole thing as a joke, the Gazette reported, others did not find it funny. At one point the Toronto Star even called the police asking for more details. After a week of furor, Principal Ronald Darby announced that the school had investigated the affair and that "corrective and educational measures for all involved" were to be taken.

The head of the FBI, J. Edgar Hoover, was predicting a "crime wave" to follow the war's end, reported the Gazette. But Hoover did not share one popular view, that returning veterans would create a crime problem. "The most dangerous crime element," he declared, "is the juvenile delinquent." He attributed this to "the failure of the mother and father to properly establish a home and take care of their children."

Northampton's answer to the problem of juvenile delinquency seems to have been a demand, in January, for a recreation center for this newly defined element, "the teen-age group." Proposals for a Youth Center were launched and representatives sought from Northampton High School, St. Michael's High School and Smith's Agricultural School. Soon a "Teeners' Own Club" was operating at the Community YMCA with regularly scheduled dances, each with a special theme such as a "Flower Dance."

Another controversy arose that spring, sparked by a January 4 letter to the Gazette from a "A 4-F Worker" protesting the "pressure once more building up for legislation which will 'force' 4-Fs into war work." He wrote, "As one of this group who is not engaged in essential war work ... I am all for such legislation provided it be similar in form to the existing military draft laws in protecting both my career and my personal property." What he wanted was "an equal chance to that of the returning veteran after the war is over."

A month and half later, datelined Germany, came an answering letter from an irate soldier named Ralph Finn. "Just who does he think he is, anyway?" demanded Cpl. Finn. "I personally have been in the Army for over three years, overseas for over a year, and in Europe since D-Day ... To read where some 4-F is scared to leave his nice, cozy, non-essential job to help the war effort is too much for me ... I personally don't care if I have a job when I come home. The only thing I want is to get home, alive, to the ones I love. After I get there I'll see about getting a job."

Cpl. Finn does not mention the fact in his letter, but he had been awarded the Purple Heart for wounds received as a member of the 30th Infantry Division that saw hard fighting following the invasion.

On the same day, March 23, that the death in combat of Pfc. Edward Mazuch of the 5th Marine Division at Iwo Jima was reported, the International Silver Company of Florence received the coveted Army-Navy E award at a ceremony held in the high school auditorium. Among those present was Elsa Boudah Cox, the wife of Technical Sgt. Henry Cox and mother of two young sons, Gerald and Allen. For over two years she had worked long, hard hours on an assembly line in what the employees called "the bomb shop." Here they manufactured the casings for the magnesium incendiary bombs ordered by the Boston Chemical Warfare Procurement District.

Letter to the Editor

One of the Daily Hampshire Gazette's overseas subscribers, Cpl. Ralph Finn, a wounded survivor of combat with the 30th Division, wrote an irate letter to the editor in response to a complaining comment by a 4-F at home in Northampton, who was worried about post-war employment opportunities in competition with returning veterans.

Factory F, one department of International Silver, had recently cast its six millionth magnesium casing for "the giant matchsticks" that, with round-the-clock sorties by B-17s and B-24s, as a Gazette reporter wrote, "have left Berlin, Schweinfurt, Saarbrucken, Munster and Kiel a veritable mass of flames." To this list should be added Hamburg, Dresden and eventually Tokyo.

Only 3 percent of the nation's war plants won the E award, so this presentation was a source of satisfaction to employees such as Elsa Cox, who had worked, in rotation throughout the war, these arduous shifts: 7 a.m. to 3 p.m.; 3 p.m. to 11 p.m.; and 11 p.m. to 7 a.m.

"The work was not easy," she recalled. "You were on your feet from start to finish and working as fast as you could to process the casings, since we were paid on what our line turned out — not on an individual piecework basis. The group as a whole was thus motivated to work harder. Trying to change your sleep pattern from week to week was very difficult and especially so if you had young children, as I did, even though my mother was caring for them. When I developed some health problems, the doctor told my mother, 'She's plain exhausted.'"

Cox recalled the men, many of them no longer young, who worked in the terrible heat of the shop where the magnesium alloy was poured into the steel molds that produced the hexagonal-shaped sheath, or casing, for these M-50 four-pound "matchsticks."

Once the magnesium bodies had passed inspection at Factory F, they were shipped out to a loading plant for final assembly. Air Force personnel received these "matchsticks" in clusters, each containing 128 of the four-pound magnesium bombs which were cast, loaded, assembled and clustered at various plants in New England. It was these "matchsticks" that on March 9, 1945, dropped by low-flying B-29s over Tokyo, caused the worst fire in history during which an area the size of Manhattan was destroyed. One million people were left homeless, and more people killed than would die at Hiroshima the following August.

Bombs from New England Defense Plants

Clusters of incendiary (magnesium) bombs — also called matchstick bombs — being loaded aboard a B-24 bomber in England. The four-pound bombs were manufactured in New England defense plants. The magnesium casings were cast at International Silver Company in Florence.

Once again in 1945, as quoted in the Gazette, the Sales Management Survey service in New York reported Northampton as having "a higher standard of living and a stronger consumers market ... than in most other communities in the country." Per capita buying power in Northampton the previous year had been $1,118, with local retail sales of $16,081,000 in 1944 compared with $15,420,000 the previous year.

"Much of the local earnings went into war bonds and other savings ... and into debt retirement," reported this survey. "Consumer buying was largely stifled because of the lack of merchandise and restricted transportation. With the prospect of more goods available during the next year, this buying ability and desire are expected to find an outlet that will boom local business."

A study of the Gazette through 1945 reveals that American civilians were indeed anticipating — and in certain ways already experiencing — the post-war boom. On April 4, the same day that the death in France of Pvt. William "Vinnie" Karparis was reported, readers were being advised that "Some Products May Be Produced At '39 Rate By Year After V-E Day." Advertisements reveal that the anticipated post-war buying spree was already well advanced on the homefront even before V-E Day and V-J Day. After V-J Day, the pent-up demand for goods would simply explode.

In April, as speed restrictions were lifted and more gas coupons allotted, Police Chief Bernier, who had so valiantly tried to enforce the wartime speed limit, urged citizens "to use these first fruits of victory with proper humility." Fuel oil and gasoline users were warned by Frederick Farrar, chairman of the local Ration Board, to exercise the same caution as they had in 1944 concerning these still-vital war supplies.

The Pioneer Valley Association was already looking forward to a post-war tourist business that would "greatly exceed the pre-war six billion dollar annual total."

In July of 1945 in Detroit, Ford reprogrammed its assembly line and planned to turn out 40,000 cars during the summer.

Welfare cases were the "lowest in the city for many years" with only 52 cases at the end of 1944, costing the city only $23,688.96. Even the cost of operating the City Infirmary, the haven on Prospect Street for penniless old people, was down to $8,352.13 for 1944.

The Northampton Co-operative Bank advertised as usual its House-of-the-Month Club to encourage potential homeowners to save and plan for their post-war dream house. "Sketches, plans, blueprints and specifications are available at the bank for your use." Perceiving the potential of GI Bill benefits, particularly the section that guaranteed half of loans up to $2,000 for veterans' homes, this enterprising institution made the first "GI Home Loan" on January 25, 1945, and by October would announce "a steady acceleration of home loans to returning servicemen" — $35,050 up to that point.

"Be independent ... Own Your Home" the H.A. Bidwell Insurance, Travel and Real

Post-war Consumerism

Even before the war was over, American consumerism was being stimulated by ads like this one trumpeting the glories of the "New Freedom Kitchen" that would be available to the American housewife.

First Local GI Home Loan

On Jan. 25, 1945, Camille Langlais was the first WWII veteran from Hampshire County to receive a Home Loan under the GI Bill. Left to right: Langlais; Veterans Bureau Contact Representative William Lewonis; Elizabeth Langlais; and L.L. Campbell, president and chairman of the board of directors of the Northampton Co-operative Bank.

Estate firm was urging with listings such as these: "Just off Elm Street, $5,200; Woodlawn Avenue, $10,000;" and "in sight of new high school, $5,500."

Five hundred and ten completed questionnaires had come back to the post-war planning committee of the Chamber of Commerce from absent Northampton servicemen. "Homes Are Chief Plans Of Men and Women In Service" read the report. Out of the 510, "108 want to build, 118 want to purchase, 106 want to rent and 178 are undecided. Considerable real estate activity is predicted in the period following the war."

An already perceived post-war housing shortage had prompted the regional representative of the National Housing Agency to announce in July that "conversion and remodeling of existing residential units have been authorized without quota restrictions so far as materials are obtainable."

The population of Northampton had increased during the war, from 24,794 in 1940 to

Buying Spree

Pent-up demand for homes, furnishings and household appliances, stemming from a decade of depression and war, produced an orgy of consumerism when peace came.

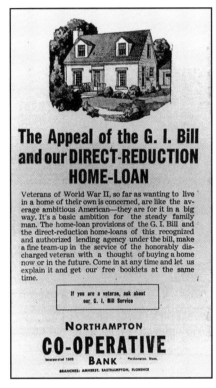

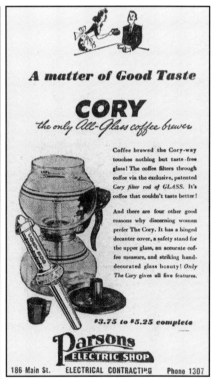

more than 25,000 in 1945, and by 1950 it would reach 29,063.

In July advertisements offered new furnaces, range burners, shower stalls and kitchen units. The Norwood Ice Co. urged homeowners to insist on new oil-heating systems, because "FULLY AUTOMATED OIL COSTS LESS!" The Northampton Electric Lighting Co. advised "New Electric Appliances Available Soon!"

McCallum's, however, was refusing to accept "deposits on scarce merchandise ... reconversion is a slow job."

It was announced that nylon stockings were about to reappear, with Propper-McCallum Hosiery Company, a local firm, ready to resume production and already "swamped with orders."

Elaborate weddings were being encouraged by Ann August: "It's Leap Year, girls. You furnish the man ... We've got the GOWNS!"

February 1945 was "Furniture Month" at McCallum's with "period sofas" on sale from $104.95 to $195; Governor Winthrop desks at $59.48; small "barrel" chairs at $63.50; and record cabinets at $45. "Elegant glo-sheen draperies" were offered at $14.95; Adirondack chairs at $6.75; and barbecue grills from $8.95 to $29.95.

Parsons Electric Shop was advertising "the better way to make coffee" with the new Silex or Cory coffee brewers.

Wartime prosperity was also evident in the entertainment field, with numerous restaurants featuring dinner and dancing. Northampton's liquor license revenue was the highest in the city's history with a total of $24,100 turned over to the city treasurer at year's end.

Then, on April 12, vacationing at Warm Springs, Georgia, and sitting for a portrait, President Franklin Delano Roosevelt suddenly said to the artist, "I have a terrific headache." Two hours later it was announced he had died of a cerebral hemorrhage. A pall fell over Northampton, as it did all over the United States.

Roosevelt Dead

President Franklin Roosevelt died suddenly at Warm Springs, Georgia, on April 12, 1945. The nation was stunned; even more so were our troops in far-off corners of the world to lose their commander in chief.

Tribute to F.D.R.

In a tribute to President Roosevelt, local merchants chose to close their stores on the Saturday following his death.

In Respectful Tribute
To The Memory Of
Our Late President,
FRANKLIN DELANO ROOSEVELT,
Stores Of The
Northampton Retail Merchants
Association
Will Be Closed
All Day Saturday,
April 14

FDR, together with other military dead, was listed on the official Army-Navy casualty list for that day. Marine Lt. Earl Tonet, out in the Pacific, heard the news over a ship's loudspeaker off Okinawa, where he was on duty with what was called "floating reserves" prior to joining the battle for that island. "There was total shock," he remembered. "We had shared so much faith in him for so long. Gloom. This was the end of an era. What do we do now? And then someone said, 'Harry WHO?'"

In Northampton, the Gazette reported "City To Join In Day Of Mourning ... Public activities to be closed down. City departments to suspend business." Some merchants ran black-bordered memorials instead of their regular ads, and Grace Coolidge — always asked to comment on great national events — made one of her rare public statements: "I hardly know how to react. The President's death is a terrible tragedy ... However, I am confident that President Harry Truman will carry forward the program of the peace just as if Mr. Roosevelt were here. I have heartfelt sympathy for Mrs. Roosevelt, 12 years earlier having been through a similar experience."

Eleanor Roosevelt had attended the funeral of Calvin Coolidge at the Edwards Church in Northampton on January 7, 1933.

In May, three Northampton men were arraigned before U.S. Hearing Commissioner James P. Moriarty in Springfield on charges of "the illegal possession and transfer of gasoline ration coupons" valued at more than 40,000 gallons. Armand Moffitt, an employee of the Northampton National Bank, allegedly had stolen coupons deposited with the bank to be turned over, as the law required, to the federal government. These stamps had then been bought for 25 cents each by a member of the Common Council, Donald O'Brien, who was also a member of the local Recreation Commission and a filling-station operator. Also involved was a third man, John Latham, identified as "an employee of a brush company." By the time these stamps reached consumers they were selling for a dollar a coupon.

During the two days that this story was front-page news, the accounts were flanked by

Navy Cross Awarded Posthumously

Pharmacist's Mate Thomas Gutowski, a Navy "medic," sacrificed his own life as he ministered to wounded comrades, and for this received the Navy Cross after his death.

Navy Cross

This medal is awarded for extraordinary heroism. It ranks next to the Medal of Honor and is the highest medal, restricted to combat, awarded to Navy personnel.

Brother Visits Gravesite

When the U.S.S. Independence *anchored off Saipan following that island's capture, William Gutowski mentioned to an officer that his brother Tom had been killed and buried there. Before long, he was headed ashore in the executive officer's motorboat, provided with a camera to record the visit to his brother's grave.*

news of the wounding of two local Marines, Pfc. Ronald Kochapski and Pfc. William Marcus, in the Pacific theater, and also of the posthumous decoration for heroism of Pharmacist's Mate 3rd Class Thomas Gutowski. Gutowski, a medical corpsman, had given his life at Saipan on June 17, 1944, when he "boldly faced a withering barrage ... deep into enemy territory ... coolly and efficiently administering to his fallen comrades when he himself was seriously wounded by shrapnel from an exploding shell. Disregarding his own intense pain, he steadfastly refused to be evacuated and continued his valiant service until he succumbed to his own wounds." He had, the citation added, "contributed to the saving of many lives" while offering up his own.

Pvt. Harold Manning, a former Gazette reporter, was at this same time home in Northampton on a medical furlough. He had been wounded in Belgium the previous autumn with the 11th Armored Division.

The Ann August dress shop, meanwhile, was urging local women to "Make The Most Of Decoration Day" with "swim suits and play suits from our wonderful collection."

The stolen gas coupon caper was not the only criminal activity in the city that year. An unnamed "Northampton retail outlet for women's clothing" was among several area concerns paying "triple damages" to the U.S. Treasury for overcharging. A youth "just turned 17" pleaded guilty to the theft of four automobile tires and inner tubes, all rationed items. Local police were on the lookout for 12,000 cigarettes stolen off a truck between Springfield and Greenfield. Counterfeit ration stamps for meat had shown up in a local market, and one housewife — apparently observing that certain women were obtaining extra sugar for non-existent home canning — protested that rationing was turning us into "a nation of liars."

Drivers going over the wartime limit of 35 mph were keeping the police busy, with 10 such offenders fined $220 in District Court on a single day.

At the Mount Tom reservation, a sailor from the U.S.S. *Bunker Hill* was beaten up and he and his girlfriend were robbed. The perpetrators tossed $1.50 back to this survivor of battles in the Pacific with the comment: "You need it more than we do."

A local man, William H. Richards, was fined $1,000 "for being accessory before the fact in two abortions," with one of the women involved "already indicted by the Grand Jury." In Superior Court, William F. Dickie, a con man from Providence, R.I., was given concurrent sentences of three to five years for forgery and larceny. In his brief three-month residence in Northampton, this "smooth talker," as the Gazette referred to him, had become engaged to three girls and also passed himself off as a former major in the U.S. Marine Corps.

A lesser transgression involved the Ann August store, which had failed, due to a workman being out sick, to clear its sidewalk following a big snowstorm. A $5 fine was levied.

Meanwhile, from "somewhere in the Pacific," Pfc. James O'Connor, an army engineer, wrote to the Gazette for help in obtaining flags of the Commonwealth of Massachusetts to fly on islands where our men had fought. A Texas buddy, he wrote, had the habit of running up the Lone Star State flag every time an island was taken, and O'Connor wanted to see his own state represented. "Keep on taking islands," was the response of Governor Maurice Tobin's office, "and we'll send a lot of these flags."

The Battle Isn't Over

Following the surrender by Germany in May of 1945, ads like this one were run to remind the American people that the war in the Pacific had still to be won.

O'Connor also reported that he had been only 100 yards from the noted war correspondent Ernie Pyle when Pyle was killed on Ie Shima island on April 18, 1945. A veteran of three years in combat areas in both the European and Pacific theaters, Pyle was with the dogfaces of the 77th Infantry Division when Japanese bullets found him.

As early as August of 1944, Northampton had already begun preparations for its celebration of victory in Europe. A full month before the final German capitulation on May 8, 1945, plans were in place in Northampton for "a day of prayer and thanksgiving with all churches open at 7:30 p.m. for special services and meditation." Local merchants vowed their readiness to close their stores when the news came.

"War Ended After 2,319 Days Fighting" read a Gazette headline on May 7.

The headline writer had momentarily forgotten the Pacific theater and the struggle still ongoing there. On May 8, however, a full-page ad appeared, paid for by the Retail

Merchants Association: "Fascism is doomed! ... Blood, tears, sweat, death — all made up this fight. And now we've licked them. Germany is conquered. But ... Hold On One Moment. The battle isn't over ... we've still got the Japs to lick. Seventy million Japanese yet to be conquered. Buy War Bonds for complete victory." An illustration depicted an American soldier with his bayonet at a Japanese soldier's throat.

Immediately after V-E Day, the east coast "brown out" was ended, and in Northampton the Public Safety Committee was dissolved. "The air raid sirens ... will be taken down in the near future," announced the committee's chairman, Edward O'Brien.

News had come on May 7 of the wounding of Tech. Sgt. Stanley Shedlock, who had earlier won the Bronze Star for "gallantry and disregard for personal safety when he evacuated some wounded soldiers, under enemy fire, in France." The following day, V-E Day itself, the death of Cpl. Urban "Slim" Fleming, who had been killed in Germany on March 26, was reported.

The great national surge of public opinion demanding quick demobilization of the American military had also begun even before the year 1944 was out. "(Secretary of War) Stimson Says Men To Be Demobilized Quickly As Possible" read a Gazette headline on October 5, 1944. Rumors had apparently been floated that the war department would delay demobilization in order to prevent sudden massive unemployment. "Absolutely untrue," said Stimson. Only the need to retain enough troops to defeat the Japanese and the availability of ships would delay the procedure, he claimed. "The Army is arranging to return those eligible for demobilization as quickly as possible."

The War Department announced, in February of 1945, its plans to release up to 250,000 men per month following Germany's surrender. Already 1,600,000 had been released, or about 90,000 monthly, with many of these releases based on "certificates of disability." Within 10 months following Germany's surrender, the United States forces in Europe would be reduced from 3,500,000 to 400,000 men.

Only three months after the surrender of Germany, the atom bomb was dropped on Hiroshima and Nagasaki, and then peace came to the Pacific theater as well. On the

More War Casualties

Sgt. Stanley Shedlock's wounding was reported on May 7, 1945, followed the next day by news of Cpl. Urban Fleming's death.

Aftermath of the Atomic Bomb

This photo of the "mushroom cloud" that rose above Hiroshima following the detonation of the first atomic bomb lives forever in the minds of all who were alive at that time.

evening of August 14, after President Truman announced Japan's surrender, Northampton wildly celebrated V-J Day. "Army personnel at camps and hospitals throughout New England will be confined to their posts for two days following the announcement of V-J Day, the Army has announced," reported the Gazette. Thus it was that the end of the long struggle was celebrated — in New England at least — primarily by civilians.

McCallum's bought a full-page ad in the Gazette on August 15:

"All America has fought and worked for the great victory! We who have worked, bid WELCOME to you who have fought. The war has been long; you have fought hard and well. It's over now, and you're coming back home again. You've dreamed about it so often ... you've compared the tragic way of life enforced on people of other nations with your own well-remembered community ... well, you're coming home now ... home to all the things you've been fighting for, and we who have worked and prayed for this great day have dedicated ourselves to continuing to work with you to keep and improve everything good offered by this country to the men, women and children who people it. You'll find many things the same. We want you to find many things better. We'll back you up in peace as we did in war ... fulfilling your every hope for the kind of security you want to make the heritage of your children."

The city of Northampton celebrated the surrender of Japan with a two-day legal holiday for almost all businesses. The Gazette ran a cartoon showing a tattered Japanese flag lying in the foreground with a rising sun in the background. At the ends of the sun's rays were drawings of American fighting men with these labels on their chests: Munda, Burma, Okinawa, Midway, Shangri-La, Java Sea, Corregidor, Tarawa, Pearl Harbor, Bataan, Wake, Guadalcanal, Iwo Jima, Leyte, Coral Sea and Buna — all places where Americans had fought, suffered and died.

The Score is Paid

This cartoon in the Gazette was published the day Japan officially surrendered on August 15, 1945. Many of the major areas where American troops fought the Japanese are listed in the rays of the sun.

Events began at 7 p.m. on August 15 with the churches open for 30-minute prayer sessions which, it was reported, were not well attended. Then there was a parade from the City Hall to the fairgrounds for a program of "speaking and prayer." Three women appeared there in costume. One wore tattered garments and had painted herself to appear wounded. She wore a helmet and sported a sign reading "Back From Batan (sic)!" The other two women — clothed in black and in "black face" — carried signs reading "We Washed Up The Japs, The Saps" and "After Tonite, Back To Island."

The real action, however, had apparently taken place up on Main Street the night of the 14th. "City Goes Wild And Woolly With Peace News Joy" the Gazette reported. "Main Street Jammed With Cars, Impromptu Paraders; Paper Torn Up, Fireworks Shot Off, Tin Pans Beaten; Serpentine Dance ... For three solid hours the Main Street area was the center of a vast tumult of shouting people, automobiles with horns blowing furiously, noisemakers, firecrackers, church bells, hand-cranked sirens and whistles. At midnight a few weary people were still celebrating amidst a litter of paper and cardboard boxes that were hurled about when the din was at its loudest."

Bottles appeared, according to the Gazette, and "victory was toasted along the curb." A false fire alarm interrupted festivities at one point, and police struggled to clear a path for the fire truck trying to make its way down Main Street.

"Among the more spectacular methods of celebration was a serpentine line of younger men and women ... laughing and shouting ... who wound down the street in a line which grew to be more than a block long." Boys and girls armed with "dinner bells, horns, tin pans and spoons, and flags," wound in and out of side streets.

Nevertheless, the Gazette observed, there were "in the midst of this riot of confusion a few islands of calm. There were older people who appeared to have suffered an irretrievable loss in the war and younger ones who had obviously fought in it and would never forget it. And on the curbstone in front of City Hall sat a middle-aged woman openly weeping."

On August 15, the OPA announced the immediate termination of rationing of gasoline, canned fruits and vegetables and fuel oil. Meat rationing was expected to end by autumn. Worries about reconversion from wartime to peacetime industry were being soothed by assurances from the War Production Board that "three or four years of interrupted supply will be required to meet the pent-up civilian demand for some goods."

The Gazette reported that area plants shifting to peacetime goods were being hindered only by a lack of raw materials. "Most plants do not need to lay off any hands. The brush company is to increase personnel."

Frank Wong

Long after the Japanese surrender, groups of "draftees" continued leaving Northampton. Frank Wong, left, headed this contingent on August 20, 1945. His brother Edward was killed the previous summer aboard the U.S.S. Princeton. Frank would serve a year in the Navy and then go to Norwich University, graduating in 1951 with both his academic degree and a U.S. Army commission. He served with the Signal Corps in Korea and Vietnam. He retired 28 years later with the rank of Lt. Colonel.

Meanwhile, the world had to digest the news of the atomic bomb. A headline had screamed on the night of August 6: "U.S. Now Using An Atomic Bomb To Hit The Japs. President Truman Makes Announcement About New Bomb Which May Open Way For New Concept of Force And Power. It Produces More Than 2,000 Times Blast of Largest Bomb Ever Used. Has Power Of 20,000 Tons Of TNT ... This awful bomb is the answer, President Truman's statement said, to Japan's failure to heed the Potsdam demand that she surrender unconditionally at once or face utter destruction." On August 7 the newspaper referred to a "single terrifying bomb which possibly obliterated a Japanese military city yesterday."

Dr. Karl T. Compton, the president of Massachusetts Institute of Technology, was quoted on August 9 describing the atom bomb as "the most portentous scientific achievement in history." Compton maintained that the bomb would "actually reduce the number of lives lost in the war — certainly for America and possibly also for Japan itself if her rulers are sensible enough to realize what may be in store for them and act accordingly."

Dr. Frank G. D'Alelio, vice-president and director of research at the Prophylactic Brush Company, was disclosed to have "played a part in the most startling development of the war, the atomic bomb." D'Alelio had that morning received his official release from the Manhattan District project at Oak Ridge, Tennessee, and was now authorized to reveal his connection with the bomb. He had also, according to the Gazette, been involved with research on the legendary "bazooka" (the portable device invented to fire small armor-piercing rockets at short range). D'Alelio was also the inventor of insulation essential to the functioning of radar.

And then, in Northampton and across the nation, began the still ongoing debate concerning the morality of dropping "the bomb" on Hiroshima and Nagasaki.

Professor Hans Kohn of Smith College told the Rotary Club: "I do not feel at ease with the use of the atomic bomb. Japan was already defeated before the bomb was dropped."

On September 19, in a letter to the Gazette, Pfc. Emmett O'Leary of Northampton, stationed in New Mexico, wrote: "Being in a small way connected with the history-

The Last of the Dotted Lines

This cartoon depicts Gen. Douglas MacArthur, who presided over the surrender of Japan aboard the U.S.S. Missouri *in Tokyo Bay on September 2, 1945.*

making atomic bomb, I would like to know what Prof. Kohn meant. ... We did warn the Japanese; they wouldn't believe us: What kind of a warning did we get at Pearl Harbor? Is it possible that the professor does not realize that if Japan held the secret of the atomic bomb, she would not have hesitated one minute in using it with full force on us? I ask Prof. Kohn to stop and think of all the American men's lives which were saved in the use of this weapon."

At the end of October there arrived in Northampton a letter from a onetime resident of this city, Fannie Ono of Tokyo, Japan. It was printed in the Gazette. During the 1920s, Mrs. Ono and her husband, who died in Northampton about 1930, had operated a shop featuring high-quality Japanese imports including china and silk goods. Children loved it because fascinating hand-carved toys also were for sale there. She wrote that she had survived the war despite "the most terrible time ... we lost everything we had, clothing, bedding, household goods, etc." She was writing to Mary Kingsley, who ran the "Mary K" gift shop at 56 Center Street, to tell her that she still remembered how the people of Northampton had enabled her to return home following her husband's death. Her letter was being carried to the United States, she said, by a U.S. Army major. Her son, George, was working as an interpreter "attached to Major General Arnold of the U.S. Army."

She closed thus: "George, Mary and Edward join me in sending you best wishes and kindest regards. Sincerely, Fanny Ono."

T. Ono, Importer

The onetime location of Japanese importer T. Ono's store is seen behind this group of Hampshire County veterans viewing the Welcome Home parade of October 12, 1946.

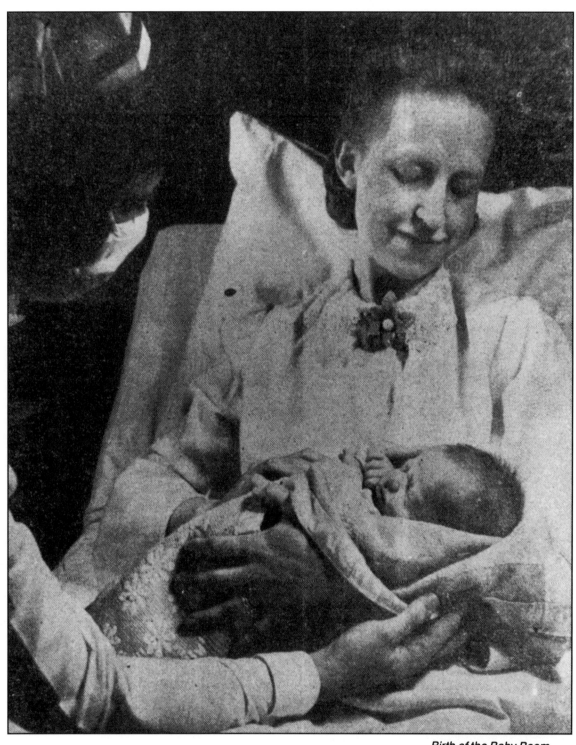

Birth of the Baby Boom

For the U.S., the fruits of victory proved to be the greatest prosperity boom in our history plus a fertility explosion that produced the "Baby Boom" generation of 76 million born between 1946 and 1964. Locally, by February of 1946, births at the Cooley Dickinson Hospital had increased 80 percent over the four-year war period. The identities of this mother and child are unknown.

1945 -1946 — The Fruits of Victory

Sgt. McKenna, writing from Tokyo in the autumn of 1945, was not the only Northampton serviceman missing the old home town. There were millions like him all over the world.

Looking ahead to the problem of eventually having to demobilize more than 10 million men and women, the U.S. Army had, back in September 1944, devised what was popularly called "the point system." Servicemen received points for the total number of months of service since September 16, 1940 (the date the Selective Service Act went into effect); the number of months served overseas; the number and kind of medals received; and the number of dependent children under 18 years, up to a limit of three children.

"The value of the point-credits will not be announced," Army officials had warned at that time, "until after the European war ends." The need for troops as occupation forces in Europe had to be considered, as well as the number of troops needed for the continuing war against Japan.

On May 10, 1945, two days after Germany's surrender, the Army announced a minimum score of 85 points for discharge of enlisted men, and the expectation that 1,300,000 men would be released over the coming 12 months. The requisite number of points had to have been reached as of Saturday, May 12, 1945.

By August 15, following the surrender of Japan, Washington officials were predicting the discharge of 7 million men during the coming year. This news was not enough to calm the anxiety of servicemen long overseas, as expressed by Pvt. Edmond Poudrier, who had returned to this country from Germany in August and then been shipped to Japan for occupation duty. In December he wrote the Gazette questioning the wisdom of keeping married men with children overseas while younger single men were apparently being spared this duty.

"This is not a 'cry baby' letter," he wrote in a second letter in March 1946, "It is a letter full of the questions which are foremost in the minds of GI dads, married men without children and single men ... questions of grave importance to thousands of men both in Japan and Germany. The Army should do more to explain its demobilization plans to servicemen," he complained: "We are told nothing until shortly before becoming eligible." The uncertainty was bad for morale, Poudrier pointed out.

Six months later, Edmond Poudrier would get his wish. He was one of eight veterans who reported in to the local draft board on August 24, following his discharge.

While Northampton men overseas concentrated on getting back home, civilians were still being drafted. In March of 1946, Northampton youths were warned "the draft is still in effect; boys must register on or before their 18th birthday." Thus groups of young men continued to leave Union Station just as they had ever since 1940.

Cecil Clark, former merchant seaman, now went to work for the Army as second cook aboard the S.S. *Sea Robin,* a new cargo ship converted into a troop carrier to bring overseas veterans home.

"Bunks were five high, and the latrines were merely long troughs — not the best of quarters," he recalled. "But our mess hall and galley were good and the food excellent. Our run was through the Strait of Gibraltar and into the Mediterranean to Marseilles. There we would pick up 1,500 men, most of them old vets of Patton's army ... many of the men were seasick; the rest played poker or threw dice ... some fellows became quite

Private Buck

A popular feature on the wartime Gazette comic pages concerned the military adventures of little "Private Buck," whose hard luck usually prevailed. Here, he finds he lacks "points" for discharge at the war's end.

Two Came Home, Three Did Not

Left to right: Staff Sgt. John Dickmyer survived the exploits of the 82nd Airborne in Sicily and Anzio, in the Netherlands and the Bulge. Lt. Earl Rodriguez survived wounding at Pearl Harbor to serve as a pilot in Europe and came home again. Aneta Kiley, Yeoman 2nd Class of the Spars (women Coast Guard volunteers), died at Chelsea Naval Hospital in July 1945. Lt. Robert Darrah, killed in action on November 23, 1944, was awarded the Silver Star posthumously for "gallantry." Pfc. Walter Siperek died in an accident in Germany in the autumn of 1945.

wealthy on the way home. Marseilles was a wild town ... one day on the street I met an old friend from Northampton, Norman Henchey, working for Stars and Stripes, the Army newspaper. He needed shoes ... and I told him I would buy some for him at home and bring them to him. This I did, and to this day I still ask him if he ever paid me the $5 for those Thom McAn shoes."

In late May 1945, Cpl. James Sullivan, who had been at Schofield Barracks in Hawaii on December 7, 1941, and had then gone on to earn battle stars for four major engagements including Guadalcanal and Luzon, was the first man from Northampton to return under the point system. Sullivan had a total of 137 points.

Lt. Earl Rodriguez, a Pearl Harbor veteran who had not been home nor seen his family in almost five years, returned in August. Lt. Col. Leon Lavallee, who had left Northampton with Company G in January 1941, returned in October, still mourning the death in Africa of one of his four sons. Maj. Charles DeRose, who had enlisted in April, 1942, and had been followed about the country by his wife and two small sons, returned in November to station WHYN where he resumed his duties as station manager.

Soldiers drifted back one by one, their names duly listed in the City News Briefs as they reported to the Selective Service Board. Forty-four reported on January 9, 1946, and 23 more two days later. After that, in groups ranging from three to nine, veterans arrived all through 1946. On June 1, the Gazette announced that William Curran of Crescent Street was "The 2,000th Local Veteran Back From Service."

To meet its developing manpower shortage, the Army began stationing recruiting sergeants in the post office lobby, as did the Navy and the Marine Corps. Not all veterans were glad to get out, the Gazette reported. Some reenlisted, including four Marines, one of whom remarked that "civilian life isn't what I thought it was going to be." Paul Brown, Lucien Fugere, Earl Lampron and James Ryan had already reenlisted in the Army.

Some local women joined their husbands in the occupation forces. Lavinia Bohnak, for example, went to Japan with her son Joseph to be with Capt. Joseph Bohnak, assigned to 24th Infantry Division headquarters. Other civilians joined the flow overseas; Claire Le Duc, a Vernon Street School math teacher, took a teaching job in Erlanger Community School in Germany.

Coast Guard Lt. Allan O'Brien, a veteran of more than three years, with two years aboard the destroyer escort U.S.S. *Mosley* as communications officer, was recalled to duty. He was obliged once again to seek a leave of absence from his high school post as a chemistry teacher. No reason was offered for his recall, but he later said he assumed the Coast Guard just needed experienced men.

Sadly, some men survived the war itself only to die of accidents or illness before discharge. Pfc. Walter Siperek died in Germany in the autumn of 1945, due to complications following a fall. Seaman 1st Class Richard Ellison, who had been aboard the U.S.S. *Begor*, one of the first ships to sail into Tokyo Bay, died of lobar pneumonia in San Diego

only a few days before he was due for discharge. 1st Sgt. Jeremiah Crane, a brother of Marine Lt. Hugh Crane, died on the way home aboard a troopship in an accident during a terrible Atlantic storm. Marine Sgt. Robert Gallivan survived combat at Guadalcanal, Bougainville, Tarawa and New Caledonia only to disappear in a severe storm on December 5, 1945, aboard a Navy torpedo bomber on a routine training flight off the coast of Florida, along with five other bombers and 27 crew members.

The families of men still listed as missing in action had long endured a special sort of anguish. At the war's end these men were finally declared dead. One such was Tech. Sgt. Michael Curtin, top-turret gunner on a B-17. Shot down on September 16, 1943, Curtin was for a long time thought possibly to have landed safely in France. At the end of August in 1945, his status was changed to KIA. Aviation Chief Radioman Parker Delaney, shot down aboard a Navy torpedo bomber near Truk atoll in the Pacific in April 1944, was finally declared dead in February of 1946.

In March of 1944 the Gazette had announced that "an unofficial shortwave broadcast from Japan" had reported that Staff Sgt. Wilfred Paquette, part of a B-25 crew missing over New Guinea as of November 27, 1943, was "alive and well and a POW in Wewak, New Guinea." This broadcast had never been confirmed, nor did any further word come through. In February 1946, a detailed report of the crash of Paquette's B-25 reached his parents after more than two years of uncertainty. The sergeant was, it stated, "now believed dead."

The war's end brought a new problem to Northampton. The number of war souvenirs sent home by servicemen caused the Gazette to warn: "Many potentially explosive souvenirs have been sent to this country, and others have been taken from war plants." The state fire marshal authorized local police, Army, Navy and Coast Guard officers "to seize and dispose of any bomb or explosive in the possession or under the control of any person." Also in the interest of public safety, "all members and veterans of the armed forces and their families are urged to register and safeguard all machine guns and similar automatic weapons brought into this country as war trophies."

In February of 1946 a large box of "souvenirs" lay unclaimed at the Northampton Post Office. The address label had been lost, and nothing remained to identify either the sender or intended recipient. How it arrived in Northampton at all, a post office spokesman said, "is something of a mystery."

For the first time in several years returning servicemen and women had to face the question of what to wear every day. Sunday suits, carefully cherished by mothers, no longer fit their veteran sons; dresses left behind by servicewomen seemed old fashioned and dowdy in contrast to their trim military uniforms. The Swiss Cleaners and Dyers on Pleasant Street ran an ad: "Attention, Veterans! your O.D. (olive drab) shirts, trousers, overcoats can now be dyed! Black, blue, green or brown." Carlson's men's store advertised: "For the Returning Veteran. In spite of the great scarcity of clothing ... men's suits

One Came Home, Four Did Not

Left to right: Sgt. Robert Gallivan, USMC, disappeared aboard a Navy torpedo bomber, December 5, 1945. Tech. Sgt. Michael Curtin, USAAC, was shot down on September 16, 1943. Aviation Chief Radioman Parker Delaney, USN, was shot down in April 1944. Staff Sgt. Wilfred Paquette, USAAC, was part of a B-25 crew that was reported missing on November 27, 1943. Donald Delaney became a radioman in the Navy, but unlike his brother Parker, he survived the war.

$23.50 up; sport coats $14.95-$22.50; slacks $5.95-$11.95."

Nearly one million foreign war brides came to this country at the war's end. Peggy Ayres Choquette, daughter of a Royal Navy officer and a former Wren, counterpart of the American WAVE, was the first of several such brides to arrive in Northampton. She and her paratrooper husband, Sgt. Lenwood Choquette, had married in 1942 just before his unit left to invade North Africa. In March 1945, she and their son John came to live with Sgt. Choquette's sister until his return. A year later, after a long wait for transport to this country, attorney John O'Connell's Australian wife Dorothy arrived safely in Springfield. Cpl. Charles Eliott and his Belgian bride Estelle were already celebrating their first anniversary in Northampton. This same year, Lt. Stanley Westort headed for New York's 5th Street Pier to meet his Dutch bride, Marianne, who arrived from Rotterdam aboard the Holland-American line's S.S. *Talisse*. They were married in Northampton's St. John Cantius Church on March 2.

The Army had conjured up a mountain of red tape designed to prevent "hasty, ill-considered marriages between lonely American soldiers and foreign women." In the autumn of 1947 former Sgt. Norman Menegat, who had accepted employment as a civilian administrator with the U.S. occupation forces in Germany to be with his German

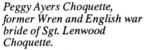

War Brides

Many obstacles and much red tape had to be overcome before Norman Menegat, a post-war civilian administrator in the German occupation, could marry his German war bride, Ingeborg, in 1947.

Peggy Ayers Choquette, former Wren and English war bride of Sgt. Lenwood Choquette.

Marianne Westort, Dutch war bride of Lt. Stanley Westort.

fiancee, Ingeborg, finally returned to Northampton with his bride. Over a two-year period Ingeborg had had to produce documents certifying that she had never been married before; that neither she nor her father had ever been affiliated with the Nazi party; that her mother was indeed her biological mother; that she had never borne an illegitimate child; that she had no police record; and that she had never had a venereal disease. She also had to undergo rigorous physical examinations. After their marriage on July 26, 1947, Menegat managed to get them both passage on the same ship, although at night they were required to sleep in separate quarters.

In June 1946, the Gazette reported "Marriages Here Nearly Double 1945 Figures." The paper was filled with photos of young women, their husbands-to-be all referred to as "veteran of Okinawa," "veteran of U.S. Marines," "veteran of South Pacific," and so on. One wedding photo showed Marine Cpl. "Peg" White and Boatswain 2nd Class Ralph

Parda of the U.S. Navy, both still in their military uniforms.

The result of this wave of marriages was the great post-World War II baby boom. In 1946, the Gazette reported that births were twice what they had been five years before. That year there were 1,084 babies born in the city — more than 200 above the previous year.

The major problem for many of the newlywed veterans was the acute housing shortage in boomtown America. Almost no housing construction had taken place during the long, grey Depression decade, and there were millions of returning veterans, all in need of homes at the same time.

On October 27, 1945, George B. O'Leary, himself a veteran and now secretary of the Northampton Chamber of Commerce, cited housing as the city's number-one problem. Many veterans, a Gazette article predicted, "may have to resort to foxholes in the Main Street Park." Local contractors could not promise any immediate relief, as building materials were still in short supply.

As a temporary solution, a "share the home" policy was proposed, and some would-be renters were said to be looking longingly at large old Northampton houses with a single occupant or elderly couple in residence. The National Housing Agency was urging such homeowners to consider conversion and remodeling to provide additional living quarters. The agency was also seeking release of building materials, without quota restrictions, for this purpose. Local applications to convert or remodel had to be filed with the Boston office of the Federal Housing Administration.

Early in 1946, the Chamber of Commerce produced a questionnaire in an effort to get a clear picture of housing conditions in Northampton. Thirty-four of the first 60 replies were from veterans living in makeshift circumstances, with 29 couples doubled up with families or friends. Half of these veterans had children, which further complicated their housing problem. Most indicated a willingness to accept temporary accommodations even if it meant living in a barracks-type or Quonset-hut dwelling. Most wanted to rent rather than to buy or build.

In April 1946, the first veteran to get a building permit was Edward Heinz, who wanted to build his house on Gleason Road for an estimated $4,500. This same month the Northampton Co-operative Bank reported it had so far made 68 new real estate loans to veterans, totaling $252,670. By the end of October 50 new houses had been started, but only about 25 were completed, primarily because of the "failure to get materials and the proper priorities."

One group of homes sold to veterans, called Cloverdale Acres, off Bridge Road in Florence, proved to have no sewers. The city refused to lay them "since the streets are only tentatively accepted." Eventually the project was completed to form a cluster of streets including Mountain Road.

In November 1946, Carrie Gauthier of the MSPCC reported how local children were being affected by the housing shortage. Evictions of rental families by new purchasers of property had become so acute that some children were being "deprived of home life and even shelter," she said. Relatives' resources were being strained to the limit, she added, and a few children had even been placed in homes for elderly poor in both Northampton and Easthampton. The Hampshire County Children's Aid Association was reporting 50 requests for shelter for evicted children.

"We have emergency shelters for cats," declared Gauthier, "but not for boys and girls." Some families within Hampshire County, she added, "are living in tents and in makeshift shanties ... it may be necessary to open schoolhouses, town halls and other public buildings to give shelter and warmth to children."

In late autumn, the local Housing Authority launched the reconstruction of six former Army barracks, each divided up into eight units to house a total of 48 veterans and their families. The federal government paid $120,000 for these barracks at Bradley Field and saw them transported to Northampton. As soon as word got out, the Housing Authority was besieged with rental requests.

Three of the units, erected on Water Street near the Coolidge Bridge, were occupied in December, with every family save one having one or more children despite the fact

Post-war Housing Shortage

One young father was so desperate for housing that he offered a reward to anyone who could come up with a rental unit for his family.

that these three-room "apartments" were designed for young married couples without babies. Another three, on Kearney Field in the Bay State section of the city, were all assigned to couples with children even before they were ready for occupancy. There was still a waiting list of 100 veterans' families. One veteran ran an ad in the Gazette offering a $50 reward to anyone who could help him find a place for him and his family to live.

Makeshift Veterans' Housing

Margaret Parda holding her daughter, Pat. In the background is a neighbor's child, Joey Peters. Some Northampton veterans considered themselves fortunate to find temporary homes in old Army barracks. "Peg" and Ralph Parda, a Marine and a Navy veteran respectively, lived in a unit near the Coolidge Bridge. "None of us had much of anything," Peg said, "but we shared all we had with each other. Those were good years. Caesar McDonald, for example, would bang on the wall and yell, 'Come on over. We've got spaghetti enough for all of us.'"

The master and journeymen plumbers' union of the city agreed to help speed up the barracks project by assigning "four or five men from the local shops ... for three days a week until the entire project is completed."

In this period a wire photo in the Gazette showed approximately a thousand veterans sleeping in a Los Angeles park under signs reading: "Homes For Vets — That's a Joke."

In Washington, John W. Snyder, federal reconversion director, had predicted on August 15, 1945, that the conversion from a wartime to a peacetime economy would take 12 to 18 months, and had also warned that "only a peacetime construction vastly expanded over anything this or any other nation has ever seen" would make jobs possible for all those willing to work plus ensure an ever-rising standard of living. "The problem," remarked another government spokesman, "is how to get the vets back to work without throwing a lot of other workers out of jobs at the same time." President Truman declared, "The emergency is as great as it was on December 7, 1941."

American industry had begun feeling the pinch as soon as war contracts were canceled following the surrender of Germany and Japan. It was expected, however, that the long pent-up demand for consumer goods would fuel the post-war economy, and Frederick Hawkes of the U.S. Employment Service told people in the Northampton area that he was expecting fewer layoffs here than elsewhere. Still, Northampton's Mayor Edmond Lampron joined other western Massachusetts mayors in urging congressmen to help keep as much of the Army's small arms works as possible at the Springfield Armory.

By the end of 1946, Prophylactic Brush Company in Florence had rehired 96 veterans who were former employees, as well as 330 other veterans. The Propper-McCallum Hosiery Co., Inc. was appealing to "disabled veterans and young women" to learn a "highly skilled trade. Earn while you learn!" Wages offered were 67 cents to 73 cents an hour for learners, and experienced operators could earn up to $1 an hour. A local "super market" was seeking clerks to train as managers, with a five-day week, free life insurance, vacations with pay and a "sickness salary."

More than 100 veterans applied for work at the post office during the 1946 Christmas rush. Civil Service jobs "Are Now Open To Vets Exclusively," advised the Gazette, based on the Veterans' Preference Act of 1944.

Robert Andrews, who had entered the Army early in 1941, been wounded at Guadalcanal and hospitalized before his discharge in 1944, was the first area WWII veteran to open his own business. In September, 1945, he started The Busy Corner Restaurant in the Goodwin block at the corner of Main and North Maple Streets in Florence.

Early in 1946, Edward O'Dea, managing editor of the Gazette, wrote an optimistic feature predicting a "Bright Outlook For Industry In City." He said that a survey of local plants disclosed that the only stumbling block to a smooth conversion to peacetime production was obtaining raw materials. Local plants that were hiring included the Prophylactic Brush Company; International Silver; Norwood Engineering; Propper-McCallum Hosiery; Grant Paper Products; Northampton Cutlery; Clement Manufacturing; Frank Bartlett and Sons; Florence Casket; Amherst Blanket; Hampshire Paper Box; Berkshire Hat Corporation and The Decker Foundry. Three local institutions — Smith College, the State Hospital and the Veterans' Hospital — "are undermanned and have been throughout most of the war period."

An article in the Gazette on December 31 cited 1946 as "A Year of Records in Massachusetts," a year that "hit new highs in population, jobs, wages, marriages, and divorces." Employment in the Commonwealth was at a record high of 1,430,000 (excluding 400,000 government, domestic and farm workers not required to report under Social Security). Citizens had paid approximately $1.5 billion in state and federal taxes.

Frederick Hawkes was discovering that few veterans were interested in work as agricultural laborers, which meant that the WWII labor shortage still persisted on area farms. Hawkes also discovered that rather than take a job, some veterans preferred to join what came to be called the "52-20 Club": under the GI Bill, veterans could draw $20 per week for 52 weeks. In May of 1946 he reported 900 veterans from the Northampton area

Transition From War to Peace

The great military machine that had turned millions of American youths into fighting men overnight now turned them loose to start new lives. Asked his previous job when he applied for unemployment insurance under the GI Bill, one Northampton resident, William Coffey, replied, "Hired killer for Uncle Sam."

V.A. Contact Representative

Leo Golash, Jr., former U.S. Army officer, served as contact representative for Northampton for the Veterans Administration.

drawing this "readjustment compensation," while "75-100 good jobs open to veterans are going wanting."

At a meeting of veterans, Hawkes advised, "The average veteran is aiming much too high. There are no openings for bank presidents or for chairmen of boards of directors. But there are many good, well-paying jobs." It was the disabled veterans, Hawkes declared, "who seem to be the most anxious and willing to go back to work."

Many veterans were attracted to the educational benefits provided by the GI Bill, and it has been said that this created a whole new middle class in the United States, made up of university graduates whose parents had never dreamed of higher education for themselves. Veterans received $500 a year for tuition and books plus a $50 subsistence check for single veterans and $75 for married ones, later raised to $65 and $90. One former Marine from Northampton studying at Boston University, however, found her $65 subsistance check inadequate and hit the press with her lament: "It just can't be done," Phyllis Lotreck declared.

Early in 1946 a survey disclosed that New England's colleges and universities were crammed by a record enrollment of 67,000 students, with thousands being turned away. Northampton High School reported four veterans enrolled at the end of 1945, three picking up where they had left off on entering the service and one taking post-graduate courses to gain necessary credits to enter college. A year later, 47 veterans showed up for "refresher courses."

Northampton was the first city in the state to establish a district Veterans' Service Center, which operated under Director Harold Kneeland in the former high school building. Here information was available concerning insurance, pensions, mustering-out pay, gratuity pay, death pensions for widows of servicemen and other benefits under the GI Bill. Here veterans could also obtain photocopies of their discharges.

On January 22, 1947, Leo Golash Jr., Veterans' Administration contact representative for Northampton, reported that 3,148 veterans and their dependents had received assistance at the V.A. contact office during the previous six months.

On October 22, 1946, Russell Smith — who had lost a leg in the landing at Anzio in 1944 — became the first amputee veteran in Hampshire County to receive a custom-

Amputee Veteran Accepts Car

Russell Smith, third from left, who lost a leg during the landing at Anzio, was presented a specially adapted hydromatic drive car by a grateful government. With him are Donald Downey, left, and Leo Golash, contact representatives for the Veterans' Administration, and Kathleen Fallon of Childs Motor Sales.

From Marine "Ace" to Mayor

Northampton Mayor Edwin Olander, former U.S. Marine Corps fighter pilot, beside his post-war residence at 21 Massassoit Street. The same house had for many years been the home of Calvin Coolidge, himself once the Mayor of Northampton.

made automobile. The 1946 Oldsmobile cost $12,000, and had been modified for use by an amputee.

WWII veterans soon discovered that the traditional veterans' organizations were competing for their membership, but many of them opted instead for two organizations of their own creation. One, the American Veterans Committee, with its creed of "citizen first: veteran second," did not endure down through the years. The other, the World War II Veterans Association, celebrated the grand opening of its club headquarters over Keefe's Package Store at 125A Pleasant Street in April of 1946.

Certain mothers of local soldiers also felt the need to organize as the United War Mothers of America, Inc., to provide hospitality and do community work for veterans in Northampton. This group was headed up by Dora Ouimet, whose son Robert had served in the Navy and son Roy had served in the Coast Guard.

In September, Edwin Olander, the U.S. Marine Corps fighter pilot who had earned the title of "Ace" when he shot down his fifth Japanese Zero, was elected mayor of Northampton, with 4,100 votes to 2,936 votes for his Democratic opponent, George D. Adler. Olander was the first Republican elected to the job since 1938 and, at age 29, he was the 32nd and youngest mayor in the city's history. In his campaign he particularly urged younger voters and those who had been in the armed services to exercise the franchise.

On December 31, 1946, another WWII veteran announced his own political ambitions when Gen. Dwight D. Eisenhower was reported "ready to run" for the nation's highest office: "I will run for President if the people of the country want me to run," the general was quoted as saying.

Not all the returning veterans were able to pick up their lives where they had left off. Tom Hogan, Iwo Jima survivor, recalled that he was "all messed up for a long time." He remembered feeling guilty, asking himself "How come I'm alive when so many of my friends were killed?" Raymond LaBarge said that it took him "a long time to settle down. It wasn't easy for me." Salvatore Polito recalled how pre-war relationships seemed strained after he returned home. "What's the matter with you? You're so different, so changed," people would say to him.

One man from Northampton leaped from the fifth floor of the Hotel Commodore in New York City; another veteran hanged himself in the Amherst police station; another shot himself in Chesterfield; while still another hanged himself at the Veterans' Hospital. One veteran, whose family had attempted to help him at home, eventually had to be taken under restraint to the Veterans' Hospital. He kicked the rear window of the police car out en route. After some months of treatment he was able to return home to civilian life.

Many WWII veterans found release in nightly "pub crawling" among the numerous bars, nightclubs and hotels in the area. A favorite hangout, Rahar's on Old South Street,

Pvt. O'Keefe, 101st Airborne

Pvt. Patrick "Pat" O'Keefe of the 101st Airborne Division, who once delivered telegrams after school to families of servicemen. At age 19, he was stationed in Joigny, France.

even concocted a special free drink for returned servicemen that consisted of red, white and blue liqueurs layered off a spoon into a glass. "And the girls were where the boys were," recalled Pat O'Keefe, a paratrooper who returned from Europe in the spring of 1946 after service with the 101st Airborne Division.

O'Keefe remembered the summer of 1946 clearly. "Excitement was in the air. There were seldom war stories. Instead, everyone wanted to be singing, laughing, smoking, drinking beer from glasses, pitchers, bottles, cans — however it came; and liquor if you could afford it. There were endless greetings of old friends back from service ... there was a continual scraping of chairs as people visited at tables where room would be made for one more ... all the old drinking songs were brought out including 'Drink-chug-a-lug' and the Yale Whiffenpoof song ... groups moved from bar to bar, particularly at closing time. Sometimes parties continued in private homes. On balance, it was a great catharsis for the war years. In a sense, it washed the war away."

During those boozy, gregarious evenings, a few veterans would absorb more than they

Northampton Police Department Circa 1935

Sgt. Cornelius O'Keefe, standing second from left in the front row, in a 1930s group photo of the local police force.

were able to handle. Court reports in the Gazette each day referred to "wet driving" offenses, sometimes under a heading such as: "Newly Discharged Servicemen Given Break In Court." In one case, two veterans, trying to shake the police cruiser following them, ended up on Union Street with their car resting on someone's front lawn. They were merely fined. In another case, when a police officer was assaulted by a still-uniformed veteran and his two civilian brothers, the civilians were each fined $35 while the "Army man is let off," the newspaper reported.

"Cops Repel Mob At Police Station ... Sgt. O'Keefe Has To Threaten With Gun," a headline proclaimed another day. "Officers Have To Use Nightsticks." This incident began at a dance in White Eagle Hall where police were called to quell a disturbance. Among the group of 25 drunken revelers — many from out of town — who showed up at the police station to "liberate" four arrested Army men were several other soldiers, a sailor and assorted civilians. When the mob demanded the four be released, Sgt. Cornelius O'Keefe drew his sidearm and, the Gazette reported, "threatened to shoot any man who advanced another step."

One topic of conversation among revelers during those summer nights concerned the strange chance meetings of local men and women that had taken place in various theaters of war around the world. During 1943, for example, the Curran brothers, George and

Meeting in New Guinea

Typical of the chance meetings young servicemen experienced around the globe during WWII was this one shared in New Guinea by, left to right, Robert Berube, Ned Sullivan and Donald LeBeau —all in the Army Air Corps and all from Northampton.

Richard, had spotted each other on different ships exiting the Panama Canal. That same year Donald Organ of Florence and Gordon Nash of Williamsburg had met at the American Club in Northampton, England. Out in New Guinea, Donald LeBeau had accidentally released a lever in the belly of a B-25 on the airstrip only to have Ned Sullivan of Forbes Avenue tumble out at his feet. Ed Olander, while censoring mail at a small Pacific outpost, had come across a letter written by Charles Woods and arranged a meeting.

The following year the Baj brothers, Matthew and Stanley, had met in England; cousins Lawrence LeBeau and Frank Shumway had met in Italy; Pat and Myron Allen had met in England; and aboard a Coast Guard attack-transport off Saipan, two former neighbors in Mt. Tom, Chester Pliska and Stanley Siwy, had discovered each other. In 1945, Stanley Golash had run into Pat Kaminski at Landshut in Germany, while on Christmas day that year four Bay State residents had met up on board a ship in the south Pacific: Albert Bourdon, John Coopee, Albert Cullen and George O'Brien. The Zehelski brothers of Hatfield, who had shipped out of Le Havre in France that same month, had discovered each other up on deck on their last day at sea. Two of the six Lococo brothers, all in the service, had enjoyed a reunion in an American Army hospital in England during the war. Charles, whose eardrums were punctured and draining, found a nurse at his bedside one morning ready to "prep" him for eye surgery. "Eye surgery?" he gasped. "There's nothing wrong with my eyes." The nurse checked her charts again and discovered that the patient scheduled for eye surgery was one Nicholas Lococo — Charles' brother. The two had unknowingly been on different floors of the same hospital.

"Finally, the summer swung into fall," remembered O'Keefe, "and those who were headed back to college were gone by the end of September. Thanks to the GI Bill, there were more young men and women off to college than Northampton had ever experienced. It had been a glorious summer ... others were getting married ... very gradually the veterans were settling down. Few ever stayed with the 52-20 Club for the full 52 weeks. Either they took jobs offered or went looking for jobs. ... By the end of the following year, 1947, Northampton had absorbed its veterans."

Despite the prevailing shortage of new cars and all kinds of appliances, Hampshire County's retail sales in 1946 totaled $28,071,000, compared to $16,794,000 in 1945. This amounted to $1,120 per resident, as compared with the U.S. average of $692, the New England states' average of $825, and Massachusetts' average of $835.

A "monumental Christmas shopping spree," according to the Gazette, literally stripped the shelves of local stores. The "surging crowds" on the sidewalks and "a continual traffic jam" in the streets required police action.

The men and women who went off to military service had left a small, pleasant New England city still blighted by the Great Depression. Now we came back, all through 1946 and 1947, some from countries devastated and starving, to a country prosperous, complacent, self-engrossed and seemingly obsessed with the pursuit of consumer goods.

Veterans accustomed to scraping their leftovers into tin cans held by skeletal children abroad now observed the stateside phenomenon of the nylon and butter lines. "Six Pairs of Nylons By Next July For Every Woman In The Country Is The OPA's Goal" announced a headline in February 1946. In April, this feverish demand hit Northampton with the arrival of the new Clear Weave shop at 116-118 Main Street. The announcement of the grand opening was on April 5, and the following day a long line had already formed, creating what the Gazette called "the Main Street gauntlet — a tribal scene." Finally, an injunction against Clear Weave was sought, but Judge Thomas Hammond instead persuaded the hosiery shop to pay for a special police officer to control the crowd.

The butter line in front of S.K. Ames, also on Main Street, was equally feverish. "Holding the Line New Main Street Sport For Spring," the Gazette declared. Sgt. Mary Daley, just returned from devastated Berlin where she had carefully saved mess hall scraps for starving children, volunteered to aid her mother by standing in the line for butter. An impatient civilian shopper turned to Daley and groaned, "You can't imagine what we have gone through here in Northampton."

Such scenes had an unforeseen effect, as shown in a newspaper story concerning one Viola Lenard of Medford, Massachusetts, recently returned from New Guinea. "In the

A Strange Overseas Meeting

Sgt. George Sears of Company G, 104th Regiment, 26th (Yankee) Division, experienced perhaps the most unusual "reunion" of Northampton residents. In a battle-wrecked German town, he and a buddy discovered three terrified young women in the cellar of a bombed-out house. One of them named streets in Northampton, described the college "Quad" and recalled favorite student haunts like Rahar's, the bar in the Draper Hotel and even Johnny Green's, another popular local night spot. She had studied at Smith College before the war.

Army I lined up for chow," she said, "but nobody was pushing and shoving to get ahead ... I don't know what the war did to people, but it changed them. Everybody at home has gone crazy over luxuries ... I did my best to get adjusted to civilian life, but after two months of it, it's no go." Lenard, who had been awarded a Bronze Star, had just reenlisted in the United States Army.

A Sergeant Reenlists

American war veterans, who came of age during the Great Depression, came back home to a greatly changed society: affluent, materialistic, consumer-driven. Some rejected the new post-war lifestyle and reenlisted in the military. Among them was Sgt. Viola Lenard of Medford, Mass., seated fourth from left, who had been awarded the Bronze Star for service in New Guinea. She shipped out shortly after this photo was taken in 1944.

Epilogue

Off and on throughout 1946, the citizens of Northampton contemplated some way of acknowledging the contribution of their World War II veterans, and particularly of honoring the 112 men and women from the city who had died in that war. On Memorial Day, Alderman Willard Hodges suggested that $15,000 be raised, through public subscription, for such a memorial.

The following August, it was announced that donation boxes for public contributions had been placed about the city and, according to Hodges, the Military Affairs Committee of the City Council, together with local veterans' organizations, would decide on the specific details of the memorial. A fortnight later, the committee announced a meeting "to discuss the means of establishing a *living* memorial." Every veterans' and military organization in the city, the announcement said, had agreed to be involved in a discussion of "the best means of establishing a living memorial and possibly honoring the soldiers in a parade or some other form of activity."

One popular early memorial proposal was for a public swimming pool. Letters of appeal were sent out to "every military and civic organization in the city," and a general committee, including 10 councilmen, was organized with Ralph Levy, chairman of the Retail Merchants Committee, as its head.

A newspaper article at the end of August said that now $50,000 was being sought "for a memorial to World War II veterans." The next day this was corrected to "the veterans of all wars" — despite the fact that Northampton's war dead through the Civil War had long been listed on scrolls and on bronze plaques in the lobby of Memorial Hall, which was dedicated to them in 1874.

Honor Roll

By the end of WWII, there were almost 3,000 names of Northampton's young servicemen and women inscribed on the wood-panel Honor Roll in front of Memorial Hall. Some were marked with gold stars indicating their deaths.

Early in September, a Veterans' Memorial Fund was finally established, with Elbert Arnold of the First National Bank as chairman of the finance committee. The money to be raised was to be "primarily for a memorial here ... and secondarily to provide ... a welcome home celebration," according to the Gazette.

"Give what you can to the Veterans' Memorial Fund. They gave. Now it is our turn to give to them. Let's make Northampton proud of her sons and daughters," declared a paid advertisement on September 9.

One Who Did Not Return

Cpl. Arthur Pruzynski is remembered today by his family through this photo taken on his last furlough home. A Northampton State Hospital building is named after him.

Three days later, another meeting was held during which a public swimming pool, a memorial building for veterans, renovation of the old high school building for a veterans' home and a complete renovation of Memorial Hall with an addition to house veterans' organizations were all suggested as fitting memorials. One local citizen, Sam Michelman, "a prominent Democrat," suggested that a monument to Calvin Coolidge would make a good memorial. Veterans' groups added further suggestions: a new childrens' ward for the Cooley Dickinson Hospital; a recreation building, with athletic equipment, in the city's center; a new memorial building similar to Holyoke's; a bronze and granite monument on the Forbes Library grounds.

A few young men killed in WWII had already been remembered as a part of a new east wing at the Cooley Dickinson Hospital earlier in the year. The Daily Hampshire Gazette and its employees had contributed toward a "modernized waiting room and adjoining admitting office" on the first floor in memory of their onetime employee, Pfc. William "Vinnie" Karparis. The Northampton Cutlery Company and its officers gave a room in memory of Lt. Charles Ksieniewicz. Butler and Ullman, Inc., provided a semi-private room in memory of 1st Sgt. Bernard Jackimczyk. Former fellow workers of Pvt. Francis Ansanitis at Propper-McCallum hosiery gave a bed in his memory, as did the mother of Sgt. Benjamin Angotti in honor of her son.

At the Northampton State Hospital, a new building was dedicated in memory of Cpl. Arthur Pruzynski, the first hospital employee to go off to the war. Pruzynski died in

Door-to-Door

When funds were slow coming in for the city's official "Welcome Home" celebration for Northampton's returning service men and women, Mary O'Keefe went door-to-door and raised more than $300.

Germany in 1945. While that building still stands and is in use today, the post-WWII east wing of the Cooley Dickinson Hospital was converted to offices in the late 1970s, and the names of the men once memorialized there are gone with the wind.

As time went on, the concept of a memorial to all the dead of WWII likewise apparently went with the wind. What the city of Northampton ended up with instead was a lavish Welcome Home celebration staged on Saturday, October 12 — Columbus Day, already a legal holiday. Even this endeavor initially was hampered by considerable controversy as well as a lack of donations. One soldier's mother, Mary O'Keefe, wife of police Sgt. Cornelius O'Keefe, grew impatient and herself solicited money door-to-door, raising more than $300.

Finally, the event was held on a grey overcast day dampened by light rain. Heavier rain in the evening cancelled the "gigantic display of fireworks" planned for Look Park.

"One thousand strong, local veterans of Army, Navy, Coast Guard and Marine Corps service marched at the head of the colorful procession that left Northampton High School shortly after 10 o'clock," reported the Gazette that evening. "They halted briefly at Memorial Hall while veterans assembled at the Honor Roll to pay their respects with a volley of shots to their comrade dead, and then proceeded to occupy the Main Street bleachers erected especially for their convenience." More than 30 musical units performed in the parade, and civic and business groups mounted colorful floats. Flowers were dropped from the air by planes from the aeronautics school at LaFleur Airport. Disabled veterans rode in cars, and a group of "Gold Star Mothers," women whose sons

Remembering the Dead

During the big "Welcome Home" parade at war's end, Northampton's men and women WWII veterans paused at the Honor Roll to remember their 112 comrades who were lost in that conflict.

had been killed, sat in a special section reserved for them in front of City Hall.

Among those who marched that day was a four-footed Marine veteran, King 310, with his fellow Marine and handler on Okinawa, Lucien Vanasse.

The parade ended at the Three County Fairgrounds, where U.S. Senator David Walsh and Congressman Charles Clason gave addresses that were mercifully short due to the "driving, wind-swept rain" which started to fall as the parade ended. The program included a turkey dinner for all the veterans, prepared by women of the Edwards Church. They had to stand in line to be served, a familiar story to most of them.

What Price Glory?

Pvt. Edward Rydenski was killed in France on August 19, 1944. In 1947, in the city where he was born and raised, his name was rejected as a street name because of the "ski" at the end of it.

Hero of the Battle of the Streets

Joseph LoBello had the courage to point out precisely why certain Northampton residents were rejecting new street names like Rydenski and Conz even though they were intended to honor men killed in the war.

After this big Welcome Home bash, proposals for any sort of permanent war memorial apparently died out. The following year they would be revived, however, in what turned out to be a lengthy and ultimately shameful controversy that grew out of the renaming of certain local streets.

Early in 1947, Fire Chief Gerald Dalton went before the Northampton Planning Board to warn that the city's duplicate street names posed a danger when his department had to respond quickly to an emergency. A few days later, the Veterans of Foreign Wars proposed that new street names be selected from the list of Northampton men of WWII "who paid with their lives, regardless of nationality, creed or color."

One street proposed for a name change was Maple Street, since there was also a Maple Street in Florence. Joseph LoBello, treasurer of the Boston Fruit Store at 235 Main Street and a resident of Wilson Avenue off Maple Street, suggested that it be renamed after Staff Sgt. Alfred Conz, who had grown up at 32 Maple Street in the round house that was a familiar city landmark. Conz's plane had gone down off Italy on August 22, 1943.

At a Planning Board meeting on March 8, Stephen Pilat, the decorated former platoon sergeant who had once wiped out a seven-man nest of German snipers in Germany, proposed that Northampton's Spring Street be renamed for Pfc. Robert Finn, who had been killed in Italy on October 5, 1944. Another veteran proposed that Water Street in Florence be renamed for Pvt. Edward Rydenski, who had been killed in France on August 19, 1944. One meeting participant, Arthur Donovan, however, suggested that the name Rydenski was "too long and confusing." Three days later, a letter to the Gazette from Robert Bean proposed that Spring Street in Florence be renamed after Pvt. Lawrence Cave, who had gone down before a German machine gun nest in France on July 9, 1944.

Soon afterward, attorney Edwin Dunphy, chairman of the Planning Board, told the Gazette that "in order to prevent confusion" the board would not announce its decisions on names "until the new street signs are prepared and ready to be installed." He added that using some names of servicemen killed in the war would be considered.

On June 25, 1947, the Gazette announced: "Names of 24 Streets Are Changed; New Signs Are Now Being Erected." The article explained that "the names of some of the oldest streets in the city were changed and although there was no official explanation ... it is known that some of them were named for World War II heroes of the city."

The account went on to say that in addition to Cave, Conz, Finn and Rydenski, street signs bearing the names Curtin and Ryan were ready to be installed. Tech. Sgt. Michael Curtin's plane had gone down over France on September 6, 1943, and Lt. James Ryan had been killed in a training accident in May that same year.

Then on July 10, the Gazette disclosed that residents on the new Conz, Curtin and Rydenski streets were protesting their street names to the Planning Board. Petitions had been circulated and signed, although "at least one veteran of World War II on Rydenski Street has refused outright to sign the petition circulated on his street." The next day it was reported that residents of Cave Street in Leeds, formerly Center Street, were also expressing dissatisfaction with their street's new name.

Dunphy was reported to be "besieged with protests by irate residents of some newly named streets." Out of 32 residents of Conz Street, 28 signed a petition refusing to accept a name change. Some residents of Curtin Street, formerly Holyoke Street in Florence, proposed their street instead be renamed O'Donnell after the late mayor. Others proposed the name Straw for Tech. Sgt. Willard Straw, killed in France on November 30, 1944.

The "Battle of the Streets" raged on through July, to the point where Alderman George McCarthy filed an ordinance with the city clerk proposing to take away altogether the Planning Board's authority to change street names. His measure, moreover, provided that "street names as of January 1, 1946, would be retained and no changes made except on petition of two-thirds of property owners on the street concerned; also, renaming authority would be returned to the board of survey."

Fate of the Cave Street Sign

To express displeasure over the naming of Cave Street for Pvt. Lawrence Cave, who was killed in action in France, someone mutilated the sign at one end of the street, and, at the other end, uprooted the sign and left it on the ground.

Representatives from the streets involved were then invited to come up with new names that were acceptable to them. Eighty percent of the residents of Rydenski Street voted to change their street's name to Ryden Street, and even presented their check for $15 to the Planning Board to pay for the cost of changing the sign and the city maps. This maneuver roused the ire of Charles Tomaszewski, "formerly 324th Infantry," who wrote the Gazette: "The residents of (Water) Rydenski Street in Florence have demonstrated poor taste in attempting to slight the late Edward Rydenski, his family, and all the 'ski's' whose names appear on the honor roll, by calling it 'Ryden' Street. ... Theirs is so small a concession to make in contrast to the dead who gave their all. ... We all must sympathize with the families of those men who are being antagonized by these shameless proceedings."

A clue to the feelings of those families is found in a letter from the parents of Alfred Conz, published in the Gazette on July 22:

"With reference to the change in the name of Maple Street, there has been so much controversy ... that we feel we should make public our views on the subject. When the proposal was made to rename the street in honor of our son, who was killed in the war, we felt that it was a fine gesture to his memory and to the sacrifice he made. He had lived his entire life on the street and, we always thought, was liked and respected by all the residents who knew him. For the past 10 days or so, however, there has been so much criticism and bickering over the change to 'Conz Street' that out of respect to our son's memory we ask that the name 'Conz Street' be withdrawn without further discussion. The voters and residents of the street are now in a position to choose another name for Maple Street.

Yours very truly,

A. M. Conz, Ida M. Conz"

Joseph LoBello, who had first proposed the name Conz Street, observed: "I don't want to think that the objection to Conz and Rydenski as street names is because they are foreign-sounding names. I hope it isn't true."

Symbolic of this whole affair is a photo that appeared in the Gazette on November 1, 1947. Ostensibly as a Halloween prank, someone had mutilated the Cave Street sign at one end of the street; while at the other end, both post and sign had been uprooted altogether. Thus the name of Lawrence Cave lay in the dirt.

That autumn, the City Council tabled the plan to take away the Planning Board's authority to rename city streets, and the controversy gradually subsided — but not without wounded feelings left behind.

In January, 1948, new street names were once again announced in the Gazette. The names Bardwell, for Lt. Allan Bardwell, killed in action in Germany on May 4, 1945; Conz, Finn, Keyes, Ryan and Straw had been selected or retained. Set aside, however, were the names Cave, Curtin and Rydenski. Cave Street in Leeds became Upland Road; Holyoke Street in Florence from Locust Street south became Berkshire Terrace rather than Curtin Street; and Rydenski Street became Willow Street.

On December 17, 1947, the wooden Honor Roll that had stood in front of Memorial Hall throughout the war, inscribed with the names of Northampton's servicemen and

The Honor Roll Heads for the Scrap Heap

On December 17, 1947, the wooden Honor Roll in front of Memorial Hall, a dominant Main Street feature all through WWII, was dismantled and turned over to the Board of Public Works for use as scrap lumber. Gold stars marked 112 names as those of war dead.

women, was dismantled. The materials were taken to the city yards to be used as scrap lumber by the Board of Public Works.

In 1947 the people of Florence dedicated a memorial to their veterans of World War I and World War II, and "in honor of those who served in all other wars and in memory of those who have died in the armed forces of our country." Soil from seven WWII battlefields was added to the site of this memorial at the intersection of Park and Meadow streets.

In Leeds Memorial Park, opposite the Leeds School, citizens added a WWII memorial to an already existing one for WWI. Later, memorials for Korea and Vietnam were added there as well. Today the four bronze plaques on four stones bear the names of those from Leeds who served. The names of those who died are starred.

Unlike those of Florence and Leeds, the citizens of the rest of Northampton for many years did not create a tangible commemoration of their war dead since the Civil War. The names of those young people of Northampton who died in the Spanish-American War, World War I, World War II, the Korean War and in Vietnam were remembered only by their comrades and surviving members of their families. There were blocks of stone here and there, with all-purpose inscriptions such as "to the veterans of all wars," but nothing with the names of the dead, with one exception. The 500 parishioners of St. John Cantius Church lost 20 of their sons, and they chose to remember them with a granite memorial, listing their names, in front of that church on Hawley Street.

However, the same event that led to the writing of this book — the sparsely attended ceremony on the 45th anniversary of Pearl Harbor — also led to the formation of a private group, Northampton Remembers, Inc., which erected in front of Memorial Hall a granite monument listing not only all the 112 Northampton men and women who died in World War II but also those (heretofore unlisted) who died in the Spanish-American War, World War I, and the wars in Korea and Vietnam.

***

"Old soldiers never die, never die, never die,
Old soldiers never die, they just fade away."

These are the last lines of an old song that we who served in the Army during WWII learned early. Some of us even altered the last line: "Old soldiers never die. Young ones do."

The obituary pages of American newspapers today attest that, as a generation, we are indeed fading away. It is touching to see how frequently these obituaries include references to battles, ships, squadrons, theaters of war, divisions, military decorations for valor and the like.

As young people growing up here in Northampton during the 1920s and 1930s we were fascinated by the old Civil War veterans who appeared each year — in ever dwindling numbers — in our Decoration Day parades in May. They rode in open cars and waved their broad-brimmed dark-blue campaign hats at us as we stood along Main Street. Finally only Alphonso Witherell was left. And on May 30, 1943, like all those of us who had gone off to serve in WWII, old Mr. Witherell failed to appear. The following February he died, the last man in Northampton of the Grand Army of the Republic which had once numbered more than 400,000 men.

One of these days the last man or woman of Northampton's WWII veterans will likewise fall out of formation. Who, one wonders, will this be?

Northampton Remembers

The monument to Northampton's dead in five wars was built by Northampton Remembers, Inc. The dedication was conducted on October 18, 1992.

What was the last thing to unlearn?
Not the acceptance of superior word,
Nor the cancelled Self nor the wrath,
Nor the habit of apes,
Nothing like these.
It was a knavish, yardbird trick
Of living in each separate mite of Time —
And thanking God for it.

After Being Discharged
by Howard Griffin

Photography and graphics credits

Allen, Leonard: 132 (bottom left)
Ansanitis, Edward: 46 (bottom center)
Associated Press: 4 (bottom), 5 (top & bottom right), 8, 9 (top right), 10, 15 (bottom right), 17 (top right), 18, 19, 21, 24 (bottom), 127 (top right), 150 (center), 153 (bottom)
Atwood, Roger: 82 (right)
Balicki, Janet LoBello: 175 (top right)
Banister, Marvin: 62 (left)
Beckman, Kenneth: 70 (center)
Begin, Bernard: 112 (center)
Berube, Robert: 169
Bishop, Russell: 131 (second from left)
Bitner, George: 115 (center right)
Bonneau, Joseph: 70 (top left)
Borowski, Charles: 71 (bottom right)
Brooks, Philip: 121 (bottom right)
Bruscoe, Dorothy Hibbard: 28
Cave, Morris: 104 (top right)
Chabot, Victor: 77
Clarke, Cecil: 48
Coogan, Felixa: 22 (top), 25, 42
Corbett, Mary: 98
Coyle, James: 107 (center right)
Cox, Elsa: 118 (all)
Crane, Helena: 126
Daily Hampshire Gazette: 5 (center right), 6 (top), 12, 16 (left), 17 (bottom), 29 (bottom right), 33 (both), 34, 35, 37, 39 (top right), 40, 43 (all), 44 (center left), 45 (top right), 46 (center left & right), 47 (top right & center right), 55 (both), 56 (both), 57 (all), 59 (top), 60, 65, 78 (bottom left), 79, 83, 85 (both), 86, 87 (left), 94 (all), 96 (bottom left), 100 (all), 104 (top center), 108 (top left), 113, 116 (top left), 120 (all), 121 (top right), 123, 124, 128, 131 (left, center, right & second from right), 134 (first, second & third from left), 135 (bottom), 138 (top left), 139 (bottom left), 143 (both), 144 (center), 146, 147, 148 (both), 149 (all), 150 (bottom left), 152, 153 (both, top right), 154, 155, 156, 158, 159, 160 (all), 161 (all), 162 (top & bottom left), 163, 165, 166 (both), 167 (top), 170, 174 (bottom), 175 (top left), 176, 177, 179
Dialessi, Stacia: 134 (right)
Dragon, Veronica: 67 (top right)
Driscoll, Helen: 59 (bottom right)
Duga, Anna and Paul Jr.: 39 (bottom right)
Fabisiak, Anna: 129
Feldman, Joseph & Ethel: 80
FitzGerald, John E., Jr.: 111
Foley, Patricia: 164
Forbes Library: 7 (top right), 9 (bottom), 13 (both), 14 (all), 15 (bottom left), 52, 53, 58 (all), 61, 117 (center), 121 (center), 125, 142, 157, 168, 172
Garvey, Richard: 4 (top left), 11, 30 (top left)
Greenberg, Stanley: 95 (top right)
Grimes, John & Joanna Hathaway: 96 (top)
Gross, Edward: 57 (center)
Gustavis, Robert: 73 (top)
Gutowski, William: 75, 151 (both)

Hammel, Marie: 110
Historic Northampton: 5 (center right), 51, 78 (top), 114
Hogan, Thomas: 30 (top center)
Hood, Lucille: 62 (center & right)
INS/UPI: 84
International Silver (a subsidiary of Syratech Corp.): 114
Jarzembowski, Joseph & Mary: 102
Kolodzinski, Charles: 68
Kremensky, Claire: 54 (top left), 58 (all)
Ksieniewicz, Mary: 88
Kuczynski, Caroline: 32 (center left)
LaBarge, Raymond: 47 (bottom right)
Labato, Anthony: 104 (bottom left), 133 (center)
LaCasse, Cynthia Simison: 93 (center right)
Lockwood, Allison McCrillis: i, ii, iii, 30 (bottom left), 171
Lococo, Samuel: 101
Lovett, Irene: 93 (top right)
Mahoney, Ruth: 132 (top center)
Manning, Daniel: 81 (center left), 93 (center)
Manwell, Edward: 136 (both)
Martin, Jane Anne: 7 (bottom right)
McDonald, Charles: 97
McDonald, Polly: 127 (bottom right)
McGinnis, Pat: 127 (bottom right)
McGrath, William: 73 (bottom right)
McKenna, Dennis: 141 (both)
Menegat, Norman & Ingeborg: 162 (center)
Morey, Russell: 135 (top right)
Morin, Origene: 90 (left)
Mysorski, Marjorie: 76
Nanartonis, Connie: 31
Niedzwiecki, Mr. & Mrs. Myron: 115 (bottom right)
Niemczyk, Constance: 72
Northampton High School Year Book: 4 (top left), 11
Oborne, Robert: 22 (bottom left)
O'Brien, Allan: 29 (top right)
O'Connor: Michael: 133 (top right)
O'Donnell, Irene: 81 (center right)
O'Keefe, Patrick: (bottom right)
Olander, Edwin: 67 (bottom right)
Pattrell, Kenneth: 137 (center)
Phelps, Sophie: 46 (bottom left)
Polito, Salvatore: 95 (bottom right)
Pope, Arthur: 44 (top right)
Pruzynski, Anna: 173
Qua, John: 69
Raymond, James: 71 (top center & right)
Rice, Johanna: 174 (top left)
Ruddy, Daniel: 117 (top right)
Sakrison, Ray: 91

Shaughnessey, Eleanor: 50 (both), 103
Skibiski, John Jr.: 116 (bottom)
Smith Archives: Chap. 1 Frontispiece, 6 (center left), 15 (top right), 84, 87 (right), 119 (top right), 144 (top left), 145 (all)
Smith, Beulah: 105 (both)
Sniezko, William: 138 (bottom), 140 (top)
Sullivan, Dorothy: 112 (top left)
Talenda, Mitchell: 140 (bottom left)
Tonet, Earl: 30 (top right), 99
Union News: 16 (center), 119 (center), 122
United States Army: 26, 27, 36, 38, 45 (bottom right), 49 (center right), 54 (center), 64, 89, 92 (left), 97 (center), 106 (both), 108 (center left), 109, 137 (top right)
Vanasse, Lucien: 130 (bottom left)
von Klemperer, Elizabeth: 63
Wall, Lola Conz: 32 (center right), 104 (top left)
Wells, Constance: 139 (top & bottom right)
Whitbeck, Elizabeth Dunn: 82 (left)
Willard, Doris: 32 (center), 66
Woicekoski, Augie: 23 (top right)
Wolak, John: 23 (bottom right)
Yates, Ann: 115 (center right)
Young, Dorothy: 24 (top left)

Map Acknowledgements

Maps of major military installations on Oahu, page 20:
Copyright 1991 by Scholarly Resources Inc. Reprinted by permission of Scholarly Resources Inc.
Maps on pages 41, 128 & 130: from Delivered From Evil: The Saga of World War II by Robert Leckie.
Copyright 1987 by Robert Leckie. Reprinted by permission of HarperCollins Publishers Inc.
Maps on pages 74, 90, 92, 107 & 108: By Martin Gilbert from The Second World War by Martin Gilbert.
Copyright 1989 by Martin Gilbert. Reprinted by permission of Henry Holt and Company, Inc.

Index

Bold type indicates photo

Aaron, Dan, 144
Abbott, Jere, 144
Adam, George, **11**
Adams, Abner L., **125**
Adams, Anna (Duga), **39**
Adams, John M., **125**
Adams, Samuel, **39,** 40
Adamski, Joseph C., **125**
Adler, George D., 167
Agar, Herbert, 15
Alberts, Leonard, **125**
Albino, Felix, 131
Allen, James L., **125**
Allen, Leonard ("Pat"), **132,** 170
Allen, Myron, 170
Ames, William ("Bill"), 115
Andre, Jesse, 9
Andre, Maybell, 116
Andre, Muriel (Adams), 115, 116
Andrews, Robert, 165
Angotti, Benjamin, 173
Anisowicz, Chester S., **125**
Ansanitis, Francis, 13, **46,** 173
Arel, Rudolph, **11, 132**
Arnold, Elbert, 173
Asaka, Toshiori, 140
Atwood, Roger, 81 **82**
Avirett, William, 63
Bailey, Mary (Phillips), 54
Bailly, Ambrose E., **125**
Baj, Matthew, 170
Baj, Stanley, 170
Baker, Bruce, 72
Balise, John 132, **134**
Banister, Ruth, **62**
Bardwell, Allan, 177
Barnes, Francis E., **125**
Barnes, Leroy F., **125**
Barrett, Raymond, F., Jr., **125**
Barrymore, Ethel, 121
Barth, William O., 42
Bauver, Harold, 97
Bean, Robert, 175
Beastall, Harold Y., 123
Beckman, Kenneth ("Ken"), 69, **70**
Begin, Bernard, 32, 77, **112**
Beliveau, Elaine (Bonneau), 70
Benny, Jack, 29, 30
Benoit, Joseph, 130
Benoit, Ted, **14**

Berle, Adolph, 34, 127
Bernier, George J., 33, 53, **54,** 55, 85, 146, 148
Berube, George, 132, **134**
Berube, Robert, **169**
Biddle, Francis, 53
Bishop, Russell, 129, **131**
Blanchard, John, 137
Blitz, **65**
Bohnak, Joseph, 160
Bohnak, Lavinia, 160
Boland, John E., 86
Bombard, John, 112, **131**
Bona, Ugo, **11**
Bonneau, Joseph, **70**
Borowski, Chester, **71**
Bouchard, Armand, 23
Boudway, Richard, **47**
Bourdon, Albert, 170
Brickhill, Paul, 68
Brown, Paul, 89, 90, 160
Bubrowski, Julian, 50 **102,** 103
Budgar, Leonard, 29
Budgar, Louis, 29
Buinickus, Stacia, **118**
Bush, George, 100
Butor, Adolph, 103
Byrne, John ("Jack"), 108
Cadieux, Beulah (Smith), 78, **105**
Cadieux, Edmund, 78, **105,** 106
Cadieux, Linda, 78, **105**
Cahill, Christopher, **143**
Campbell, John, 75
Campbell, Louis L., **148**
Camposeo, Joseph, 132
Cantwell, Thomas, 44
Car, Peter M., 42
Carhart, Gregory, 10
Carradine, John, 121
Carrier, Louis M., 143
Carroll, Madeleine, 109
Cave, Lawrence, **104,** 175, 177
Chabot, Victor, **77**
Chalmers, A. Burns, 86
Chamberlain, Neville, **5**
Champoux, Neil, **46,** 63
Chase, Mary Ellen, 121
Chereski, John, 50
Chiang Kai-Shek, 11
Chiang Kai-Shek, Mei-Ling, 38

Choquette, Lenwood, 50, 162
Choquette, Peggy (Ayers), **162**
Christian, William, 144
Churchill, Winston, 8, **9**, 13, 62, **64**, 65, 74, 99, 124, 132
Ciekalowski, William, **143**
Cimini, Frank, 103, **104**
Clapp, Roger F., 85
Clapp, Ted, 9
Clark, Cecil, **48**, 108, 159
Clark, Mark, 103
Clark, Robert, **78**
Clason, Charles, 174
Clifford, John, 75
Clifford, John P., **125**
Clifford, Margaret (Dwyer), 61
Coffey, William, **165**
Compton, Karl T., 156
Conant, Paul, 14
Connell, John, 138
Conz, Alfred ("Ted"), **32**, 103, **104**, 175, 176
Conz, Archangelo M., 177
Conz, Ida M., 177
Conz, Lola (Wall), **32**
Coogan, Felixa (Sieruta), 41
Coogan, Thomas, 129
Coolidge, Calvin, 150, 173
Coolidge, Grace, **15**, 44, 55, **58**, 61, **124**, 143, 150
Coopee, John, 170
Cox, Allen, 146
Cox, Elsa (Boudah), **118**, 146, 147
Cox, Gerald, 146
Cox, Henry, 146
Coyle, James ("Jim"), 107
Crabbe, John M., **125**
Crane, Hugh ("Hymie"), 30, **126**, 130, 161
Crane, Jeremiah, 161
Cross, Melvin, 112
Cullen, Albert, **11**, 170
Cunningham, John, 49
Curran, George, 168
Curran, Richard, 168
Curran, William, 160
Curtin, Michael, **161**, 175
Dahmke, Ley William, 86
D'Alelio, Frank G., 156
Daley, John, **112**

Daley, Mary (Corbett) **98**, 99, 170
Dalton, Gerald, 175
Damon, Isaac, 85
Danforth, Vernon, 25, 26, 138
Darby, Ronald, 146
Darrah, Robert, **160**
Davis, Herbert, **15**, 62
Davis, Irving, **39**
Davis, Nancy (Reagan), **84**
Deinlein, Leonard, 79
Delaney, Donald, **9, 161**
Delaney, Parker, 9, 161
DeRose, Charles, 160
Devine, Joanna (Pucylowski), 119
Dialessi, Stacia (Lipski), 135
Dickens, Charles, 91
Dickie, William F., 152
Dickmyer, John, 73, 74, **160**
Diemand, Katherine, **118**
Dodd, Marion E., **124**, 143
Doenitz, Karl, 46
Donovan, Arthur, 175
Donovan, Catherine, **118**
Doolittle, James, 37
Dornberger, Walter, 99
Dowlen, Jack H., 41
Downey, Donald, **166**
Ducharme, Donald, **32, 66**, 67
Dunn, Elizabeth (Whitbeck), 81, **82**
Dunphy, Edwin, 175, 176
Dziubek, Walter, 10
Eliott, Charles, 162
Eliott, Estelle, 162
Elkins, Dorothy (Young), **24**, 25
Ellison, Richard, 160
Eisenhower, Dwight D., 49, 91, **97**, 106, 132, 167
Fallon, Kathleen, **166**
Farrar, Frederick, 148
Feder, Sid, 103
Feeney, William, 112
Feldman, Ethel (Cohen), **80**
Feldman, Joseph A., **80, 125**
Fennessey, Donald, 47
Fenton, Daniel F., **125**
Finn, Bernard, 103
Finn, Elizabeth, 143
Finn, Ralph, **146**
Finn, Robert, 175
Fisher, Wilbur, 20

FitzGerald, John ("Jack"), 16, 109, **111**
Fleming, Urban ("Slim"), **153**
Florio, Michael, 46, **121**
Florio, Vito, 46
Forbes, Esther, 121
Fox, George, 65
Freeman, Jane, 124
Fugere, Lucien, 107, **108**, 160
Fungaroli, Joseph, **11**
Fussell, Paul, iv
Gallaher, Elizabeth (von Klemperer), **63**
Gallivan, Robert, **161**
Gare, Edward J., Jr., 56, 86, 119
Garvey, Edward, 10
Garvey, Michael, 115
Garvey, Richard, 29, **30**
Gauthier, Carrie, 118, 146, 163
Gavin, James, 104, 106
Gay, Hobart, **49**
Geary, Joseph E., 53
Gesiorek, Joseph, 49, 132
Gilbert, O. A., 42
Gilligan, Ramona, 30, **50**, 78, 89, 90, **103**
Goebbels, Joseph, 8, 121
Goerdeler, Karl, 123
Goering, Hermann, 121
Golash, Leo, **166**
Golash, Stanley, 170
Gomez, Pvt., 93
Good, Alexander, 65
Goodsell, James, 65, 66
Grant, Alfred, 9
Graves, E., 42
Greenberg, Stanley, 94 95
Grew, Joseph, 17, 19
Grimes, John, **96**
Grogan, James, **45**
Gulledge, Charles, 128
Gustavis, Robert, **73**, 74
Gutowski, Thomas, 75, **151**
Gutowski, William ("Bill"), **75**, 151
Guyott, Ann, **118**
Gwiazda, William F., **125**
Hall, Basil D., 79
Hall, James C., 86
Halsey, William ("Bull"), 37
Hammond, Thomas, 170
Hanson, Justus, 116
Harrington, Llewellyn, 128
Harrington, Marcella May, **145**

Harrison, G.G., 139
Harrison, Joseph L., 83
Hartman, Joseph ("Joe"), 67
Hathaway, Joanna (Grimes), iii, **96**
Hawkes, Frederick, 58, 164, 165, 166
Hayes, Charles, **46**, 47
Hayes, Frank, 23
Haynes, Lewis, 135
Hebert, Ludovic, 133
Heinz, Edward, 163
Henchey, Norman, 160
Henchey, Thomas J., **125**
Heyne, Ella, 116
Hibbard, Raymond ("Buddy"), **28, 75, 100**
Hickey, Alice, 115
Hill, Adelaide (Cromwell), **144**
Himmelsbach, Richard, 65
Hinds, Gailon, 143
Hitler, Adolf, 3, 4, **5**, 8, 14, 65, 89, 98, 107, 108, 121, 123, 131, 132
Hnojowy, Doris, **118**
Hodges, Willard, 172
Hogan, Thomas, 5, **30, 128,** 167
Holmes, Richard, **31**
Homma, Masaharu, 25
Hood, Donald, 34, 81
Hood, Donald, 138
Hood, Lucille, **62**
Hoover, J. Edgar, 146
Hopkins, Julia B., 86
Hornbeak, Katherine, 29
Horvat, Anthony D., 128
Houle, Larry, **14**
Hover, Ellis, 93
Howes, Wallace, 116
Hull, Cordell, 4
Huntoon, Richard, 128
Hurley, Thomas W., Sr., 55
Ice, Ferdinand, 143
Jabanowski, Ralph ("Jabber"), **11,** 91, 93, **94**
Jackimczyk, Bernard, 13, **115,** 173
Jackimczyk, Veronica (Dragon), 67
Jackimczyk, William (Pete), 13, **67**
Jackson, Robert L., 41
Jacob, Carey, 15
Jason, Helen, (Driscoll), **59,** 60
Jekanowski, Harry, 83
Jerome, Theodore ("Bud"), 125

Jodl, Alfred, 132
Jones, Rufus, 29
Kalinka, Fred, 107
Kaminski, Patrick ("Pat"), 170
Karloff, Boris, 85
Karparis, William ("Vinnie"), **131**, 148, 173
Kathericus, William F., Jr., **125**
Kecy, William, 41, 42, **43**
Keefe, Richard W., **125**
Kelley, Edward ("Ed"), 134
Kelsey, Edward, **11**
Kenderski, Bruno **115**
Kennedy, Joseph, 6
Keyes, Robert, 13
Kiley, Aneta, **160**
King, Franklin Jr., 54
King, 310, **130,** 131, 174
Kingsley, Mary, 157
Kinner, Richard, 57
Kinney, Robert ("Bob"), 16, 109, **110**
Kirby, William F., **125**
Kisielewski, Lillian, **118**
Kneeland, Harold, 166
Kneeland, Raymond, **11**
Knight, Robert, 125
Knox, Frank, 10, 17, 26
Kochapski, Ronald, 151
Kohn, Hans, 156, 157
Kolodziej, Jan, 20
Kolodzinski, Charles, **43**, 44, 63, 67, **68**, 132
Konoye, Fumimaro, 17
Koop, Allen V., 119
Kosteck, Martin, 121
Kowaleski, Elizabeth, **118**
Kozloski, Thaddeus, 21
Kraushaar, Otto, 33
Krol, John, 9,10
Kross, Anna, 145
Krueger, Walter, 113
Ksieniewicz, Charles ("Hooker"), **88,** 89, 91, 173
Ksieniewicz, Charles (son), 91
Ksieniewicz, John, 91
Ksieniewicz, Mary, 91
Kurzydlowski, Henry, **94**
Kusaka, Shuichi, 86, ?fc,10>87, 119
LaBarge, Raymond, **47,** 48, 167
Labato, Anthony, 103, **104, 133**

Lafoe, Henry A., **125**
Lajoie, Rene P.**125**
Lampron, Earl, 160
Lampron, Edmund, 81, 164
Langlais, Camille, **148**
Langlais, Elizabeth, **148**
Larkin, Oliver, 4
Latham, John, 150
Lavallee, Leon, 7, **12,** 13, 160
Lavallee, Raymond, 13
Leary, William, 13
LeBeau, Donald, **169**, 170
LeBeau, Lawrence, J., **125**, 170
LeBeau, Raymond, **93**
LeDuc, Claire, 160
LeDuc, Francis, **94**
LeGallienne, Eva, 121
Leland, Allen, 56
Lenard, Viola, 171
Lerche, Ralph, 79
Levy, Ralph, 172
Lewonis, William, **148**
Lincoln, Eleanor, 54
Lindbergh, Anne (Morrow), 7
Lindbergh, Charles, 7, **15,** 33
Lipski, Stanley, **134,** 135
Little, Jean, 122
Liversedge, Harry, 129
LoBello, Joseph, **175**
Locke, Margaret, 15
Lococo, Charles, 170
LoCoco, Marion, 59
Lococo, Nicholas, 170
Lococo, Samuel ("Sam"), 100
Loftus, 123
Loiselle, Maurice, **43,** 44
Lojko, Stanislaw, 113
Londergan, John, **40**
Lopez, Pilar, 121
Lord, John, 113
Lotreck, Phyllis, 166
Loudfoot, Robert, **14,** 112
Lucey, James F., **125**
Lyman, Florence, 15
Lyons, Robert, 100
MacArthur, Douglas, 25, 26, **156**
McAuliffe, A.C., 109
McCarthy, George, 176
McCarthy, John, **94**
McConnell, Sarah, 122

McCrillis, Allison (Lockwood), **i, ii,** 29, **30,** 87
McCrillis, Sarah (Sharpe), i
McDonald, Charles ("Caesar"), **11, 97,** 109, 164
McDonald, William ("Bumps"), **11, 127**
McGrath, Harold, **73**
McGrath, William, **73**
McKelligott, Maurice J., **125**
McKenna, Dennis, 140, **141,** 159
McKinley, Earl, 59, 60
McKown, Kenneth, 30, 31
McNair, Lesley, 95
McVay, Charles, 134
Maday, Anthony, 135
Mahoney, John, 85
Mailloux, Francis, **43**
Malinowski, Edwin, 65, **125**
Malinowski, Joy (Brennan), 65
Manning, Dan, 32, 80, **81,** 92, **93** 104, 107
Manning, Helen (Kukulka), **81**
Manning, Harold, 151
Manning, Ibie, 93
Manning, Pat, 93
Manwell, Edward, **136,** 137
Marcus, William, 151
Massey, Jane, **118**
Mathias, Rudolph, **4, 5**
May, Andrew, 63
Mazuch, Edward, **51, 129,** 146
Menegat, Ingeborg, ("Inge"), **162**
Menegat, Norman, Jr., **125, 162**
Michelman, Samuel (Sam), 173
Miller, Bernard, **139**
Miller, Blanche, 27, **139**
Miller, Dorothy, 55
Miller, Joseph, 25, 26, 138, **139**
Mleczko, Helena (Crane), 30
Mleczko, Stanley, 30
Moffitt, Armand, 150
Mooney, Sgt., 63
Morey, Russell, 135
Moriarty, James P., 150
Moriarty, Joseph, 57
Moriarty, Robert, 57
Morin, Origene, 89, **90**
Morrow, Elizabeth (Cutter), 7, 144, **145**
Murphy, Mrs., P.J., 122
Murphy, Steven ("Steve"), 101
Musante, David, ii
Mussolini, Benito, 3, **5,** 65
Mysorski, Ben, **76**
Mysorski, Marge ("Babbie"), **76**
Nagumo, Chuichi, 19
Nanartonis, Connie, **31, 94,** 99, 105
Nash, Gordon, 170
Nehring, Margaret, **118**
Neilson, William Allan, 7
Netto, John, 13, **115**
Newell, Helen (Lucey), 79
Newell, Ruth, 79
Newell, Stanley, 25
Niemczyk, John, 71, **72**
Noble, William, 46, 86
Nolan, George, 13, **112**
Nolan, John, 9
Oborne, Robert, 21, **22,** 25, 81
O'Brien, Allan, **29,** 160
O'Brien, Daniel ("Dan"), 29
O'Brien, Donald, 150
O'Brien, Edward, 54, 153
O'Brien, George, 170
O'Brien, John, **125**
O'Brien, John F., 77
O'Connell, Charles, 25
O'Connell, Dorothy, 162
O'Connell, John, 162
O'Connor, James, 152
O'Connor, Michael ("Mike"), 121, **133**
O'Connor, Robert, **7**
O'Dea, Edward, 165
O'Donnell, Irene (Wade), **81**
O'Donnell, James ("Jim"), **81**
O'Donnell, Walter N., **53,** 176
O'Donnell, William, **127,** 129
Okamura, Sonoko, 33
O'Keefe, Cornelius, 77, **168,** 174
O'Keefe, Mary (Walsh), **174**
O'Keefe, Patrick ("Pat"), 77, 97, **167,** 168, 170
Okolo, Blanche, **32**
Okolo, Chester, **32**
Okolo, Caroline, 96
Okolo, Joseph, **32, 96,** 112
Olander, Edwin, Jr., 7, 31, **67, 167,** 170
O'Leary, Emmett, 156
O'Leary, George B. 163
Ono, Edward, 157
Ono, Fannie, 157
Ono, George, 157

Ono, Mary, 157
Ono, Tadanori, 86, **157**
Organ, Donald, 170
Organ, Hank, 101
Osborn, Francis, 4, 15
Osga, John, F., **125**
Osgood, Rachel, 47
O'Shea, Donald, **11**
Ouimet, Dora, 167
Ouimet, Robert, 137, 167
Ouimet, Roy, 167
Owens, Roger, 122
Paddock, Martin, 56
Paquette, Wilfred, **161**
Parda, Patricia ("Pat"), **164**
Parda, Peg (White), 162, 163, **164**
Parda, Ralph, 162, 163, 164
Patch, Howard R., Jr., **125**
Patton, George, 131
Pattrell, Kenneth, **137**
Paul, W.S., 111
Paulson, Fred, 9, 143
Pease, Robert, 87
Perkins, Frances, 59
Peters, Joey, **164**
Piepiora, Michael J., **125**
Pilat, Stephen, 112, 113, 175
Pliska, Chester, 170
Poling, Clark, 65
Polito, Salvatore, 94, **95**, 96, 167
Pomeroy, Shirley, 62
Pontbriand, Henry R., **125**
Pope, Alexander, 121
Pope, Arthur ("Art"), 42, **44**, 45, 134
Poudrier, Edmond, 159
Poudrier, Edward, 112
Powers, brothers, 101
Powers, Charles, P., **125**
Powers, Patrick J., **125**
Powers, Thomas Jr., **125**
"Private Buck", **159**
Pruzynski, Arthur, **173**
Puchalski, William, 13, **46**
Punska, Joseph, 143
Pyle, Ernest ("Ernie"), 152
Qua, John, 32, 69
Raymond, James ("Jim"), **71**
Remarque, Erich Maria, 3, 5
Rice, Francis, **34,** 43
Richards, William H., 152

Rider, Maurice David, 4
Rochelau, Robert, 133
Rodriguez, Earl, 23, **160**
Rommel, Erwin, 49, 51, 65, 92
Rooke, Margaret, **6**
Roosevelt, Eleanor, **79,** 150
Roosevelt, Franklin, 3, 4, **5**, 7, 10, 13, 14, 15, 16, 27, 33, 37 **64,** 65, 124, 127, **150**
Ruckeyser, Merryle, 7
Ruddy, Daniel ("Dan"), **117**
Ruskowski, Tallis, **125**
Rutkowski, Bruno, 101
Rutkowski, Mitchell, **100,** 101
Ryan, James, 160, 175
Rydenski, Edward, **175,** 176
Sadoski, Frances, **118>fc,8>**
Saito, Hirosi, 4
Sakamaki, Kazua, 25
Sakrison, Ray, **91,** 93
Sampson, Francis, 97
Sarrasin, Wesley J., **125**
Szarkowski, Thomas Jr., **125**
Scarborough, Thomas, 143
Schmitz, Matthias, **87**
Scott, Hayden, 128
Sears, George, **170**
Senuta, George, 131
Seymour, Claude, 123
Sharpe, Allison, i, **ii,** iii
Sharpe, Sarah (McCrillis), i
Shebak, Joseph, 25
Shebak, Michael, 101
Shedlock, Stanley, **153**
Sheehey, Francis, **50,** 116, **131**
Sherrod, Robert, 129
Shirer, William L., 3, 5, 8
Shockro, Harold, 77
Short, William J., 85
Shumway, Frank, 170
Sicard, William (Billy), 56
Sieruta, Felixa (Coogan), 41
Sieruta, William, 46
Sieruta, Zigmund, 21, **22,** 25, 41, **42,** 63
Sikorski, Wladyslaw, 62
Simison, Donald, **93**
Sinclair, Alvin, **100**
Siperek, Walter, **160**
Siwy, Stanley, 170
Skibiski, John, 30, 60, **116**
Slater, Charles, **43**

Smith, Gavin, 42
Smith, Holland ("Howlin' Mad"), 100
Smith, John, 86
Smith, Russell, **166**
Smith, Sidney F., 56
Snape, Edward J., **125**
Sniezko, Caroline, 27
Sniezko, Helen, 27
Sniezko, Stanislaw, 27, **94**
Sniezko, William, 25, 26, **138,** 139, **140**
Snyder, John W., 164
Stalin, Joseph, **5,** 89
Stiles, Meredith, **145**
Stimson, Henry, 153
Stokesbury, James T., iv
Stone, George W., **125**
Straw, Willard, 112
Streeter, Robert, 112
Strong, Albert, 75
Strong, Esther (Holway), 54
Subocz, Joseph, **47**
Sullivan, 109
Sullivan, James, 160
Sullivan, John, 57
Sullivan, Ned, **169,** 170
Sullivan, Patrick ("Pat"), 57
Susco, Mitchell, **11**
Switalski, Chester, 50
Szarkowski, Stanley S., **125**
Talenda, Charles S., 27, **125**
Talenda, Edward, 27
Talenda, Emelia, **114**
Talenda, Mitchell, 25, 26, 27, 77, 114, 138, **140**
Talenda, Walter, 27
Taylor, Norton, 21
Tebbutt, Roy, 103
Tencza, Frank, 123
Terauchi, Hisaichi, 136
Tessier, Henry, **125**
Thompson, Malvina, **79**
Tobin, Maurice, 152
Toda, Martha, 33
Tojo, Hideki, **17,** 100, 141
Tomaszewski, Charles, 176
Tomlinson, C.F., 42
Tomlinson, Juliette, 60
Tonet, Earl, **11, 30, 99,** 100, 101, 137, 150
Toomey, Winston, **69**
Toomey, Mrs. Winston, 69

Torrey, Merrill, 55
Trow, Nancy, 41, **121,** 122
Truman, Harry, 136, 150, 156, 164
Tsuchiya, Hichiro ("Patches"), 140
Tuit, Frank, **134**
Underwood, Herbert, 61, **79**
Valentine, Norman, 119
Vanasse, Lucien ("Joe"), **130,** 131, 174
Van Doren, Mark, 121
Von Braun, Werner, 99
Von Paulus, Friedrich, 65
Wainwright, Jonathan, **38**
Waldron, William J., **125**
Walker, Frank, 21, 41
Wall, Richard ("Dick"), 29
Walsh, David I., 14, 15, 60, 174
Washington, John, 65
Watsa, Robert, 121
Weaver, Sgt., 129
Webster, Harry, 145
Welch, William, 9, 10, 33
Wells, Durbin, 10
Westort, Marianne, **162**
Westort, Stanley, 162
Wheeler, Burton K., 14, 33, 53
Whitham, Challenger, **11**
Wiggins, Lewis, 125
Wildner, Carl, **37,** 38
Wilkins, Roy, 124
Willard, Doris (Ducharme), 66, 67
Willkie, Wendell, **10,** 13
Wilusz, Chester, 130, **131**
Winchell, Walter, 29
Witherell, Alphonso, 178
Witty, Nathalie, 56, **57**
Woicekoskie, Augie, **23**
Wolak, John, **23**
Wong, Edward, 57, **113**
Wong, Frank, **155**
Wong, Helen, **57**
Wong, Lou Shee (Mrs.), 113
Wong, Violet (Partridge), **57,** 113
Woods, Charles, 170
Wright, David, **11**
Yamamoto, Isoroku, **19,** 38, 39
Yokoi, Shoichi, 101
Yoshio, Tetsuro ("Cyclops"), 77, 140
Young, Thelma, **118**
Zaborowski, Frank, 61
Zehelski brothers, 170